I Remember...

Marilyn

By g. Peter Collins

LS 214 56 / 920/MON

Foreword

Who "Marilyn Monroe" was and what she may or may not have meant to anyone else who knew her closely, is NOT the subject of this book. This is not intended as a diary of *competition.*

She and I became special to each other at a time when our individual lives were in turmoil, not unlike such a relationship between any two human beings on the face of this earth.

What memories of her may remain with Joe DiMaggio, Arthur Miller, or any known or unknown persons who may have been touched by her, cannot possibly be explored in this diary.

Had she lived beyond that tragic day in August of 1962, perhaps all sorts of things might have been different. She didn't, and they aren't.

As far as I am personally concerned, we all lost in what may be termed the final game. Who loved her more or who loved her less is an unimportant issue.

Rather than fight a verbal duel for her affections, it is best we remember the guilt we must all share mutually.

For however we felt, and for as much endless devotion we now all pledge individually and together, on that August night, so very long ago, she undertook her longest journey alone.

For me, no amount of soul searching will ever erase that sad, simple fact.

To Marilyn,
in fulfillment of a promise...
To Janice and Bobbie for
brightening the years between...

To a very special collection of friends
who helped me overcome
insurmountable odds;
and..
To Kathy,
for unflinching loyalty, love
understanding and devotion.

Introduction

With the possible exception of certain actual dates and times committed in error due to the amount of calendar years that have passed since the incidents described herein actually occurred, the following story is true.

To preserve the rights of privacy for certain individuals, either living or dead, who may have played a part in this story by innocent association, their names have been altered in respect of that privacy.

It is the hope and intention of this author that by allowing you to share in what was once an extremely private relationship, you may come to a better understanding of a girl whose reputation throughout the years has been so clearly misunderstood.

Peter Collins

Prologue

It was a period of change. Something was in the air, but it wasn't anything you could put your finger on. Historically it was the end of the first five decades of this soon passing century.

It was a time when women still wore dresses, and men, shirts and ties. It was a time when cars each had personalities of their own.

It was a time when New York City smelled of the mixed odors of Juicy Fruit gum and hot dogs, when merchants of pretzels and chestnuts roamed the streets with their small but profitable businesses on wheels.

Radio City Music hall operated on a 7-day-a-week schedule, still offering a super stage show with a first run film.

It was also a time when arguments within the city were settled most often without bullets. It was, in effect, a quiet before the storm.

1959 was a year that saw the death of Buddy Holly and Lou Costello, and in a grander sense, the death of music and laughter, at least as we had come to know it.

Families still existed as did many of the first generation seniors who had found their way here in the late teens and 20's. Rebellious unrest and confusion were still below the surface, but coming to the the top as the decade counted down its last days.

For many, it was the end, but for so many others, the beginning.

Morals taught early on could still be referred to, but as the clock ticked on, about all that was left was referral.

It was a time when"the bomb" hung over all of our heads, and the uncertainty of tomorrow prompted us to live only for today.

What seemed most important through this period of right, wrong, and otherwise, and was to have someone to hold, someone to understand, someone to care.

Long before the internet, computers, cellular telephones and elaborate fax machines, communication between two people existed in the holding of a hand.

For me, September of that year, 1959, would begin the most impossible of journeys with the most improbable partner.

It is a journey I expect to complete at a much later date.

Chapter One

Marilyn - It Begins

The weather forecast had predicted "a chance of showers," but had mentioned nothing about a typhoon.

As a result of the suddenness of the storm, the Stage Delicatessen was even more crowded than usual, as many strangers to it arrived more for shelter than for food or atmosphere.

The noise level continued to grow and finally had become so loud as to become silent. It was apparent that everyone had so much to say, that no one was taking time to listen.

Her voice, as soft and gentle as a whispered night's breeze and so in contrast to that room of screamers, cut through this volley of noise like a steak knife through butter.

"May I sit down?" was all she said. And yet, despite the verbal storm that raged around us, her question came through almost as though being dubbed-in by an expert sound technician.

I gave the bearer of the voice the casual glance I would have given any, acknowledged her question with a nod of affirmation, and returned to my trade paper. Then, as though struck by some second thought, or perhaps an 8 second delay in my mind, I performed the always comical double-take, made most comical when it honestly happens. Imploring the very worst of manners, I found myself staring at her, unconsciously permitting my brain to catch up with my eyes.

She looked back at me while patting the remains of water from her face with a tissue. As she wore only light make-up, the scenario of horror that had befallen many women that night had not touched her. The kerchief she wore about her head, as well as her jacket, offered the only proof that a storm was even occurring in that the traces of water seemed only minimal. Catching her glance to me, snapped me out of my momentary trance, and forced from me an apology that was definitely in order.

"I'm sorry," I began, "I didn't mean to stare, but you look so much like...."

Before I could finish, and upon seeing my embarrassment, she smiled.

There are all kinds of women in the world. They come in a variety of sizes and colors. Behind each of them is a mystery that becomes most individual. This was the intention of the creator, and it is among life's only certainties. Hindsight makes experts of us all. If we could relive a special moment, a second in time perhaps, and see it for what it really was, and know it for what it was to become, we would possess the knowledge we do not. Unfortunately, we can't, and so often see it only long after it happens.

For me, none have ever, before or since, possessed that smile. I imagine this lends credence to the "chemistry theory." I didn't know it then, but with Marilyn, it was my long overdue answer. The serendipity of our separate journeys had ended.

Her eyes were blue, encircled with specks of grey, which under certain light, would go hazel. Her lips, full and eager. Her face and skin were delicate, with only a trace or two of human blemish, and her trade-mark blonde hair, was tucked beneath a dark kerchief for more than obvious reasons. All could have been camouflaged...all but that smile, which came from way deep down somewhere, and as real as the rain that kept pounding on the roof.

"It is you!" I said.

To which she replied, "I hope so!"

Somehow I should have been more sophisticated about

all of this, having been surrounded by it daily. I had seen more than my share of "movie stars", and many in off-screen looks that would have disappointed their most ardent fans. Something about many of them echoed of falsity, of pretense, of illusion substituting for reality, but not so with Marilyn. If anything, the opposite applied.

Used to my open-mouthed reaction, she handled it like a well seasoned pro, by totally ignoring it, giving my awkwardness a chance to regroup. Conversation began as though we'd been friends for years.

"That's some wind out there." She said. "Nearly blew me off my feet."

As she was about five-foot-five, and smaller in stature than her screen image, that comment was probably more fact than fiction. Curiosity finally overcame me.

"Are you here alone?" I asked, with that thought seeming slightly dangerous to me.

Without asking, suggesting , or implying, she took a sip from my coffee, shook her head affirmatively, and uttered a simple "um ummmm."

"Isn't that risky?" I asked, while simultaneously pointing to my cup of coffee, and suggesting one for her in body language.

She nodded, and I signalled Max who had already begun observing, and was quick to deliver.

"Oh no." She answered. "I go lots of places alone. I'm not afraid. Most people are really nice, especially when you just act like yourself."

Before I could ponder or react to that statement, Max made his appearance, glanced at me, then to Marilyn, laying the cup before her and recognizing her much publicized face. His eyes opened wide, and a "Jack-O'lantern" smile exploded onto his face. A slight hum erupted from his throat, but he held his composure. His expressive eyebrows gave me finally, a look of admired approval.

He would tell me on a later night, in a different time, and under an entirely tragic set of circumstances, that he knew, in an instant, that I had hit the jackpot. If only there had been more Max's in the world.

Observing his performance as closely as I, Marilyn again smiled, sipped her coffee, and went on; "What's your name?" She asked, light-heartedly and at a disadvantage.

"Peter." I said. "Peter Collins. I'm a writer, and one with obvious bad manners. " She reached over the table, offering me her hand for a shake, which I accepted.

"Well, Peter, I'm Marilyn, Marilyn Monroe. I'm an actress!" As our hands touched, the urge to laugh engulfed us both, which we did, offering us a polite compliment to each other.

I suppose it would be a matter of over-statement, or at least its suggestion would be, but factually, against things we cannot prove, but do so well remember, the simple touch of her hand began writing the words of our contract. It is, of course, hard to see in a state of bewildered infatuation, so therefore it goes unnoticed. Whatever your feelings, you are certain they are for other reasons. Magic only returns to haunt you after the fact.

"Kind of a rough night to be taking a walk, isn't it?" I went on.

"I just came from a lecture on modern plays at a theatre just around the block." She answered. "It wasn't raining when I got there, but boy, when I got out ...Whew! I just followed the crowd!"

Her eyes followed me, almost as though in study, and after sipping from her coffee, she went on:

"What do you write?"

Feeling somewhat inferior to the then current writer in her life, I answered , " Actually, at this point, I re-write."

Her face formed a logical frown, for which an explanation was in order.

"You see," I began, "A studio buys properties that are sometimes conceptually workable, but may lack something. Maybe the dialogue doesn't sound just right, or the settings are inappropriate. Maybe in the head of the original author, it played well, but in reality, it falls apart. Lines have been written that actors just cannot say, period. It's that simple, and happens all the time."

"That sounds fascinating!" She exclaimed with a smile born of genuine interest.

"It can be." I answered, recognizing that "fascinating" might have been a good deal more than it was. "At the very worst, it's a good place to start."

For a brief moment, she seemed lost in thought, and then slowly repeated a word that had intrigued something inside her.

"Conceptually," she repeated, first slowly, then at a normal beat. She rolled the word over her tongue and then smiled again, seeming to come out of her momentary, self-induced, trance. "That's a nice word. I wish I could speak like that."

Now it was my turn to smile, as her comment was such an honest one. There wasn't an ounce of pretension in Marilyn, not from the start.

"It means 'the idea'." I said, adding to the rapture of her new discovery. "The original concept, the intention of the author."

"I like it." She continued and repeated, "Conceptually, sounds almost sexy."

With a shake of my head in approval for her mastery of the word, and finding humor in her additional appraisal of it, something no one else could possibly have thought, I smiled, giving her an "A" for what seemed an accomplishment to her. There was something so incredibly warm about her that rather than face her for the moment, in what was a building reaction, I instead glanced out of the window.

"Are you waiting for someone?" She asked.

"No." I replied, returning my attention to her. She didn't know, of course, that there was no one I could have been waiting for at that time. No one. "Just thanking the storm." I said, in conclusion.

"That's sweet." She answered, again in possession of that smile. "Do you come in here often? The man who served the coffee seemed to know you."

She didn't miss a beat.

"About three nights a week." I answered. "I go to an acting work shop, and always stop here afterwards. It's more of a habit."

As though finding common ground, her eyes widened, "I do the same thing." She began, "Go to an acting workshop, I mean. I don't go as much as I used to, but it has helped me."

She continued, "Kinda helps put you in touch with yourself, don't you think?"

It hadn't helped me do anything of the kind, but offering a negative against all of her positives, would have upset what she apparently believed. As an alternate to an unnecessary explanation, I just nodded my head and offered, "I suppose."

"Are you studying to become an actor?" She asked, still wide-eyed.

"Oh God, NO!" I answered quickly, almost gagging on my coffee.

Whether it was the answer that came so quickly or the near choking on the coffee with the answer, she found a moment to giggle at my reaction. In an attempt at regaining composure, I proceeded along more subdued lines.

"I'm just trying to get a fix for all sides of this...this..business, or whatever you call it. I think you should do that to succeed."

I hadn't even finished the words when the corniness of them already came back to hit me in the face. What a lame, pretentious speech. I knew what I had meant to say, but it didn't come out that way.

Marilyn had a knack for editing a phrase and understanding what you, or anyone, would have meant. She left the weakness of any word or group of words behind.

"It's too bad more writers don't feel that way." She went on, completely ignoring the bravado style in which the words had come out.

"It would be better for us, if they did. You should see the scripts they hand me. Some of them are un-readable. I guess that's where YOU come in."

I agreed with a nod. She began loosening her jacket, keeping her eyes fixed on mine. She was still studying me. Now, a bit more comfortably, she made her face into a frown and dropped her chin a bit.

"You sound so serious." She said, mocking her own voice by dropping it a few octaves. "Aren't you awfully young for all of this?"

Had anyone else asked me that question, the hairs on the back of my neck would have risen to the occasion, but with her, even that sore spot was different.

"That's what THEY keep telling me." I answered with a sigh of disgust in my voice. "Morning, noon, and night."

"Who's THEY?"

"The people I work for, the people I work with, people in general." Rather than begin a tirade on this sensitive subject, I decided in favor of explaining it to someone who might just understand.

"I've been doing this, in one form or another, since I was seventeen, and that alone seems to boggle their minds. I know, to them, I should be going to drive-ins, eating "steamed" warmed over hamburgers, and ravishing some cheerleader, searching for our hormonal destinies. I don't know what the hell they think I should be doing." I concluded. " Anything but this I guess."

"Seventeen." She repeated, and again rolled the word around, but this time for a different reason. "I started modeling just about then, of course that was years ago...."

There was the beginning of a hint in that remark, that I felt I'd better throw back at her for exactly what it was.

"Oh, hell yes." I answered quickly. "How can you remember that far back?"

She caught it, giggled, and let it go by. The next question was a bit more serious, but possessed the same undertones.

"How old are you?," she asked, finally unable to conceal her curiosity.

"Twenty two, going on fifty."

The immediate silence was deafening. Those two blues pierced straight through me. For the moment, the subject was dropped, but would return on a different day, to be answered forever.

Over the passing years, many have asked me what she was like, not knowing of how close we had become. I would give answers that almost anyone with half a brain could have guessed, but when I could feel details coming forth, I'd clam up. Now, unclamed, so to speak, I can remember my first impression of her, and the word that comes to mind is "electric." That particular night would not have been the one to judge, as fantasy and infatuation were my guides. Based on her first words, and observations, I can dispute, for all time, the misconception that she was ever a "dumb blonde," because that is what she never was from the beginning.

Marilyn had a way of putting YOU in center stage, and making YOU feel important. She saved her own chest pounding for her agents and lawyers. You couldn't lie to her, or to yourself when she was around. Her sincerity made you sincere, and to perform in less fashion, would have been an insult to that special trust. There was no way you could look into those "blues" and tell her anything but the truth. Of course, on other occasions, that would be a painful task.

She was animated, and spoke with body language to accent everything she said. You would have had to be deaf, dumb and blind not to pay attention.

I can remember that first encounter, and my first impressions, which were less than spiritual. It was fascination in its finest hour, and no thoughts of "tomorrow" entered my mind. Within all of us is a built-in biological lust. To say it was absent on that first night would be a bold-faced lie.

Long before Marilyn became the so-called "legend," she had an aura about her that prompted all of the right thoughts at the wrong times.

She was the greatest actress that ever lived "off screen," as she could often portray that which she could never have been. She was honestly shy, but could portray a bravado that would dwarf the Ringmaster at Ringling Brothers.

She had been involved with men from childhood on, yet within her was an innocence that made you think of a 12-year old on her first date. She was fascinated by everything and everyone. And yet, in this year of 1959, she had come to distrust most of those around her.

The stepping stones on our mutual paths to this dot on the map, had become huge boulders, and the "April Showers" of our defeats had become flash-floods. We were ready for each other by simple subtraction. Our dreams had been similar, and the results the same. We had not included human error, and in that, had both become something we weren't.

One of the fine strings that would bind us closely together was our mutual ability to talk and listen, speak and be understood. We were in the process of beginning just that, when an unprovoked incident broke the spell.

They weren't dangerous, but they were definitely drunk. The male counter-part of this middle-aged couple who had obviously indulged in too much "evening," literally fell onto our table. The female member of the duo tried in vain to pull him away, but he had already spotted Marilyn from his prone position, and in his inebriated condition, began to grope for her, using all of the classic, over-used, less than clever, less than appealing phrases. He began reaching for her as a baboon reaches for a banana. As a natural reaction, I rose to full six-foot four, and pulled him up to a standing position. The venom in his eyes was clearly an effect of the drink in his system, as that same bourbon or scotch that was currently raising hell with his liver was making him something he probably wasn't. As calmly, but as firmly as I could, I "handed" him back to his mate, who then assisted him from the place. Max had been watching from behind the counter, his hand on a baseball bat he had stashed for those occasions when logic wasn't enough to end an argument. I thanked him for his intended support with a nod, and then returned back to Marilyn, who presented me with my first mystery.

She had positioned herself against the wall. Even the chair on which she sat was shaking.

We had been seated across from one another, but this rather strange reaction changed that. To achieve eye level, I grabbed a second chair and pulled it toward her, seating myself and instinctively grabbing her hand. It was ice cold. The look in her eyes darted from my hand to my face, and back to my hand, as though challenging what was only a gesture of reassurance.

"What's the matter?" I asked, observing her trembling. With no answer, I continued to rub her hand, not so much out of affection, but rather to return circulation to it.

She was in a near-quiet trance.

"Hey." I went on, "Marilyn...Marilyn..."

One more look at my face, and with no hostile sign of withdrawing my hand, composure began returning to her expression.

Finally, after the longest minutes in history, she whispered, "I don't like to be pawed...."

"They were just drunk. Too much party..it's okay, really."

I assisted her in reaching for her coffee, and steadied the cup in her hand. As tobacco was still our "friend" in those days, I offered her a cigarette, which she accepted. After a few drags, her eyes seemed to drop in a gesture of timid guilt.

"You must think I'm crazy." She began. "Here I tell you I go everywhere alone, and the first big lug who comes along, I cave in...."

I don't think "crazy" was the word, I think "frightened" would have been a much better choice. The fear in her eyes was very real. This was no performance. It was the first time I would see what I would soon see so much of - two distinctive sides to one girl, constantly at war with each other. Thoughts of lust went right out the window.

This was not the "Marilyn Monroe" who immortalized "Diamonds Are A Girl's Best Friends", or "Sugar Kane" and her Ukulele.

She wasn't the girl whose close-ups melted the film, as she sung to a hidden lover, planning her husband's demise, or the hapless dizzy neighbor of a befuddled Tom Ewell. This wasn't any of those people. This was a girl as fragile as fine china, who had explained more of herself in that one terrified reaction, than in any mountain of words.

An idea suddenly hit me, and I stood to put that idea to work. At that motion, she grabbed my sleeve. The fear had not yet completely passed. I reassured her with my other hand touching hers, that I wasn't going anywhere.

As quickly as I could, I stole a couple of chairs from the next table, and placed them strategically in front of ours, building a "wall" of sorts. Max watched and approved. I then quickly sat beside her.

"Nobody's going to drop in on us again, tonight." I said, hoping to put her mind to rest. I believe it worked.

My own mind was racing a mile a minute. Brooklyn, and its streets, had come in handy. The defense had been an instantaneous reaction. Perhaps, in Marilyn's Glendale California, no such reaction had ever been necessary. Maybe, just maybe, that explained the reason for those two red lines ending up here.

She had been, so often, the target for grabbing, pawing, and pulling apart. There are many ways to commit rape, with the physical one being the easiest to understand. What, after all, is a "queen of the screen," but a commodity used to turn a profit. How important had she become to the bean-counters who bought and sold her as one would a table and chair.

A pattern began that night, that neither of us could have made part of any organized plan. As there were no thoughts of a tomorrow, no plans were discussed. Things just happened.

Life is a carousel.

In a Brooklyn of so very long ago, I spent a good deal of growing-up time in a place called Coney Island, then the unchallenged greatest amusement park in the world. In this place of wonder there were thrill rides that would take more than your breath away. Sometimes they'd take your lunch with it. Roller Coasters, Ferris Wheels, a thing called The Parachute Drop, all of these were geared to scare the living daylights out of the strongest among you.

As far as I was concerned, they had wasted a lot of steel, wood, and tracks, because the ride that effected me was the innocent-looking "merry-go-round." I suppose, the writer's curse was already in my blood, because I seemed to be the only one frightened by this tame, simple, musical resting place.

The fear came from seeing something in it that did not meet the average eye, and I have continued to see proof of it all through my life.

The horses on those original carousels wore the look of torment. These were not the smiling faces of the later Disney versions, but the original concepts, and there was nothing "smiling" about them.

They all seemed possessed of a private demon, and their paths had been carefully charted...they would never be able to out-run that demon. The only peace they would ever find was when the ride stopped, and that loud music ceased.

They were running a race they could never win.

We step on this carousel at the very beginning, and for a time, it seems to weave its magic spell, as we learn more and more as we grow. We soon discover that the more we learn, the less we know. And if we've progressed at all, it is only back to the beginning. We can never get off that carousel as long as life continues, as the circle we have designed for it will not free us to change.

Once in a while, however, it will slow down, and the heart pounding music of bass drums and bells will soften to strings. For that time, it will indeed be restful, but before long, that time will pass, and the beat, will again, take over.

When it is finally silenced, so too are we.

For some, the ride goes on for a very long time. For others, not so long. Those we touch while sharing the ride, are those we leave behind. Whatever we accomplish on the ride is left for others to remember.

The human condition, when considered in any relationship, has been a study that has baffled the greatest minds of this, and all preceding generations. No two of them are ever the same. What may take some years to cultivate, under no guarantees, will take others only seconds. The "love at first sight" variety, is sometimes born of a necessity that can not be seen in its time. If this particular brand of excitement is to end suddenly in the bed of disappointment, then it does, quickly and painlessly. If it is to last, it often does under the newly introduced term of sorrow and loss.

There was never any formal "getting to know you" clause between Marilyn and I, as it seemed, from the first second, all of that was behind us. Being with her was comfortable, was easy, was something that seemed most natural. Oh, there would be turbulence, and a few rocky moments, but even they appeared only part of the big picture, and as normal as breathing.

The seed to this had been planted on that first night, and would be nourished very quickly, unknown to each of us then.

For that moment on my carousel, it was a time to grab the brass ring, which for me was gold, and to hold it for as long as I could.

You must try and understand that the girl I am speaking of was not the subject of world attention, not the poster girl, or "any sailor's dream." Not the one who now smiles at you from a postage stamp, or who has been immortalized in song and prose. THAT girl is a product of hype, of a need for an image. THAT girl is unreal, and was, even to herself.

The one of whom I speak, bore none of those attributes,

and was constructed of a very real substance. What either she or I did as a profession had little to do with any of it, other than the logic of being able to share that profession's pitfalls and traps.

Simply put, for Marilyn and I, a huge clock ticked over our heads, and it was a clock that offered us only seconds, but was kind enough to permit us to make, in those seconds, what some try to in a lifetime. A dispensing of preliminaries was not a luxury for us, but rather a necessity.

After the episode of the two drunks, the evening progressed uninterrupted. We became lost in mutual dialogue, and in that, failed to observe the crowd thinning, the rain being reduced to a trickle, and the wind to a breeze. As would become our unconscious custom, the rest of the world somehow magically disappeared. Unfortunately, for some around us, that same world was very real. After permitting the last second, Max would remind us that somewhere there was a wife and kids who waited for him, and that it was getting late.

We both apologized for the oversight, and now, out of our mutual trance, glanced around to notice that aside from the cleaning crew, we were the only ones left in the place.

In a near automatic gesture, probably prompted by the hour, and the dizzying endless dialogue, we agreed to continue our talk on the next day. The plan was to meet by a certain statue in New York's Central Park around 4pm.

With a final hand-clasp, I saw her to a cab and walked a few blocks to where my car had been parked. The air had been scrubbed by the previous storm, and the short walk gave me the opportunity to inhale a few deep breaths of it.

The streets of Manhattan had been cleaned by the rain, and, indeed, sparkled in the literal sense as well as the physical one.

Driving the 26 miles or so to my beach apartment afforded me the benefit of clearing my still coffee-wired brain. As was so usual in my life, things had happened fast...almost too fast. Reality began to sink in.

As a boy, in Brooklyn, I had lusted after Virginia Mayo in the film THE SECRET LIFE OF WALTER MITTY. There was no threat to Miss Mayo, at the time; as I was only nine-years old. I only knew that I "wanted" someone like that, but wasn't yet certain as to "why." I had also made up my mind that I would never be the character of that film who dreamed of being something he wasn't. Well, to this date, I had already proven that bit of fluff was true.

On that drive home, I began to wonder, if, in fact, Walter Mitty hadn't taken over. It all suddenly seemed so unreal.

In the year 1959, the person known as Marilyn Monroe, was clearly a known world image, and the subject of a million dreams by as many men, and possibly even women. On a scale of one to ten, she was twelve.

I was not yet privy to the path that would be laid out before us, and considered, then, only the immediate, which sounded, with every heartbeat, like an overwhelming impossibility.

By the time I reached my beach-front apartment, I had completely sold myself on the concept that this small moment in time, this accident created by the weather, this "Walter Mitty" illusion, would clearly fade at sunrise.

I was not yet ready for a truth I could not have conceived, and adamantly fought against it.

Chapter Two

The Gold Ring

Nothing can be more disruptive than the human delusion, and sooner or later, we all fall victim to it. We think we have the control switch that guides our lives in our hands, when in truth, no such switch exists. An even simpler truth is the fact that none of us really know what the next moment will bring.

Gazing into the bathroom mirror on that next morning gave me a chill. I had become used to the stranger who sometimes looked back at me, but what I faced, for the first time, was confusion. I didn't like it. Even if my daily activities had brought out the fraud in me, I had, at all times, been aware of that deception. In that awareness, I could control it.

The memory of too many cigarettes and too much coffee can be erased with a good dose of Colgate and Listerine, but other memories remain, as no such medication or cure is available.

I had already abridged my mother's "Golden Rule" to a simple "do unto others ." Period. And, right, wrong or otherwise, it had worked. My head had been filled with the pride of accomplishment, and just how I had succeeded in all of that, seemed unimportant. What I now didn't need was a sudden attack of conscience, however camouflaged with the scent of Chanel Number 5.

The business of motion pictures is a difficult one at the very least. It is a business that promises with the right hand, and withdraws those promises with the left. It deals with "unreality" as a commodity, and yet, the methods to reach that unreality are based on cold hard facts.

The "Mr and Mrs John Does"of the world, who dream of what it must be like, cannot possibly fathom that answer. It is beyond any reasonable explanation. This illusion-creating, and for all it builds, it equally destroys.

It had always been my desire to become part of the business, but never part of the illusion, or, at least I had never seen myself as a victim of it. The night before had been nice, and now it was over. We had said a lot of things about a lot of subjects, and probably succeeded in ridding ourselves of some private fears by the simple act of sharing them. That was all that happened. This next morning, with my head filled with self-induced doubts, I did all I could to try and return to a reality that had temporarily vanished from my mind. The "Wise Old Owl" in Disney's BAMBI had called it "TWITTERPATED," and that is one thing I didn't need to be.

When a prize-fighter sets himself up for a fight, he begins to mentally "hate" his opponent. All but George Foreman, that is. It would not be possible to "like" the other guy, when in a few hours he would be paid to beat his brains out. He psychs himself into this state, and remains in it until the fight is over.

I began just such a campaign as I shaved, and while I did not hate the lady from last night, I began to despise Marilyn Monroe for being able to make me lose my grip.

She was a "movie star," the same kind of person I saw daily. Her success was something to be proud of, but did not call for a worshipping at her shrine. All that cute stuff, and that act of being frightened over a couple of drunks so that Prince Shnook could come to her rescue, what a performance!

If Marilyn had represented everything "beautiful," I made sure that before I left that apartment, I would think as much about *ugly* as I could.

I damned myself for talking so much. In that state of twitterpation, I had told her things that no one knew. I began swearing, using words I hadn't heard since

Brooklyn, and saying them over and over again. This sudden nervous breakdown came courtesy of my letting up on my guard for a few lousy hours.

I was so up-tight about people at the office snickering about my age, and me in general, what in the hell would she be doing this morning? Gaffaw came to mind. I imagined she would be telling some maid about her adventures with this "kid" last night, and how nice it was, on occasion, to indulge in complete fantasy. How she hoped that I really wouldn't go to the park, as that had been a part of the fantasy. After all, I was a nice kid.

Driving into town, the negative scenario continued, as I began to think of her as just another "movie star" who couldn't utter a word without people like me. If we didn't write it, they couldn't say it.

She had a great set of knockers, and a never-want-to quit ass. I should have let it go at that.

As the day went on, as days do, I decided she had occupied too much space in my brain and in order to rid myself of this incredible delusion, I would actually go to the park. By her non-appearance, I would never be forced to wonder.

Returning from lunch, I passed a theatre advertising its latest attraction, SOME LIKE IT HOT in big bold letters. The marquee boasted, *HELD OVER*, So and So *SMASH WEEK!*

There she was, playing her ukulele, surrounded by cutouts of Tony Curtis and Jack Lemmon in drag.

What the HELL had been on my mind.

My attache case had become my "blue blankey" and whether I needed it or not, it always went with me. That day, it went with me to the park.

Well, there I was, at the designated bench, by the designated statue, and at the designated time. To look and feel less a fool, I opened my case and pretended to be working on something.

Central Park, in the late 50's, was still a haven within the city, an oasis of green grass and trees nestled in the midst of a concrete jungle. It was a place to stroll, to sit and reflect, or to ride on a horse-drawn carriage with your best girl. During the daylight hours it was quite a safe place. Night-time, of course, demanded more caution, as certain elements had already begun to crawl about the many tree covered paths.

This day was in early Fall, around the end of September, and aside from a light breeze which was already tossing some fallen leaves about, it was very pleasant. Some children were playing ball a short distance from the bench, and an elderly couple passed me, hand in hand, reminding me that some plans DID work.

Sitting there, a vulnerable target for anyone to observe and find amusing, I pretended to make notes on the script before me. It was 4:15.

I suppose I continued to wait out of some sadistic design of stubbornness.

I began to remember the "in" stories of Marilyn, told and written by those who claimed to know, and a media I was convinced didn't lie. She was unreliable. She was always late. She drank and did drugs. She slept with whomever she fancied. From these "accurate" accounts, the picture of a first-class-bitch began to form. Well, this was one guy who wasn't falling for it.

Very few people, if any, kept their word, especially in this industry. Promises were made and forever broken. As the mental picture of this "true" Marilyn began taking shape, the thoughts of a rendezvous became comical.

Just about the time I had finally decided that I had qualified for the title "World's Biggest Idiot," and looking at my watch to observe, 4:45, one of the children who had been playing ball, gave that ball a good kick. My eyes followed the ball as I suppose something to set my mind to other than my current, unpleasant situation.

Watching the antics of a possible future NFL star, seemed as good a place to start as any. The ball first soared into the heavens, and then dropped just next to the feet of someone who seemed to be running in my direction.

The sex of the runner could not be determined from this distance, but what WAS clear about whoever it was, they'd never qualify for the Olympics. He or she kept bumping into their own knees.

A sudden bell went off, and at the same instant, a huge hand flicked on a light-bulb in comic-book style. What was it she had said,

"They keep talking about my sexy walk, but if they only knew, I just can't walk naturally in those tight dresses. My knees are constantly bumping into each other!"

It was the smallest of physical handicaps, but what if, just suppose, that "walk" had been sped up? What would be her appearance on a "run?"

In a near trance, I began walking toward the approaching runner, leaving my script and attache case on the bench.

It could have been some guy named Frank, out for an afternoon jog, even before that particular name for it was given. If it had been, he would have run right by me, laying the final straw on the growing stack.

I could now see that the figure wore a bomber jacket, Korean War vintage, slacks and medium high-heels, and sported a kerchief. This took care of the "Frank" theory.

The speed of my walk increased, and finally, within a few feet of the runner, there was no doubt. Out of breath and panting, Marilyn tried to speak.

"Do you know how many statues and benches there are in this park?" She wheezed. "I counted at least 10!"

It felt odd to me that a life that had been centered around "words" found not one to use for that moment. Not ONE.

The fact that she was out of breath was no performance, and in a subconscious move, I placed my arms around her, offering her something to lean on. It all seemed so very natural.

A lump in my throat the size of a baseball formed in the next split second, as she reached her arms around my waist and rested her head on my chest. There was nothing artificial or staged about it. Out of reflex, my right hand stroked her kerchief-covered hair. My God, what was happening?

With her head placed firmly against my chest, she mumbled something about not following directions, about being sorry, about being late, about all kinds of things. I didn't hear any of it, but could feel the vibration of her voice throughout my entire body.

Thoughts raced through my brain at a million miles a second. What a fraud I had become. In an instant I had given her a label that belonged to me. The day had been spent in condemning something inside of me, and, for lack of an honest target, it had been misdirected to her. Everything was indeed backwards, and by warped, frustrated, self-design.

What I had been trying to destroy was a truth by surrounding it with lies. Deep down, something inside me kept screaming, "no," but I thought, perhaps if I protested enough, the screams would stop. The self-induced anger, the swearing, the accusing, and the belittling, all faults of mine, not hers.

I knew, as we stood in that position for only a few brief moments, that all I had read and heard were the lies.

She had kept her word, and for that, this moment stood on its own. The rest of my accusations fell into place behind that one.

Cruelly, but deservedly, the shame of my own small-minded lack of trust came back to slap me hard across the face. At this point in time, Marilyn was looking for a friend, and the reasons for that search were her own. No trumpets or Heavenly choirs were there to give this encounter a back-up, as none were needed. Looking, again into her eyes, made me clearly aware of how I had already abused that friendship, and the reasons for that abuse seemed as childish as the age I kept refuting.

If this day in the park stood for nothing else, it taught me a much required lesson. Her simple act of keeping a promise, made me suddenly and acutely aware of the many I had broken. I had presumed all around me to be weak, selfish, and self-centered. When, in fact, that description fit me to a "T."

The coldness I had been passing off as "sophistication", the manipulating of all those around me, the private jokes I had made to myself at the expense of those in the work-place, all ceased. Whatever cockeyed plan I had thought I'd put into motion, was torn into little pieces. It hadn't been a very good plan anyway.

Had it all ended on that day, the memory of that moment would have been among my most precious souvenirs of a world that, before Marilyn, had seemed filled with useless self-induced contradiction. If you find your-self in such a world, it is your responsibility to make it better. I had done more than my share to make it worse.

On the previous night she had said, "People in my position are a target for everything, and so often we are accused of doing things we could never do. It goes with the job."

Well, my wise new blonde friend was right. The proof had been in my own actions.

During our time together, which began on a rainy night

in New York City, when the world was young, and was given its first credentials on this late Fall day in the park, to a time that is not yet here, no lies would ever come between us. There was simply no need for them.

The city, for all its cold and unfeeling appearance, can be instantly converted, under a different set of circumstances, to a place of warmth and contentment. The carousel slows, the lights dim, and the level of the music quiets.

The initial embrace, our silent salute to friendship, gave way to a comfortable stroll between two people whose identities and private drives were temporarily placed on the backburner.

Talk began of the industry, that driving force that had ruled her life, at this point, a good deal longer than mine.

Marilyn was extremely perceptive, an ability that only punctured more holes in the "dumb blonde" scenario. She began speaking of a time when she too had suspected everyone, as though being able to read the last eight hours of my life on a page I hadn't written.

She had begun with the same kind of wide-eyed innocence as possess us all, along with a trust of people that had proven itself to be false. They weren't going to be what she wanted them to be, and she paid dearly for that lesson.

By this year of 1959, she had sorted most of it out. "Trusting everybody to be what they are is foolish. Not trusting anybody, even more foolish. All you can hope for is an ability to tell the difference."

"Sometimes you think you're actually having fun." She went on, "Then you realize that all you're doing is giving that fun to someone else. You're not gaining anything from it. On top of that, you realize that even THEY aren't having any fun. It's like a game, and the rules change every second. The worst thing about this game is you never win or lose, you just keep playing."

"Why?" Was all that came to my mind.

"Because, by the time you realize all of this, there's nothing else you can do. Kinda dumb, eh?"

No, it wasn't dumb, at least not the appraisal of it, because that is exactly what I had been doing, playing a game. She knew it. In fact, she probably sensed it the night before. She knew the look on my face at her arrival to the park was born out of the suspicion that she wouldn't show. There had been many "parks" for her when those suspicions had been proven right. When I had so convinced myself that she might have been laughing at me, that is the last thing she had been doing. I think, now, she would have come to that park on crutches if she had to. Memories of those who hadn't were still too firmly etched in her mind.

She began to talk of a girl named Norma Jeane, speaking of her as though she might have been a neighbor. The dialogue came to rest on another girl named "Marilyn Monroe." She now had my complete attention.'

"She's a character." She said. "A fictionalized, make-believe character. She doesn't exist. Bugs Bunny! No one seems to be able to separate us, and that becomes very irritating. I'm not HER ! I created HER, and now neither she or they will leave me alone."

My bewilderment must have been obvious, and repeating the words, "Bugs Bunny?" only made it more so.

"Yes!" She snapped, almost defensively. "Everybody expects ME to be HER, and for that reason, when I ask for a serious role, no one hears me!"

Seeing the growing questions on my expression, she stopped in her tracks, and looked me squarely in the eye.

"I'm going to show you something." She began, " And I want you to remember it, not just for me, but for everything you do in this business."

She began removing her kerchief. As she made ready

for the performance, she tossed her hair, shaking it loose from its restraint.

"First, you have to remember all those nice people who have been passing us, waving and smiling, and minding their own business. Now, let me show you how SHE changes all of that!"

She placed her hand on my chest in a gesture suggesting that I just stand right where I was, which I did. She then began to walk from me. All she did was *walk* a few feet.

That walk, those hips, and the traces of a disappearing sun radiating off her blonde locks as though a "key light", set the stage.

People began crowding her, some from out of nowhere, literally falling out of the trees. Her name was whispered among them all.

"Marilyn!" "It's Marilyn Monroe!"

A hundred words of fanship from as many people, and the numbers grew. She began signing autographs with pencils, lipsticks, anything they could find.

Fortunately, as the crowd continued to grow, a mounted policeman entered the scene, and, recognizing her, began to separate them. She looked over her shoulder to me, and winked. Her point had been most graphically made. For that second in time, I had almost forgotten who she was. But this exhibition was quick to remind me.

There she was, "Sugar Kane,""Lorelie-Lee," "Rose," all of them. The metamorphosis was damned near frightening. At the policeman's insistence, the newly formed mob began to disperse. She turned, and came back to me, re-affixing her kerchief. Before tightening it, she turned once more to the crowd, and blew them a kiss..a "Marilyn" kiss, which none of them would ever forget. The "icon" returned to the girl, and the girl returned to me, making me feel, for the moment, as tall as a mountain. I suppose my inner feelings of wonderment were hidden under my look of ignorant surprise, because, as though realizing the impact of the performance, she was quick to give me the benefit of that most genuine smile.

She looked at me with that smile, and near compassion in her eyes.

"Don't look so frightened," She said, reassuringly. "I'm still me, honest."

Some things defy description, and no words can even suggest the barest of explanations. I had never seen anything like that in my life. If ever there had been the proof of illusion versus reality, this had been it.

"They love you." I said, finally snapping out of the trance I had been in. " All of them!"

"Sugar," she said, a slight sigh in her voice, "They love HER. They don't even know me. I just proved that."

"Yeah, I guess you did." I said, snuggling her arm under mine.

"Don't let it scare you." She went on. "It comes with the package."

A different sound to the next words began leading up to something.

"Is it too much for you?" She asked. "Is this the end of the walk?"

That statement was the combination of seven of the loneliest words I'd ever heard. For just a flash, I felt like holding her tightly, and, for some unknown reason, I felt the strongest compulsion to cry openly.

From this day on, she would bring those same feelings to me. I could lift her, high above my head, and hold her there for all the world to see. In direct opposition to that, I could envelope her within my arms, shielding her from anyone or anything. No one is ever supposed to feel these desires, and for a reason. The pain lasts far too long and never, really, ever goes away.

In answer to her question, "God, I hope not!" was all I

could say.

I knew I had to get us both out of this, and it seemed the best way to accomplish this was to lighten a bit, still offering a truth in the bargain.

"I just need to come down off that mountain...give me a second." I said.

She laughed. "Mountain?"

"Yeah, mountain." I said, joining her in that laughter. "Is that where you are, on a mountain?" she continued. Still in possession of that smile.

"Oh yeah," I continued, now mocking myself. " Way up there and of course YOU can't image why....." I looked her squarely in the eye, "I'm sure you've *never* been told this before, but you DO have an effect on people."

The game continued with her "aw shucks" attitude feigning the obvious. "Noooo!" she whispered, hardly able to contain the pretense.

"Yessssss!" I answered, completing the charade. "But it's okay now, I'm back on the ground."

In a good deal lighter mood, we continued our walk, stopped and bought a pretzel, which we shared. Along with a multitude of subjects came new names to me. Milton and Amy Greene whom she called "former friends", and Lee and Paula Strasberg, current ones.

With every smile came a frown, as it seemed each and every relationship had it's down side. She and Greene had formed a partnership, with BUS STOP and PRINCE AND THE SHOWGIRL resulting from it. Harsh words had come between them, and accusations of mistrust had been fostered by that ever-present Arthur Miller. Her decision to believe Miller had made her unhappy, but she was never able to bring herself to apologize to two people who had genuinely cared. She also suggested that while Lee Strasberg had become her mentor of sorts, that Paula, her friend, was also picking her pocket. History records that Paula gave much of herself to Marilyn, and was indeed a strong shoulder to lean or cry on. This was fact, but fact alone never completely convinced Marilyn. Perhaps Paula HAD borrowed some money, but more than likely had repaid whatever the sum in time, loyalty and friendship. Knowing all of this, Marilyn still remembered the money. The years had done this to her.

Once so very trusting, she now felt the opposite. It wasn't Paula, or Milton,..it was everybody. It was a statement of contradiction against what she had just suggested to me only an hour earlier.

Along with all of this self-confession came an inquiry that had begun the night before. It started by her suggestion that "I wish you had been here ten years ago."

My first reaction was to counter with the absurd. "We'd have been a great couple then." I said. "A 22 year old bombshell and a 10 year old kid. That would have made the papers."

Recognizing the seriousness of her approach, I canceled the wise cracks. There was some 11 or so years between us, and now was the time to clear that up, win, lose or draw.

The question had been posed as an answer, and one we had been sliding into for a few minutes. I cradled her head in my hands, zipping up her jacket to ward off an early evening chill.

Still holding both she and the zipper, I looked directly into her eyes. "I knew a couple once, who were the same age." I began. "They were miserable together. The calendar is a prop, used to remind us of when our bills are due, nothing more."

She smiled slightly, perhaps at my ignorance of the larger issues, and just as perhaps accepting that which she felt was a dodging of those issues. And they were some issues. Just moments before we had been talking of the profession, of stage productions vs. the movies, of people who cared and of people who didn't. The husbands and the close friends had come up in that conversation. It now became clear as to why.

She had felt, and dared verbalize that feeling to the subjects, that both DiMaggio and Miller had already hit their prime, and were now on the downside. Both had been older than she, and both had already lived their moment in the sun. In her verbal abuse of Miller, she had spelled it out in large letters. "Why do I always get somebody too late?" were the words she used.

She had had a relationship with actor Marlon Brando that had begun when both were new to the Actor's Studio of Lee Strasberg. That relationship had covered it all - from A to Z, but had lasted beyond the dim lights of the bedroom. They had become friends. She adored the music of Frank Sinatra, and, for a time, that too had become a fast paced limousine-infested relationship. She and "the swinger" had swung. Somehow, that too continued as a friendship.

My 22 years of age frightened her, but yet, something was there and had to be dealt with.

The 50's, and indeed, the early 60's presented an archaic "double-standard" no longer important in the 90's. For a man to be seen, and indeed, marry a younger woman, was considered a sign of virility, and was quite acceptable. For a woman to attempt the same, was considered anything but. To a society that wore blinders, this was generally viewed as "the robbing of a cradle," as "a desperate attempt" to retain youth that was gone.

As just about anything but what it may have been.

Miller would have seen it as the following scenario:

I had never hit a home-run in my life. Nothing that even approached a Pulitzer Prize had been offered to me. I was at the beginning, with the "end" nowhere in sight. I was tall, dark, and fairly attractive. Certainly no Adonis, but able to compete. The key word here would have been "young." Imagination relating to our private hours could have filled in the blanks. It would have been a double slap in the face.

"Trust me," I said, as those eyes kept searching my face. It wasn't me she had to trust, it was herself.

Miller had been writing a screenplay dedicated to her. Within the pages of that screenplay, a role had been created just for her. Regardless of the state of their current marriage, this role was important to Marilyn. A chance to break the "Bugs Bunny" mold. Any word of her cavorting about with a young man would have been Miller's final straw. The concern seemed quite legitimate. An exhibition of this sort would have been the final rubbing of salt into the wound.

It was then that the "conspiracy" began. It was clear, to both of us, that we wanted to see each other again, and maybe, even as much as possible. For a time, the "age" thing was put on hold, at least between us. As neither had a crystal ball, thoughts of how far this would go or when it would end, never came into the conversation. Any premature day-dreaming in that area would have been just that.

Marilyn was constantly being photographed with subjects that ranged from screen personalities to bartenders and lifeguards. This fact became an asset. Insinuations by the media and the public that she had bedded these snapshot pals was commonplace. It actually provided a diversion. It was then, and because of that, we mutually agreed that no cameras would ever follow us.

Once that script had been finished and that production done with, things might be different. But for now, a new plan was formulated. Whether it was right or wrong wasn't the issue. The game had to be played with these rules, or it couldn't be played at all.

"Sparks" existed between us, but no roaring public bonfire could be staged. Nervously, Marilyn gave me her phone number, a place she shared with Miller somewhere on 57th street. It was out of mutual trust, and I assured her as I gave her mine, that trust would not be abused. She had no way of knowing that. Had I been an opportunist looking for something extra, it would have been a tool to that extra.

She had always been trusting of people, and quite often, that same trusting had come back to haunt her. Here she was, doing it again. Only later would I learn just how very much that gesture meant to her. After all, we had then only known each other a few hours. "Forever" was indeed miles away. Something inside her seemed to suggest we might be good together, but then, suggestions can be false. The heat of a moment can often fog common sense. All we had shared that day was some dialogue and a pretzel. Hardly sufficient grounds for a commitment.

Another taxi entered our lives and again she was gone, leaving me in a state of confused euphoria. It had all happened so very, very fast.

I can remember swinging my briefcase in the wind, as the mood of change was already all about me. The joy of her had sunk in, but not yet, the responsibility.

All I knew then, on that late afternoon in a Fall season so very long ago, was that someone special had come into my life, and her name was Marilyn. Just how permanently she would remain in my life, just how, in fact, she would become my life, was not then my privilege to consider.

Chapter Three

The Velvet Curtain

It was probably the first time my co-workers had ever seen me bound into the office in the eighteen or so months of my tenure, and their looks of suspicion were justified. If only I could have told them what had happened, or better, what its effect had been on me, it would have eased some of their unspoken questions. I couldn't and didn't, thereby leaving them with the outside possibility that perhaps I had been visited by three spirits as had been one Ebenezer Scrooge on that fateful Christmas Eve of Dicken's lore. The secretaries, typists, clerks, and mail-room attendants who so often smiled at me, were shocked to find that smile returned. I even waved at some of the "suits" I so often ignored completely. One secretary who had particular "eyes" for me, and who made every effort to seduce me with favors from advance "previews" of upstairs office plans to bending and leaning provocatively in my direction whenever the timing was right, seemed puzzled. In that bewilderment, her voice, the one I know she must have borrowed from Lauren Bacall, squeaked rather than dripped.

"Here are the two copies of the script you requested," she said, after which she damned near ran off.

I know, in the re-telling, this must all sound foolish, but foolish is the only thing it wasn't. For me, it was the freedom of returning to something I had always been. Marilyn had been the catalyst in my own chemical equation, and one that had been suffering a great imbalance. It wasn't "moon, June, spoon," it was something far more realistic than that. Poets might call it "the wings of love," but for me, on that morning, "the shoes of common sense" would have better described it. Something between us would bring this on from time to time for both of us. We'd take turns. Serious biographers, those who honestly seek whatever truth might be, would later discover, and document, that in late 1959 and early 1960, Marilyn would on certain days "bring the sun in with her." That she would be the Marilyn everyone knew she could be. That at times like this, all bowed to her much deserved "royalty." These same researchers and biographers have tried, but can't seem to pin-point "why", and in their questions, have attempted educated guesses. I am certain that if they and I ever compared notes, we would discover that those same unexplained times of pure beauty would coincide, in some small way, with one of our recent times together. The "magic" that happened between us had nothing to do with moments of passion, of wild and crazy love-making, of anything the human eye could see. To each other, we represented the security of positively knowing that, at least, one person honestly gave a damn. It was that simple. She had begun that ritual in the park, and as a result, my "walking on air" scenario the following morning. My time to repay that feeling of "ummph" would come later and would be directed to her when the need arose. What would be would be, but for that morning, she had become a most missing ingredient in my life. A solid, unquestioning, non-judging friend. I was most fortunate to have two of something most people have none of, friends, the other being Bob, with his friendship having begun in high school.

Although she had personally come to despise it, Marilyn's creation had made people laugh, sing, and generally feel good about themselves. Mine, born out of warped ambition, had made them miserable. Leaving it behind was no great effort, as it weighed on me like an anchor. Mark, the senior member of our "ghost team" had many times been the victim of that same warped ambition, and this "Christmas in October" attitude of mine was seen by him as a new approach to what he had come to feel, was my old killer instinct. He approached me apprehensively. I could see him out of the corner of my eye, and waited for him to be near enough to feel the full impact. Before he could even begin to dampen this day with another "doom and gloom" speech, I suddenly turned and spoke his name loudly.

"Mark!", I said, startling him out of a few years growth. He backed up a few feet. It was a different kind of game than Marilyn had suggested, and one that gave me pure joy. After the shock of my turning to say "Boo," which is essentially what I had done, substituting the word "Mark" for "Boo" itself. I handed him one of the copies of the script I had been given, with a simple, calm, "here."

"What's this?", he mumbled.

"It's your copy," I said, pouring my coffee and adding the one lump of sugar. His voice grew in suspicious intensity,

"What do you mean, 'my copy'?"

I turned from the coffee dispenser, sipped a sip, and made the announcement. "We're doing it together."

Waiting for the angle, or the punchline, or at least the other shoe to drop, he followed me closely into the shared writer's office. Looking over his shoulder, he whispered loudly, "What the hell is going on?"

My attitude had, indeed, looked like a set-up, and so obviously against type, he did deserve a straight answer void of flowers and violins. I placed my attache case down onto the community desk, turned to him, and removed what must have been, a broad grin.

"Ok," I began, "I know you think this is some kind of a sick joke. I don't blame you. Believe me, it's not." His eyes scanned my face, watching and waiting. As he arched his eyebrow, I continued;

"I read your draft last night, and it works. Not only have you made the author's intentions clear, you have definitely improved on them. In fact, you have taken a piece of crap and turned it into a workable blueprint. Changes I could make would be minimal. We have to finish it together. I ordered the two copies this morning. The office is aware of it."

Hitting Mark across the mouth with a steel pipe would have created a less surprised look. In a state of near-shock, and with no further words, he slumped into his chair, gave me one more look, and opened to page one. Nothing else was said.

That night I managed to work undisturbed, munching on a hamburger and french fries from the nearby Pig 'n Whistle beach front restaurant. I saw the changes necessary in the script very clearly. The words flowed. I would discover, as time went on, that Arthur Miller had considered Marilyn a distraction to his work. Someone to cloud his mind. Whatever prompted such thoughts belonged to Miller. They were private and not for public opinion. Each of us reacts to one another in a different, individual, way. What may be gravy to one, is poison to the other. It is never honestly a question of right or wrong.

Thoughts of Marilyn flashed in and out of my mind, but never clouded it. As a matter of fact, they sharpened my abilities, made things more clear to me. Her presence became an incentive more than a deterrent. Whatever silent demons haunted Arthur Miller belonged to him. Whatever happened between "I do" and "we don't" was for them to decide. Their relationship had begun for all the wrong reasons, none the least being a re-bound from a guy named DiMaggio. "Joltin Joe", the "Yankee Clipper" had made his name on the baseball fields of my youth. As a ball player, he was the best. What had started for he and Marilyn as a home-run season, had ended with "three strikes and you're out." Miller, who had long pursued her, was simply there for the fall, and caught her with his near fan-like adoration. The romance between Marilyn and Joe was a physical one, and in that, it was good. Joe was, however, no mental giant and his background included an education of where women belonged. It was this unrealistic double-standard that destroyed them in 9 short months. DiMaggio had had his moment in the sun, and somehow had deluded himself into thinking the same applied to Marilyn. In this appraisal he was wrong. If part of his unconscious scenario included Marilyn playing Mrs DiMaggio serving spaghetti to a room full of his friends, he was ill-advised.

Miller, on the other hand, had been a successful play-write, and his use of big words impressed Marilyn. Perhaps too, she saw him as a father figure, something she had so long been without. Well, sadly you don't marry your father. Miller was dazzled by Marilyn. He wanted her. He thought he wanted the whole package. In return, Marilyn made the effort of trying to please him. She became close to his family, tried to study his religion, tried to become the Mrs Miller he had envisioned. As she began slipping away from him, he desperately held on now performing for her more as a hired stooge than a husband. Once that happens in any relationship, it's time to move on. Whether out of loyalty, desperation or need, Miller chose not to close the book, and instead lingered an hour too long. Promising to write a script for her was their only reason for continuing. As Marilyn had already confided, "love" was never the issue. She had convincingly talked herself into something. It was a something that died long before meeting me.

Marilyn would always speak of Joe with gentle fondness, but of Miller with disgust. In those comments could be found the truth of it all. She and I had just begun. What had gone on before was history. I had no visions of her serving spaghetti, or for that matter, my wearing an apron offering her breakfast in bed. Somewhere between the two, maybe we had a chance. I had not yet given it a name , but whatever it was, at this point, no harm could come from it.

A major decision faced me on the next morning, and one that forced my attention from Marilyn and my work. My first brush with "love" had proven to me again, that the word was clearly an invention of greeting card companies and florists. The word only seemed to apply to my mother and grandmother who practiced the interpretation of the word with no strings attached. Their's was a kind of love that permits mistakes and allows for human weakness. This man/woman thing seemed riddled with complications and misinterpretation, most of which came back to slap you across the face.

Marilyn had already discovered this to be true, and so had I.

My first marriage had produced a daughter, a lovely child who, like all children, hadn't asked to be born. When, for all the reasons, right or wrong, the honeymoon was over, she had become what all children become, a casualty. My former wife had begun entertaining thoughts of returning to school or re-entering the world of classical music, while I pursued the ambition that raged within me. We would spend some time together with the little girl, but "some time" isn't really enough. My former wife's parents knew this, just as they had known, all along, where this Cinderella story would end. Of course we didn't listen, as youth never does, and one night under a hot summer moon in the back seat of a 54 Ford, the decisions were made for us.

They now had put another suggestion on the table. They had offered to adopt our daughter and give her what they knew we couldn't. I had been unjustly wrestling with the idea, but to refuse the gesture would have been more an act of selfish bravado than of sense. I had agreed to sign the opening petition, with the proviso that I could back out for a period of 6 months. I saw it as a positive move for my daughter's welfare, and put the traces of any male ego in my pocket.

Poetically, Marilyn had always wanted a child and had not been able to carry one to full term. Here I was giving one away with the stroke of a pen. Had things been a bit further down the line, perhaps I would have refused, allowing Marilyn that chance at motherhood. Between she and my former wife, both great ladies in their own right, the child would have had the love of two mothers. What a different scenario it would have been. My first task of the next day was the signing, which I did in spite of the attorney's comments about "my getting off easy." It was around 12 pm, and feeling just a bit empty of heart, I retreated to the local cocktail bar nearest the office. The frequent watering hole of those who labored in my profession as well as some from the wacky world of advertising on nearby Madison Avenue.

A Black pianist there had the "touch," and a voice like ol' Nat Cole himself. It was generally relaxing. I have never been a drinker, but on that day, the screwdriver tasted good. My mind was a mixture of thoughts ranging from Mark and the script, Marilyn entering my life, and my daughter departing from it. With the gentle strains of "Pretend" and "Mona Lisa" in the background, I tried to sort it all out.

Back slapping is an art practiced daily in the business of films, and those who do it best, artists of the lowest caliber. Before I could begin to place my thoughts in the order of importance, one of these practitioners squirmed onto the bar stool next to mine and offered me that "oh so obvious " greeting. After the pretense of surprise at seeing me here, along with the few predictable current jokes, this character, as do all of his kind, got right down to it.

His name was Jim, and by some magical force, he always knew what was going on in his department, foreign sales, and indeed all departments. He had that special gift of understanding the untold story of everyone who ever so much as slipped on a banana peel. He never needed to produce any concrete evidence of anything, because, as I said, he had that gift of "just knowing."

Within the nearly two years of my association with this studio, I had made very few friends. This was by choice. Most of my co-workers had years on me and saw me as a threat of some sort, offering friendship as a blind for envy and disgust.

As I worked at home on an independent contractor basis, most of these victims of paranoia knew little about me. They just knew I was there, that I was a writer of some kind, had a brand new shiny red convertible, and got paid well. With little for them to gossip about, I am certain they manufactured suggestions for the facts that were missing. Personally, as long as the subject was me, I viewed their entire subversive behavior with complete indifference. If the subject was someone close to me, it became a different story.

One of the few men I did come to call friend, was a middle-aged poster artist named Arnold Albinski. He was an old world master, and had been with the company virtually from the beginning, which at this point was about 40 some odd years. He was currently fifty-five years old, having begun in the silent period as a teenager, much like myself. His art was stunning, and the posters resulting from it, equal to fine paintings. I admired his work, and he admired my guts, obviously seeing some of his youth in me.

As a pianist from childhood, I understood and appreciated the music of the Masters. So too did Arnold. The two ingredients that bound our friendship were our love for film and our love and appreciation for music. These two distinct creative arts bridged the gap between age 22 and age 55. On those days when nothing seemed either to make sense, or be worthwhile, he and I would discuss Schubert, Mozart or Beethoven. He was a gentle man of the cleanest integrity. Now, on this already cloudy and somewhat confused day, Jim, the back-slapper, was relating to me a story of why Arnold Albinski had been asked to resign. He knew we were friends, and thought "I should know." Being such a wonderful guy, he probably saw it as his civic duty to be first to tell me.

"He drinks," he began, "and then there was that woman....." He continued to babble on offering his interpretation, which of course was warped, degenerate, and filled with negative condemnation. I mentally switched him to "off" as I knew from the now muffled dialogue what had really happened. Arnold had been in "love", here we go again. She had been a woman several years his junior, but it had lasted for ten years. He had made the colossal mistake of adoring her, and for that she had taken full advantage. When the bubble burst, which it so often does in affairs of the heart, she was gone with not so much as a "fare-thee-well." It was superficially unprovoked, and it was extremely painful. By the very nature of it all, an artist lives by his or her emotions walking a fine tight thread over pits that others wouldn't even see. They work into endless nights in creating a beauty that is seldom appreciated. Whether they pursue their art in performance, painting, music or writing, theirs is a lust that is never completely fulfilled. They are always pushed to the maximum as only that maximum will ever offer them the kind of peace only they can feel. The loss of a loved one even to the average person, can be devastating. To the artist, it can be the final act. Maintaining whatever inner strength he could muster, Arnold continued to work. He also began to drink, at first to numb the pain, and finally to obliterate it. His assignments began arriving late and under par to his capabilities. Finally he made the biggest mistake of all, he confided his troubles to those he thought were friends. The more he cried in his beer, the larger the dossier became. The very ones he had trusted, those he had called out to for help, were among those who pounded the first nails.

Marilyn would later call it, "my hard edge", that protective layer that sometimes erupted from my Brooklyn heritage. Maybe she was right, because just for a split second, I entertained the thought of putting this man on the floor. This blow hard who found it so necessary to inform me that Arnold had been asked to resign along with his personal knowledge of why.

Being six-foot-four, thin, but with a decent build, I could have easily struck a blow for integrity during that midday demonstration, but in deference to the proprietor and the soft-voiced piano player, I elected otherwise.

As I have already said, my being the subject of gossip rolled right off, but an attack on a friend, not so. Arnold Albinski may not have been an international beauty, but as surely as Marilyn had been abused, so too was he being abused. It amounted to the same thing. In Marilyn's case, they reached for her body. With Arnold, they attacked his soul. If you thought about it, and lived through it, and possessed even an ounce of awareness, you could see, in these last days of the 50's, the ending of more than an era. Words like SELF-PRIDE, INTEGRITY, and HONOR would soon be retired to the book shelf. Self-esteem would go along with them as the soon-upon-us 60's would promise a freedom from all of this, and deliver its promise in spades. By the 90's we would learn the most painful lesson of all. Freedom, as with everything in life, has its price.

I couldn't see Arnold that afternoon as his secretary, while he still had one, had informed me that he was on an all-day project out of the building. It was probably just as well, because that day had already taken its toll and perhaps, as a result, our conversation might not have been all it should.

I decided, I'd seen enough of Manhattan for that day. After all, in a few short hours, I'd written-off a daughter and a friend. That was enough.

By the time I reached the quiet peace of my small but tidy beach apartment, I felt exhausted, drained. It was around 5 pm, but it felt like midnight. Climbing slowly the small stairs outside my door, I heard the ringing of a phone. The day was not yet over. It continued as I opened the door and flung my briefcase onto my small couch. Purposely moving with the speed of Steppin Fetchit didn't seem to quiet it. Its persistence finally won.

My former mother-in-law possessed all of the feminine charms of a bull moose when angered, and although I knew a heart lurked under that Neapolitan armor-plate, I also knew I wasn't going to be the one to find it. Of course she had been right to try and quelch the relationship between her daughter and myself, but the very fact that she tried so hard was among the reasons it continued. The one thing that you never want to tell "youth" is that they "can't." It's a certain guarantee that they will, if for no reason but to prove you wrong.

Now she was on the phone, and again telling me I'd better not THINK about backing out of the petition I had signed, as though that thought had even crossed my mind. Again she was waving a verbal finger into my face, proving she hadn't learned much in that department. This time, however, there would be no fight. In an effort to ease the tension through the wires, I asked her why she still felt compelled to scream at me over the phone? For that attempt I was rewarded by a quick hang-up.

With other things than her temper tantrums on my mind, I slipped out of my jacket, threw my loosely fitted tie over a chair and withdrew a Coke from the refrigerator. With a bottle of that most famous soft-drink in my hand, I sat just looking out over my ocean, glancing to the left at the children's carousel still in operation as the season was not yet over. The shafting of Arnold Albinski kept coming to the forefront. There was nothing I could do for him other than offer a few words of condolence. His credentials kept zooming in and out of my brain, and a reminder that even forty years meant little in a business that considered everyone expendable. Combining the loss of his wife and his career, and mixing it lightly with the temperament of his art had me puzzling as to what he would do. It also made me wonder what I would do under the same bleak set of circumstance. No answer appeared, but before it had time, again the phone rang. Assuming it was a second barrage from my first caller, I answered it awaiting round two.

To my pleasant surprise it was my former wife, whose voice relaxed my apprehension. She was either aware of her mother's call or knew that bull moose well enough to know she would. As she had been doing from the day we met, she apologized for "Mother's" behavior. I assured her it wasn't necessary, and after a few words of comfort in both directions, she bid me a pleasant, worry-free night. One thing she did so well was care.

In the third act of trying to relax, I took a hit off my Coke, and dosed my face in cold water from the tap in the sink, making up my mind that nothing would move me out of here right now.

Between the traffic in and on the way out of the city, the events of the day, and the climax of a severe telephone chastising, the day had been full enough. Once I locked the door to my private safe haven, nothing but nothing would motivate me into setting foot even one inch beyond that door. I thought of taking the phone off the hook, but then, it was the only method by which either my mother or grandmother could reach me should an honest crisis occur. What the hell. I left it alone figuring I'd heard from the worst of them who was left?

It rang again, almost in answer to my question. This time I answered just a bit more gruffly as I was becoming more than casually annoyed. "House of melody and madness, it's your three minutes." The voice on the other end seemed unsure of my identity.

"Peter?," was all she had to say.

I wasn't certain, although I should have been, and answered the only way I knew how.

"Yes"

"Hi" came the voice. No further introduction was necessary. With a most certain lift to my spirit, I returned the same.

"Oh Hi"

"Are you busy?" Marilyn asked.

I managed a simple "No" rather than to elaborate on what had transpired, and before offering additional dialogue, the question came.

"Can you come and get me?," she sighed, with more than a hint of frustration in her voice Completely unprepared for this kind of question, and in near shock over the words, I answered in what seemed the only logical way I could.

"Are you alright?"

Without even a slight pause, she answered, "I'm alright, but I have to get out of here. I need to see you."

I think it was the word "need" that did it.

During our time, I would become used to phone calls of this type and substance, but this was the first and I wasn't sure of just what it all meant. There was an urgency to Marilyn's question that could have been answered in one way only. So much for barricading myself in against the world. On a night I honestly don't think I would have walked across the street for a hot dog, there I was, back in traffic returning to the very city I had just left. So much for resolves.

The air was still quite warm, and with the top down, it really wasn't as much a chore as I would have imagined. Traffic on the Long Island Expressway had thinned as it was too late for those who may have been heading home, and too early for those who may have been going out for the evening.

With the strains of Paul Anka and Connie Francis on the radio, I began thinking that maybe I was stepping into something over my head. Had it been anyone else, there may have been reason for such thoughts, but it seemed with Marilyn, somehow we had already gotten by all that. She hadn't demanded that I come for her, she had asked. What, after all, are friends for? The "mystique" of Marilyn Monroe had already been put to rest in the park only a few days ago. This was simply the act of one person calling to another. It was no big deal. As agreed, I arrived at the curb just outside The Stage Delicatessen and waited. I could see Max slicing his world famous sandwiches through the window. As this was the beginning of the dinner hour, business was brisk. What a gold mine this place was. As the top of the car was still down, he spotted me, waved and then turned toward someone behind him. He then offered a "wait-a-minute" gesture with his hands which made me think for a moment of just how many New Yorkers spoke with hand language.

Carrying that thought a bit further, I wondered how the city could exist without this hand language. Whether you spoke or kept silent, your hands always kept moving. Where would we all be if some unseen invisible force suddenly tied all our hands behind our backs? Before I could elaborate on this temporary nonsense, Marilyn suddenly burst through the door.

Her clothes and makeup were a mixed match, and a startling one at that. Her face, fully made-up was the "Marilyn" face. Her contrasting wardrobe was a pair of slacks and a jacket that would have been more suitable for a hike in the woods than a night on the town. A kerchief covered her head, and sun-glasses, lightly tinted, her eyes. It was the look of someone who may have started going some place, and then changed her mind. Of course, Marilyn had already become an expert at just that. It wasn't as though she offered disrespect, she just, sometimes, got tired of doing what others expected her to do. For that moment, I had no idea what all this meant as we were still learning about each other, but, here we both were so what else mattered?

She slid into the car and offered me a glance, followed by the request, "Just drive", which I did to Max's wave. Almost immediately after pulling from the curb, she removed those sunglasses and her kerchief allowing her hair to blow in the early evening breeze, freeing her from the restraints of both. With the lights of Broadway in the background and all around us, and she in the foreground, I yearned for my Rollie stuffed somewhere in my closet. Two of the greatest sights the world had to offer, with the greatest of the great seated beside me. Driving in Manhattan offers enough confusion when you know where you are going. When you don't, that confusion is intensified. For the first few moments she continued to glance over her shoulder as if expecting someone to be following. For those moments, I chose not to ask any questions. After circling Times Square three times, however, the logical question could not be kept silent.

"Where are we going?", I asked, in what seemed a reasonable question.

"Just away from here," she said, offering an insufficient answer.

"Any particular place in mind?" I continued.

"Can we just go home?" she said matter-of-factly forcing my hand to suddenly squeeze the steering wheel. Trying to remain calm and honestly only imagining what she meant, logic still continued.

"Whose home?", I asked, not wishing to offend.

With that came a look that would become most familiar. Marilyn had overcome the hand-language with eye language. Those blues, greens and light grays said it all.

With a lump in my throat the size of a bowling ball, I swung out of the loop and headed for the Queens Midtown Tunnel, narrowly missing a bus in the process. With the music of The Platters "Great Pretender" providing an underscore that would forever remind me more of she and I than anything since or before, we headed out to the island.

As images of Marilyn appear in all parts of the world in this ninth decade of our soon passing century, it must be difficult to perceive of such a scene. There must appear to be a dream-like quality to it, something un-real and un-touchable. This unreality is only as a result of where the world has suddenly placed her. She wasn't any icon or legend back then. We were both active in the same business, so even though she was definitely a known personality, even the term "movie star" didn't do her justice. This wasn't something you buy, an ashtray, a plate or a poster. This was someone you cherish. Someone who breathed just like you do. Someone who made you feel

ten feet tall and able to conquer anything. This was someone very real in a world that had become less.

Inviting her into my small apartment first affected me
as would inviting Queen Elizabeth into my bathroom.
Marilyn soon ended that worry, as there wasn't an ounce
of pretense to this girl, not a trace of snobbery. She
removed her jacket and immediately moved to the window to observe my ocean, commenting "This is very
peaceful, I'll bet it's a big help to your work."

Picking her jacket from the chair I hung it in the closet
offering her a double-edged answer.

"Not only my work, but somedays, my life"   This particular day would have been the best example of that. As
there was no book of instructions on what to do next, I
slumped down into a chair and just observed her gazing
from the window. She turned from that gaze, smiled and
playfully asked, "Do I make you nervous?"

I answered with a directness that surprised even me,
"Yes!"

Under the jacket which now hung in my closet, she was
wearing a loose fitting sweater and no bra. Apparently
when she changed her mind about whatever she had
been readying for, she changed her mind about that little
article of clothing as well. This, of course, helped make
me nervous. Had I been worldly and sophisticated, I suppose I could have handled all of this with dispatch, but
for the moment I was Tom Ewell in The SEVEN YEAR
ITCH. Had I known then what I would come to know,
Marilyn was well aware of this. She played at it. She
enjoyed it because she knew you did.

She would then do something in the very next minute
that would contrast and compliment the teasing she may
have begun. On this night, she simply moved from the
window, and knelt beside me, leaning her head on my
knee. I found myself stroking her hair in an automatic

gesture as though I had done it a thousand times before. It was her saying, silently, "I am me, and it is by choice that I am here. If what I am makes you happy, then I'll be happy knowing you are."

The blonde hair, of course, was her own creation. It came as part of the package. On the surface you would hardly consider it having any special merit of its own, but strangely it did. On the nights when she wasn't there, it became a strong and very real part of her memory. During the longest night of all, the one that still exists, so often do I desire to stroke it again. Perhaps, in the grander scheme of things, someday I will.

"Are you mad at me?" she asked from her kneeling position on the floor.

"Mad at you?"

"For calling, and assuming you'd drop whatever you might have had planned...." she said.

The thought of having anything planned that would even compare, much less be more important than this, brought a smile to my face that seemed to please her.

"There's a question for which not enough time exists to answer." I said, not even aware of saying it but rather thinking out loud. "What are friends for?" I concluded.

She hugged my leg for that answer. Unconsciously I had answered one for myself. The whole thing had happened so fast with almost no time to think about it. And now, in the most unlikely of settings, it all seem so damned natural. What was, for an instant, overwhelming, was now simply gratifying. There was such a wall within me, such a fight against commitment as to become selfishly contradictory to all the laws of life. Somewhere, the author of this scenario had grown tired of watching me hit that wall with a pea-shooter and frustrated over my constant rejection of the only thing in life truly worth having, that same author had brought out the heavy artillery. As frightened as I was, I could feel the wall shake. We remained in that position for a long time leaving all words for someone else. Through all of this outward cloak and dagger drama, we had forgotten dinner, and frankly, under the circumstances, that didn't seem strange. Considering the natural desire that was all about me, it was difficult to suggest an intermission, perhaps it was a cop-out, perhaps the last few bricks on that wall. It would be the last intermission I would ever suggest.

The Pig 'N Whistle restaurant was only a short stroll from my apartment and it offered the "best hamburgers in the world", or so the sign said.

We selected an outside table just beyond a group of trees that shielded us from prying eyes. The music of the carousel could be heard in the background. People of all ages came and went. Many walked right by us. Some even smiled. The approaching shadows of evening prevented detection. As there were no key lights, no cameras, and no confusion, there was no reason to think that the two people who sat eating hamburgers, french fries and onion rings, were anyone other than two very normal, average people. Somewhere I knew we had left "Marilyn Monroe" behind, and Norma Jeane seemed very pleased by that.

No questions had been asked or answered regarding the start of this night, and I suppose Marilyn felt now was as good a time as ever to explain.

"They call them press conferences," she began, taking a healthy bite out of her hamburger, "but they always end up brawls. The first questions are about whatever your next project might be, but in a matter of minutes, they're asking you the color of your undies. They hear only what they want to hear and make mountains out of the mole-hills they see."

"Is it always like that?", I asked.

"Yes", she continued, chewing on a french fry. "They're constantly leading you into questions that can be answered in any of a dozen ways and twisted to suit them. If you talk too much they say you've been drinking. If you say too little they think you're hiding something. If you become angry with them they consider it moody, and if you give up and go along with whatever they suggest, they call you a whore. I just didn't feel like going through that tonight!"

"So you cancelled the interview", I said in what seemed only logical.

Looking suddenly smirk, she answered, "No!" She raised her nose toward the Heavens in a gesture of defiance. "They're all waiting for me at the hotel."

"They're all..." I began to repeat her statement

She giggled a simple "um umm," half at my reaction of surprise.

Trying with difficulty against that giggle to remain controlled I suggested "Won't they be slightly angry?"

"Everybody's always slightly angry at me anyway," she continued, "it'll serve them right!" She would lower her eyes, drop her head slightly in preparation, build for the moment and then let go with the broadest smile you ever saw which often climaxed with a laugh. It was at times like this I would find myself laughing with her. It was catching. For all the heart break that had been hers, and in mutual worlds that had been so serious, we presented to each other, the cure of laughter. It was one of our relationship's greatest assets.

All things between us were answered if given the time with neither ever asking. The laughter had cleared the air for a moment of truth. I never asked. It just needed to be addressed and removed from this most special night. "Old grumpy grumps is in Connecticut, doing whatever Arthur does in Connecticut. Sugar, there's nothing there for me anymore, just in case you might have been wondering."

The thought had crossed my mind, but for more than one reason, I had assumed as much. I knew if it became important, we'd look it in the face.

Somewhat dreamily Marilyn went on, " I don't really think there was ever anything there. Maybe I thought there was, maybe I wanted to believe there was. I was once an idealist, just like you, oh yes. When I first started I wanted to please everybody. I should have said "no" more than I did, but saying "yes" seemed to make them happy. Even the duds, and there were a large number of them. You want to show them you care, even when you don't, and make them feel like they're all the things they think they are, when they're not. Then you have to prove *you're* all the things they think *you* are. That's an impossible job, because you're no different than anybody else. They wait for bells to ring, and maybe for some of them, they do. They get all mixed up in this image thing. Once in awhile one will stick around and become a sometime-friend. The rest, you hardly remember their names."

As had become our custom, we continued our talk through the completion of those world-famous hamburgers, and as a means of allowing those less-than-world-famous onions to settle, we took a stroll on the beach.

Marilyn seemed determined to "talk it out", clear the air of what I may have heard or considered. Words that would form a giant broom to sweep it all away. Conversations drifted in and out of every subject from the orphanage to "Diamonds Are a Girl's Best friend."

"Friends are the most important thing a person can ever have," she said, as the gentle breeze from the ocean rustled her hair, " and they're the hardest things to find. Lovers come and go, and most of them make you feel like you need a bath when they're gone."

As though a genie, finally released from a jar the words

continued. I could feel her need to say them, and saw no reason to interrupt.

Some things were comical, others less so. She would use profanity to highlight a point, generally out of distaste, as though the words themselves provided ammunition for her displeasure.

"There's always somebody around with a camera, waiting for you to bend over, or burp, or show something." She went on, "Every man they spot you with is an "assumed" lover. They never ask, they just "know." That's why, for now at least, we must never go where any camera can find us. Pictures can create storms if they lie or tell the truth. Either way you lose."

Marilyn may not have possessed a mastery of the English language, but through her own experiences, had discovered life with all its tricks. Sometimes, she'd even take the place of the magician, and pull a few tricks of her own.

On that beach, so very long ago, she spoke of it all. She was articulate, candid, and well aware of her own shortcomings. Her most recent triumph, SOME LIKE IT HOT, seemed burned into her memory as incidents that had occurred during this film's production had nearly defeated her. She had been pregnant and feared for that pregnancy as it had already defeated her. It would have been Arthur Miller's child. In itself this was a contradiction as both she and Miller had already begun to fight openly. She became desperately torn between her desire for a child, and what would be the fate of that child if it had survived. For the cameras, Miller's adoration of her was faithfully recorded. The reality was something else.

She became totally confused. Having been there before with DiMaggio, she remembered what it was like to fear every waking hour. Those from her personal life and those from her career pulled at her from different directions. Everybody was telling her what to do. She began forgetting her lines, showing up late. The more this was made an issue, the more an issue it became. She sought the temporary relief of pills, and then booze. Rather than making her problems "go away," these two substitutes for reality only intensified them.

There was discord between she and her co-stars Tony Curtis and Jack Lemmon, as well as a nerve-wracking battle of wits with her director, Billy Wilder. A multi-talented man, Wilder committed the unpardonable sin of any director and lost touch with his star. Unable to recover from the pills of the night before, she would keep Curtis and Lemmon waiting for hours on the set, dressed in women's attire for the film. Wilder would complain of severe back aches and lack of sleep. Lame jokes were circulated about the set and most were aimed at Marilyn. The more hostility fired at her, the more she would forget her lines, her movement, her character. Wilder then resorted to placing cue sheets in and about the set for her to look at. While this sometimes worked, more often it only made her more nervous. Re-take after re-take created even more friction between she and Curtis who were supposed to be lovers in the film. In the background, Miller kept giving her speeches about "being a professional" while coach and friend-of-sorts, Paula Strasberg whispered to her to have the shot taken again. Waiting for all this to resolve itself, even the bit players kept themselves amused by getting drunk. Wilder knew that Marilyn was the money and began spoon feeding her lines upsetting the flow of action for the co-stars. His comments of "never working with her again" reached her ears and hurt her deeply. The kinder remarks by Jack Lemmon after the film that "she was a troubled girl" to the biting and stupid remark by Tony Curtis that "kissing Marilyn was like kissing Hitler," only intensified that hurt, and made things even more confusing. It seemed to her that even those who had something "nice" to say, did it left-handedly.

The film, almost miraculously, became a solid hit despite the swamp of intrigue in its production. If ever the theory of "the illusion of film" was made clear, this was the example for all time.

The public would embrace this hilarious comedy and the stars who made it so. Wilder would add it to his already distinguished credentials. What appeared on the screen was gold. Wilder had been correct in his appraisal as this had become a "Monroe" film. The methods to reach that gold were forgotten by most, as the reviews were most favorable and offered applause to all involved. They were not forgotten by Marilyn.

Contrary to the opinions of many, Marilyn did NOT blame everybody for faults she knew were hers. She blamed circumstance. History will remember SOME LIKE IT HOT as being one of the top films of the century. It will forget its cost to all involved.

The light breeze had grown cold as the night now engulfed us. I found myself zipping her jacket protectively as you might to a child before sending them off to school. As we walked back to my apartment she remarked, "I know it's silly, but sometimes I wish I could start all over again. Things would be different, but I guess we can't do that, can we?"

"Oh I don't know", I said, in an attempt to lighten the mood. For that remark, made so matter-of-factly, she clutched my arm. "Do you think we could?," she said only half-kiddingly.

"Why not," I answered, kissing her lightly on the forehead. Time does have a way of making things seem more clear. Sometimes things said and done most casually, have, within them, a solid truth that escapes us on the first go-round.

I was not a retired baseball hero, or a multi-awarded Pulitzer prized playwrite. I had not yet paid my dues, but was willing. The very youth that had made me feared and also the subject of paranoid jokes, was on my side. When the smoke cleared, that was a fact that defeated them all. Perhaps, in the most incredible of incredible circumstances, I could inject a transfusion of some of that youth back to Marilyn giving her a second chance at something she had never had.

On the way back to my apartment, we stopped at a convenience store, fore runner to those that exist today and not yet given that name, to pick up a couple of bottles of wine. Not being certain of the next step, I allowed the scene to play itself, void of any director or script.

Upon entering my apartment, Marilyn excused herself for a moment. Contrary to the concepts omitted in the films of the 50's, even super-stars had to use the bathroom once in awhile.

I sat my energized body into my chair and gazed out of the window going over the words I had just been hearing. Marilyn had presented to me a wisdom that I could not have known, and had made me acutely aware of just how little I did know about an industry I had been convinced I could conquer. In the purging of her soul, I had learned in a few short hours, realities that had never entered my mind. If youth would be my gift to her, wisdom would be hers to me. We would have, indeed, been an unbeatable couple.

The sound of the shower from the other room first startled me, but then, I thought, "why not?" She was washing off the world. I took this opportunity to move into the kitchen, withdraw two glasses, and improvise a wine bucket from a salad bowl. Not used to entertaining at home, this crude improvisation would have offered no competition to Cary Grant. Like Dracula, I never drank wine, but she had requested it. From that night there would come many things I hadn't ever done, many feelings I had never felt. The heavy artillery was working as I observed the last traces of infatuation pack its bags. There was no time to think of retreat, and frankly, no thoughts of it. If there had been, they would have been interrupted by her appearance in the kitchen. She had removed a shirt from my closet and now wore it as her only clothing. She was clean and scrubbed, and stood there arms extended as though making her entrance on stage accompanying that entrance with a verbal "Ta Taaaa." The scent that I had already associated with her permeated the room. By the brand it was Chanel Number 5, but to me when it mixed with her own body chemicals, it reminded me of a field of lilacs off at a distance. More importantly, what ever it was, it was her.

She came to me, unafraid and I hugged her for just being there. After a moment she moved to the wine, smiled at my improvisation, and poured two glasses. I leaned on the sink just watching her. "Jesus forgive me," I said. "You are certainly something else."

"Yes I am," she replied, handing me my glass.

The wine was good, and the company the best. Finally the words stopped. We sat on the bed toasting each other and those who weren't there whom we felt deserved it.

Had this been a movie, and I the observer, I would have asked "What the hell are you waiting for?" but it was not.

Seated only inches from me was the stuff of all male dreams, and what was I doing? Pouring wine.

For the last few hours I had been listening to stories of those who had found themselves in a similar situation, and also the result of those stories. While there was no question that I wanted her, thoughts of being just another chapter in a book of frustrations crossed my mind.

She knew it. As usual, she was wiser than all of that. I began shaking my head affirmatively as though translating without words, "Ok, here we go, chapter 12." She cupped her hands under my chin and pulled my face close to hers, kissing me lightly, gently. With a smile, she then backed up to observe the reaction. I returned the gesture. From that came another, and another, a testing of the waters. Now laying side by side, the next one lasted. The wall was gone and the carousel stopped completely as did the world.

If love making releases frustrations, then years were released that night. Her lips were as soft as rose petals opening toward the sun, that same sun that had turned them white hot. Her body as smooth as silk, a feel of velvet. As we became familiar with each other, the moments alternated from tenderness to savagery and back. I never so much wanted to swallow a person whole. With every conclusion, would come only a brief intermission, and a new beginning. Immediately grateful for a stamina I didn't know existed, I also found a second to thank my youth. Just what drove her was a mystery. She seemed inexhaustible. Both now soaked in perspiration, it continued. We were literally melting into one another. It can not be translated to the written word. When the final spark of energy had been drained from both of us, we just lay there staring at the ceiling and alternating glances to each other. Sometimes at the most wonderful moments, the dumbest things come to mind. I thought for sure that I would never be able to walk again, and probably neither would she. Someone would find us, weeks later, smiling and dead as a doornail. What the media would do with that!

"You're wrong", I said, still in that frame of mind.

"Wrong?," she questioned in half groggy fashion.

"Definitely!," I continued. " I know I heard at least a

thousand bells!"

She laughed, "Is that all?! I must be slipping!"

I reached for her and pulled her close, kissing her light-ly on the forehead. She fell asleep almost before I had pulled the covers over us. I still hadn't found a name for it, but for now, that seemed unnecessary. All that seemed important was that she was sleeping soundly. All of the tensions, the memories, the victories and defeats were put away, at least for a time. Just as importantly, if not more so, no pills were required.

So often we seek solutions when no problems exist. We look for answers that are just in front of us. We are called "animals of reason," because, I think, that is the one thing we never seem to do.

With all the plans, and all the useless ambition, all the make-believe, all the baloney we feed each other, looking reality in the face seems the hardest thing to do. For me personally, in both remembering and still feeling, my answer to it all slept beside me on that night and would for nights to come. It is, at last, my one indestructible truth.

Chapter Four

Reality Under Fire

Even the lightning bolts of ecstasy give way to the dawn of a new day, and while the scent and memory lingers on, the hum-drum of reality slides neatly back into place at the sign of the new sun. Marilyn and I had agreed never to say "goodbye," but instead had chosen the phrase, "until next time." We parted on that next morn near 57th street, and both returned to, what had become, our lives, knowing or at least hoping there would be other days and nights.

The events of the past few days had been slightly over powering, so much so, that by this new day, I began again to question it all. At 22 you still cannot see as clearly as perhaps 32, or even 42. I knew how I felt when she was with me, but when apart, things took on a strange aura of impossibility. What at once seemed desperately real suddenly seemed impossibly contrived. Her star may have slipped a bit, but it had, by no means, fallen. What would be her reason for ME? Sex? Well, okay, but by her own admissions there had been plenty of that already. Someone to talk to? Maybe. Love?, oh please, in 5 days? Only in story books.

I suppose these thoughts were the hangovers of defense. There was an ugly rational about it all. She was safe if this, in fact, was a passing fancy, if in no other way than by simple denial. Who, after all, would have believed the virtual symbol of sexual desire would have selected a "nobody" fledgling writer to run off with? I wouldn't have in the best of days. I decided to place this flight of fantasy on the back burner, and try and see it in its true perspective. It was fun! It was nice. Something to someday tell my grandchildren as they fed me my Geritol. By then they would say, "Marilyn who?," and the memory of that one great night would return to be last and finally my own.

Long before the late great film director Tony Richardson would frame so beautifully the plight of the defamed artist in a scene so well constructed in his production of THE LOVED ONE, a scene in which an aging film director simply dives into an empty pool, realities of this sort were already a part of this industry. Arnold Albinski was a prime candidate for such a scene, and that thought, whether valid or invalid, occupied my mind as the first piece of business for that day, dwarfing, for the moment, my recent impossible fling. His studio was located on a different floor than those I frequented graphically separating "art" from "unimportant hum-drum." On my entrance to his "gallery," I found him already putting his studio in order. Arnold was "old" world. He "ate" and "slept" tradition. His was a world of integrity and flare already removed from what the actual world had become. I found him neatly arranging the tools of his trade surrounded by vivid colorful examples of his work. He stopped immediately upon seeing me and as was his custom, greeted me with a hug.

There was little need for words as my expression had already announced the reason for my visit. The men and women of his generation were made of stronger stuff, and weeping and whining were not part of any of it. Whether right or wrong, they accepted, at least on the surface, the inevitable, and dealt with it proudly. As we moved into his studio with both of us admiring his work now staring down from the frames of another time, he seemed more concerned over my somewhat beginning career than his own which, in effect, was ending.

Almost Christ-like he seemed so willing to forgive those

who had pounded the nails and put off their actions and rumors as their own weaknesses, more to be pitied than scorned. For myself, and had it been to me that the slings and arrows had been targeted, I would have subscribed to the "punch 'em in the face" approach as my retaliation. Not so with Arnold.

I asked him what he intended doing now, as 55 by no means was old. With a smile and casual flick of his hand, he suggested possibly Europe..perhaps honest art, and maybe more visits to more concerts. There was no inference to diving head-first into an empty pool.

In his concern for me, he pleaded that I profit from this by never permitting it to happen. He underlined, most emphatically, that I "watch my back," and that I never bring my personal life into this building. The term, "building" of course used to refer to my job in general.

Between Marilyn's comments of the night before and Arnold's this morning, I indeed began to wonder why anyone, including myself, would ever want to BE in this business in the first place when its rewards were so out numbered by its blatant disregard for the human spirit.

Whether the symbol of international beauty and sex, or the aging gifted poet of a behind-the-scenes craft, both seemed reduced to hamburger in the less than grandness of it all. It was no wonder that "neurotic" had become the middle name of so many, and paranoia, the chief by-product of the whole mess.

Rather than return immediately to my own part of the building, considering the mood I was in, I elected, instead, to grab a Kaiser roll and some coffee in a nearby favorite restaurant. Again, more out of habit than need, I picked up the trades and began scanning them with my coffee and roll, not particularly caring, for the moment, what was doing "Boffo Biz in Boston."

SOME LIKE IT HOT was continuing its dizzy climb to

the top, but after hearing about its production problems, its drama within the drama, and its echoing effect on one particular lady, now wasn't the best time for me to give it the applause it may have been due.

As a matter of fact, now wasn't the best time for me to do anything especially after having just left the death cell of Arnold Albinski as he prepared for his execution. I had no way of knowing at that second, that things were about to get worse.

Within the confines of the walled world in which we labored was a certain kind of enigmatic personality known as "the gossip columnist." In earlier days, classy old dolls like Hedda Hopper and Louella Parsons, made it an art. Their "inside" scoops on "who's doing what in show biz," became popular with the fans. Many times the studios would actually encourage them to spread it around to build a certain star within the system. Being busy bodies at heart, once in awhile they would get carried away with their own importance and slip up, creating minor bouts of chaos. Beneath their outrageous hats and clothes, they were basically harmless.

But now, in this year of 1959, a new breed of insect had emerged, spawned in a cesspool and hatched from a cocoon that had survived on the waste product of man. The resulting bug was a character on the lowest rung of the journalistic ladder. Dangerous, insidious and maligning, the ancestor of those today who honestly feel the O.J. Simpson trial is an example of justice. In the name of "reporting," they infect all those who read, listen or observe their brand of verbal scum much like a cancer, with about the same result. They capitalize on human weakness, and drive it into the ground. They laugh at tributes, and find humor in sadness. Their contribution to the human race is to find fault and weakness in everything, and everyone. They are the living personification of evil as their target is the soul.

Willy was a master at his craft. A rotund little man who physically resembled comedian Joe Besser. He wore an ever plastic smile, dressed in early mail order, and was as lethal as any King Cobra. He free-lanced for a gossip newspaper that appeared bi-weekly in supermarkets, on street corners, and in back alleys. A pioneer in one of today's most successful businesses. The business of sleeze. He had a gift, much like a safe cracker, but while the thief steals only money, Willy stole lives. He was Jack The Ripper with a pen, both feared and despised, and at this moment, he was heading my way. It was by no means an accidental meeting, as nothing Willy ever did was by accident. Placing his beat-up briefcase by his side, and with no invitation, he sat his fat ass down at my table. With a bravado snap of his fingers, he ordered coffee from a passing waitress, and proceeded to stare at me with a most devilish gleam in his eye. After the standard, "good morning Peter," "good morning Willy," he got right down to it.

"I've been waiting for you Peter," he began, "habits are my best friends, and I know you have coffee here at least 3 days out of 5."

I'm convinced my reaction of disgust was responsible for changing his smile to a frown.

"What do you want, Willy," I asked, finally permitting him an excuse for his surprise.

"What do I want?', he echoed, fumbling through his poor excuse for a briefcase . "I want to show you something. "With that remark, he proudly exhibited the latest edition of his "rag" not yet on the newsstand. He would have preferred a reaction, but something inside of me shifted into protective overdrive. I gave the cover a casual look, a non-committal glance, while inside, rockets had already been launched in my brain. The headline read,

"THE NEW MAN IN MONROE'S LIFE," below which was one of those doctored pictures that showed nothing but insinuated everything. Oh it was Marilyn, dressed in evening wear and on the arm of someone whose face had been conveniently blurred. Of course it wasn't me, because no such scenario had to that point, taken place. Beads of perspiration began appearing on Willy's face as his squinty puffed-up little eyes focused closely at my observance of the picture. One spark, one tell-tale deep breath or twinge of the lip, would have been all he needed. It was a poker game and I was holding a Royal Flush, not something I wanted my opponent to see.

"Very nice, Willy," I said. "Why show this to me?" To give him a double chance, I looked at the cover again. It was typical. The "mystery picture" was in the middle flanked by insets of DiMaggio and Miller in appropriate corners. Hardly original.

"Yeah," he rasped, "Take a real good look." One of the less appealing aspects of Willy's profession was the need for his constant looking over his shoulder. He, like most of his kind, was a coward and would run at the first sign of confrontation. Those who hadn't run fast enough, might just end up sipping sewage at the bottom of the East River. It was a very real occupational hazard. Willy had done his homework and knew all about my short fuse. Word gets around. His position on the chair had conveniently placed the table between us. That too was no accident. With an internal fire building inside of me, I thought I did rather a good job of remaining calm. My voice gave me away, probably because it was coming through gritted teeth.

"Okay, Willy," I began, "I didn't invite you here, but you sat your fat ass down anyway. Now I looked at your rag, and put up with your body odor all I'm going to. It's time for you to leave."

He sat further back keeping his distance and was momentarily intimidated, but, without thinking, I was making the wrong moves. I should have laughed it off. My anger substantiated his accusative suggestions.

"It's you, Peter!" he grinned, now working up a sweat. "Maybe not the picture, but it's you. I know it and you know it." It was obvious that one of Willy's "eyes," his team of hired snakes, had seen us in the park. As innocent as that particular day was, we were together, and to a mind like Willy's, sharing a pretzel is incrimination enough.

I remembered Marilyn's speech on "cameras," and knew her inner fears of being tabloid news for any reason because of that Miller script. She had so convinced herself that this then untitled script would vindicate her from that "Bugs Bunny" image, that her fears of anything standing in its way represented nightmares to her. They were already engaged in open warfare, which included battles in public, but she felt Arthur would still try to please her, to win her back with that literary work. It was her thought that if he discovered another man in the picture, especially a younger one than he, it might have been the straw. Personally I felt it was an unnecessary game, but she hadn't asked for anything else. Maybe the whole thing was an excuse to keep us secret for reasons known only to her. Maybe all sorts of things, but the fact remained, this weasel sitting before me was on to something that could have been most upsetting to Marilyn, and that alone was reason enough to find a way out.

Willy's "shock approach" then gave way to a second, kinder, more "sympathetic" one, which I confess threw me a curve.

"We don't have to fight about this, Peter," he began. "Maybe we could work together, turn it around, let the public hear your side."

"You play a dirty game with people, Willy," I answered, "and some day it's going to come back and hit you right between the eyes."

He sat back in his chair now wearing the look of a man who is forever misunderstood. A really nice guy just doing his job. The Cobra performing to music, taking the victim off guard.

"I met her one day at the park and walked her to her acting lesson," I said, "that's it. Period. There's no story here Willy. She's had some bad breaks lately. Planting something like this is only going to hurt her."

The smile on his face alerted me to the repugnant fact that I was only building his case. Trying to appeal to legitimate reasoning was only tightening the noose, and if I didn't just shut-up, I'd only make it worse.

"Public figures expect this kid," he went on, now grinning from ear to ear, "It's part of the game. That lady sells papers. That's my job. You and she were together. What you did together will be up to my readers to decide. Thanks for the confirmation."

"Take a walk, Willy," I said, now angered at myself for assuming there was an ounce of decency in this low-life. He rose from his seated position, and gave me a wink.

"They tell me you're good at what you do," he went on, "Well so am I. If you have anything else to add, you know my number. If you don't, I'll fill in the pieces myself." As I watched his bloated hulk leave the restaurant, several thoughts came to mind, none of which offered me an answer. Marilyn was right. With or without their "Brownies" in hand, people like Willy were always ready to make mountains out of mole hills. It no longer puzzled me as to why she left that group waiting at the hotel with no apologies. Maybe to some it was a game, but Marilyn was on the edge. There was probably a time in her life when she might have laughed this whole thing off but now wasn't that time. If my life had become what she described Miller and she had become, I would have ended it. I would have walked. None of it made sense to me. No script would have been worth this. Somehow she had gotten this "serious drama" thing all twisted around. Miller may have been reduced to "puppy-dog" status in their so called home, but to the sophisticates in the world of theatre, his name still meant something. An Arthur Miller play was something that appealed to that special audience of appreciative snobs who would never darken the doorway of a theatre showing a thing called " THE SEVEN YEAR ITCH." An Arthur Miller screenplay would only broaden that audience.

Walking my beach that night only confused the entire issue. Attempting to sleep in a bed that still had her scent all about it, only made it more difficult. I thought about using that private number, but with Willy's latest edition hitting the streets on the next morning, I rejected the idea. It was certainly too late to stop the lead article, but Willy's planted intros always led to continuing articles. There had to be a way to turn this around, but at this moment, just how completely threw me.

It had been two days since Willy's unexpected assault on my senses. Since that morning I hadn't slept, and work seemed the furthest thing from my mind. The more I would try and convince myself that this was none of my business, the more it became just that. Before the die is officially cast, all of us permit the rationalization of a back-door to creep quietly into our minds. Self-preservation zooms to the fore front, and weak alibis attempt to justify the coward in all of us. We speak about caring, but only seem to perform the act when no threat is offered. We volunteer understanding when we know it won't be needed. We pledge loyalty when we feel it won't be tested. A man named Judas proved that a long time ago.

I began feeling a slight resentment toward Marilyn for bringing me into this nonsense. Friendship was one thing, but this, well this was something else. I mean, what we did was fun. We had a great couple of days and one great night, but it didn't call for this.

The justification goes on, and soon you begin to buy it. Once that happens, the problems go away and the back door opens. She'd get through it. She got through everything. She told me so. I was the one making a mountain out of a mole hill. The whole thing started looking just a bit ridiculous.

Finally on Thursday of that week, tired of thinking, plotting, condemning and excusing, I dropped off to sleep around 6pm. Tomorrow I would go back to work, and that would be that. So much for self deception.

At first the ringing sounded distant, a part of whatever I may have been dreaming in this dead sleep of exhaustion. It continued until my mind connected the fact that it was my telephone. A look at the clock through half-closed eyes denoted the hour. With thoughts of "who the hell would be calling at 2:45 in the morning" I reluctantly picked up the receiver.

"Peter, is that you?" came the tiny, near inaudible voice from what seemed like a million million miles away. The words dragged very slowly, almost "sing-song" as though the bearer of the voice had been as much in sleep as I. "I know it's late..." Marilyn continued.

I don't know what it was. Concern, a premonition, guilt, a feeling. I just knew something had gone wrong. Very wrong. My brain snapped to attention. No trace of sleep or the need for it remained.

"Marilyn, where are you..?" I asked, already slipping on my pants and holding the receiver under my chin.

"I'm sorry," she continued in that slow, terrifying rhythm, "I know it's very late..."

"Damn it, Marilyn, forget the 'late' business," I snapped, "where the hell are you?"

"Don't be mad at me," she continued.

"I'm not mad, just tell me where you are." I said, continuing to dress. Then came the worst response and one I didn't want to hear.

"I'm not sure" she said. I am certain the anxiety of my voice and repetition of my asking the same question finally got through to her. I heard the faint rustle of papers as though she were looking for something to identify her location. "The Berkeley Hotel, it says here...," she said, and then as if remembering, "Oh yes... The... Berkeley...Hotel..." Her voice was fading and my pulse racing.

"What room?," I asked now in a state of desperation.

"Room?" came the fuzzy reply.

"Your room number! Please Marilyn, don't go to sleep!! Give me your room number!"

"Oh," she continued, then after what seemed like an eternity, "631..it's room 631."

"Ok, I got it," I repeated "631. Marilyn, can you hear me?"

"I hear you my darling friend" she said.

"I'm on the way!," I blurted. From that came the deafening sound of silence. I am certain I broke at least a dozen laws that early morning as I raced through town, onto the expressway, and into and out of the tunnel. Towns, lights, houses and billboards blurred as I raced by them. My thoughts too were running a race. I cursed my own weakness, and damned my mind for being nothing I'd said I was.

It's hard to soul search when the speedometer of your car reads 110 drifting to 120, the top of the dial. The Long Island Expressway had sections of straight road, but there were also turns. At that speed, one wrong touch of the wheel and all your problems would be over. Pontiac had used in their sales pitch, "wide-track," which they claimed held your car on the road. I prayed that for once Madison Avenue wasn't exaggerating.

Subconsciously I also thanked the merchants of sleeze, because had they not made so much of Marilyn's pill habits, maybe I wouldn't have considered the grimness of this certain possibility. In and out of my thoughts came the constant prayer to someone I hoped was listening, "Please don't let her die."

I also asked for the power and faith to stop trying to label everything as though all honesty had an angle. As though whatever love was appeared on page 32 in a Sears catalog.

The Berkeley Hotel was one of those stately old digs from another age that had somehow avoided the ball of destruction and still managed to maintain a small degree of past integrity in a world that was rapidly going plastic. The tools of construction were all around it as repairs were constantly necessary. Somehow I had maneuvered down a then sleeping Lexington Avenue still at a speed far above any that were posted, and no member of New York's finest had been there to stop me. Narrowly missing a parked bulldozer, I steamed into the parking garage of the hotel in a hail of flying dirt and rocks. Entering the lobby on a run, I observed only one desk clerk reading a magazine. Either he was dead or completely engrossed in that magazine, because he didn't look up at my entrance. Rather than risk the old elevator, I decided to take the stairs, hoping against hope that the room number she had given me was correct.

There were times when youth counted for more than work or sex, when stamina fired you up six long flights of stairs. One thought flashed on me that may have come too late. Instead of riding here on my white horse, maybe I should have called the emergency hospital. Maybe this stupid attempt to keep publicity from her would cost her life.

Maybe, for all the reasons that seemed right, I had finally done the wrong thing. There was no more time to consider the "maybe's" as I reached the door to 631. Of course it was locked. Pounding on the door would certainly wake the whole floor.

Trying a stunt I had written into scripts and seen in other movies, I slipped one of my credit cards between the door and the frame by the lock. If this contrived attempt hadn't worked, I would have reverted to plan number two and kicked the damned thing down. It wouldn't work today as hotel rooms are now constructed to avoid such an entrance. By a miracle, this silly bit of theatrics worked on the door of room 631. On opening the door, I saw her, sprawled face down on the bed, dressed only in a slip, her hand clutching a pillow. I immediately sat down beside her and felt her pulse again offering a silent prayer.

A slight sigh ebbed from her sleeping body. Unexplained tears suddenly ran from my eyes, which I wiped onto my sleeve at the same time lifting her gently with my arms, holding her now in those arms and calling quietly to her.

"Marilyn, Marilyn honey it's me" I kept saying wiping her head with my hand now almost giddy with the fact that the worst had not happened. She made an attempt to open her eyes and uttered only "Hi.." before closing them again.

I propped her in a half-seated position, leaning her against as many pillows as I could find. I left her only for a moment to run cold water on a wash cloth and returned. Holding her again, I began wiping her face and the back of her neck. Glancing to the bed stand I spied the empty pill bottle with its innocent label suggesting, "Take two for sleep."

"Fuck 'em all," was all I could think to whisper to the so-called "friends" and doctors who continued to supply these God-damned things knowing the strain she had been under. I hadn't yet discovered that Miller was among them. If I had known, I would have personally called Willy and dictated the scoop he was after in the first person!

The cold wash cloth was doing some good, but it wouldn't be enough. Still seated on the bed, I grabbed the phone and dialed, hoping the clerk I had passed was finished with his magazine and could be of some help.

"Is there anywhere that I can get some coffee?" I asked. The feminine sounding voice of the so-called masculine clerk answered, "Are you serious? At 3:30 in the morning?"

At the risk of frightening this delicate creature, I suggested a coffee shop, a "White Castle," anything, to which came the uninterested reply, "Don't be outrageous!"

Feeling in my pocket and checking that I had even remembered to bring any money, and finding that I had, I suggested as calmly as I could, that I would give fifty dollars for a couple of cups of coffee, offering some lame excuse of being hung-over and needing it.

There was a sudden dead silence on the other end. To some people in 1959, fifty-dollars was a weeks wages. After a few more nervous seconds, he returned to the phone. "I'll see what I can do," he said and hung up.

I continued to soak the cloth and return to Marilyn, all the while considering the possibility that this character might have been going for coffee or perhaps the police. All I could do was hope for the former. The cold cloth was beginning to annoy Marilyn who tried to pull away from it. I didn't care because as long as she was annoyed, she wasn't asleep. Finally the knock on the door came. Moving from the bed to the door, I spoke before opening, "Yes?"

The clerk's voice answered, "I found some coffee."

At the risk of staring at a badge and maybe even a .45, I opened the door slowly. He stood there with a pot and a cup on a tray.

"It's from room service," he said somewhat timidly, "They close at eleven, but they leave this on for me. It's not very hot, but it's the best I can do."

In times of crisis, you do find some strange allies.

I gratefully handed him the fifty-dollars, relieved him of the tray, thanked him, and closed the door as he struggled to peer over my shoulder.

After pouring the coffee into the cup, I returned to Marilyn and lifted her head gently. As carefully as possible, I guided the cup to her lips.

"Come on beautiful, take a swig," I whispered, praying that she would, " Come on, just a sip."

Reluctantly she did, and then another, making a sour face which brought a smile to mine.

Never underestimate the power of caffeine. It might not have been "Chock Full Of Nuts," but it began doing the job. After a few more sips, I placed the cup on the bed-stand, put my arms around her, sat her up and lowered her feet to the floor. I then lifted her to those feet and together we began to walk about the small room. Marilyn had to weigh somewhere around one hundred and ten pounds, but under the influence, for this moment, she felt like two hundred and fifty. I placed her arm around my neck and my arm around her waist, and we walked...and walked...

"Let's you and I take a walk around the park," I said thinking of anything, however dumb, to say. At this point, I would have recited the alphabet to keep her attention.

She fought it. I tried to relate what she was feeling by remembering my own awakening process after surgery. The difference , of course, is that I had been surrounded by qualified doctors and nurses. Marilyn was surrounded only by me. I kept asking my untrained mind to do what was right and hoped it was listening. Images flashed in and out of my brain. Like so many millions of people, she had enticed me from that big screen. Her beautiful image had made people smile, and laugh, her voice had made them sing. For the short time they'd spend with her, their problems went away. She could make them dream again. To the studio she had become a multi-million dollar property. To the world, someone they felt they knew. The girl they had voted, most likely to be someone very special.

At this moment, I held her life in my hands, and none of that hype meant a thing.

Somewhere Joe DiMaggio slept, as did Arthur Miller, Billy Wilder and the rest of them. As they slept, Marilyn walked to stay alive, fighting a drug that called her to sleep.

"I don't want to walk anymore, Peter, I just want to sit down," she said.

"No, baby," I answered as gently as I could, "You can't sit down, not just yet... Come on, one step at a time." I had never used the term "baby" before. It sounded so phoney, something from a "B" gangster film, or something from the mouth of someone who might have been too hip for his own good. I didn't like it, but, for so many reasons, it fit Marilyn. It just slipped out because that is what she was. For all her gutsy dialogue, and all the battles she had to fight alone, she was the most vulnerable person I would ever know.

I made a lot of decisions that night, some without being aware of them. The streets of Brooklyn were about to pay off. The "hard-edge," the roughness, wasn't for my work. For the days and nights we would be together, no one with trouble on their mind would get anywhere near her. If they'd try, they'd wish their fathers had never met their mothers.

She continued to follow my instructions against the drug's inner calling, telling her brain that all she had to do to feel better, was to lay down and close her eyes. It was an exhibition of trust, something that almost always takes longer to establish. A supporting of one for the other, with no strings attached and no questions asked. I don't remember just how long we walked. It seemed like we made it to Cleveland. I had opened the windows of this old elephant, and the city air, stagnant or not, was helping.

Finally there was a change. A look came over her face which signaled a detour to the bathroom. Quickly kneeling by the commode, her stomach gave up its contents which included the coffee and remainder of the pills. I knelt beside her continuing to wipe her face and lips with the wash cloth "I think we've discovered a new cure for this thing," I said attempting to lighten the load, "Stale, warm, rotten coffee."

She shook her head in silent agreement.

When she had finished, I guided her back to bed, and returned to the bathroom for the clean-up. In that same clean-up I saw enough undigested pills to have ended more than one person's dreams that night. Returning to the bed, I propped her back into a sitting position. She was beginning to honestly wake. Those beautiful eyes would see again. For me, there would be no more doubts, no more excuses, and no more looking for any back doors. I didn't have to put a name to it, it had named itself.

I watched her return to me as I sat on the bed beside her, holding her hand.

"Olivier used to say, as his answer for everything, "Be

sexy Marilyn," she said, temporarily feeling an unnecessary embarrassment, "How's this for sexy?"

"To me, you never looked better," I answered, without the slightest hesitation.

She reached her hand to my face, pushing my own hair from my eyes. I hadn't thought about my appearance. There hadn't been time. In fact, there had been less time than even I thought.

"That was dumb, wasn't it," she said, now becoming more alert with each passing minute, and probably observing my concern for the first time.

"Why did you do it, honey," I said, no longer holding feelings in my back pocket. .".and this place. How'd you ever find it?"

"Are you mad at me," she asked, ignoring both questions.

"Yes," I said, in a tone less than condescending.

"All I wanted to do is get some sleep!"

"Well you damned near got a very long sleep. You up-chucked enough of those God-damned pills to knock out a bull elephant. Why?, Marilyn, honey, why?"

"I lost count," she said timidly. "Great," I said, now somewhat sarcastically. "Well you almost lost more than that!" Her eyes kept looking at me, now sad eyes, eyes that always said it all. A strong urge came over me just to hold her in my arms and whisper "it's all right." But it wasn't, and wouldn't be until certain ground rules were established. All her life she had been subjected to lectures for her behavior. Lectures from James Dougherty, her first husband, lectures from Joe DiMaggio, and, from Arthur Miller, all of whom, of course, were so well "qualified" to offer them.

She'd had enough of these lectures.

"Well one thing" I began in place of a lecture, " You don't have to worry about this age difference thing anymore. Tonight I caught up." The traces of a first smile crossed her lips. That was good enough for me.

"I must look a sight," she said, now considering the obvious.

"It wouldn't be the best time for an interview," I answered. Now smiling that complete smile, she countered, " It wouldn't be?"

"No," was the final period on that sentence.

"How did you ever find me?," she said. "You don't know?" I asked. A simple shaking of the head was answer enough to that. "You called me." I answered, "Don't you remember? " Again she shook her head, and that thought alone was a frightening one.

"That's great. This thing gets better every minute," I said now concerned more than ever. "What if I hadn't been there? What if I hadn't heard the phone? What if you hadn't reached out? You want anymore 'what if's'?" Continuing to gain awareness, she again shook her head.

"Honey, I'm no good at this," I began, "This is not something I wanted. You came along and upset a finely crafted, well-planned campaign. This "moon, June, spoon" thing is new to me, and I'm not sure I'm going to be any good at it. But, I'm going to try, and I'm going to begin right now by telling you that you are very important to me."

Again she ran her hand through my hair and I began to hope I was getting through to her.

"You still haven't told me what triggered this off, and what you're doing in this place?"

"My mouth tastes like..." she said, interrupting the chain of thoughts, and, of course, questions.

I stopped. Stepped into the bathroom, and came back with a glass of water.

"Just sip it," I said, " Don't chug-a-lug it"

As moisture returned to her mouth, she began "We had a fight, a real doozy," she continued, " It started over the stupid headlines of one of those gossip sheets. You may have seen it."

Of course I had, and indeed had met its author.

She went on..."It wouldn't have been so bad, things like that always happen, except in this article, if you can call it that, the last line said, 'to be continued'..."

That part I didn't know, but could have guessed.

"It isn't as if he was hurt. We stopped hurting each other a long time ago. We've actually run out of excuses to fight, and when something like this comes along, it gives us a new excuse. When it passes, all I want to do is sleep it off. It is the most empty feeling a person can have. I found out a long time ago, that if I go to bed, he'll come back in and continue it. I don't have enough pillows to hide under. He goes on a talking binge. He'll actually wake me up to keep talking." She took another sip of water, and continued, now wishing to make a complete breast of it. "I found this quiet hotel about a year ago, after one of those knock-downs. They mind their own business. You can register under whatever name you want. You pay them in cash, and they leave you alone. Until tonight it's been, what you would call, a workable plan."

"How does your 'just leaving' affect Arthur?," I asked, offering what I thought to be a logical question.

"When I come back, and so far I always have, there's a bouquet of flowers waiting for me." Her voice began to quiver slightly as she continued, "Peter, it's the sickest thing I have ever been part of...It's just so wrong, I can't even tell you."

"Why do you stay? Why does HE stay? Why do you continue to beat the hell out of each other?"

She licked her lips and took another swig of water. "Arthur hasn't done one thing in the last five years, and now he's working on this script. He's molded the main character around me, at least the main female character, and it's good. I think he began it hoping that it would bring us together, but now, he knows that can't happen. He's not a stupid man. I think what he feels now is that when this film is completed, we can separate with dignity. Because of that, we stay together. He says I've robbed him of everything else. If that's true, I don't want to rob him of this. "

"And all of this is worth the price?," I asked, now for my own benefit as well as hers.

"Honey, you took enough pills tonight to end your problems and his," I said now thinking out loud, "Is that what you were trying to do?"

"Oh God no," she said, somewhat frightened of the concept, "They just lose their strength after awhile, and you need more to do the job. I just took too many more."

"Right," I said, my thoughts already racing with any number of suggestions. " As I see it, we have two choices. One, now that you're ok, I walk out of here and keep walking."

"Please don't say that," she interrupted.

"Ok," I continued, "then, two, I stop those articles." Tears began to form in her eyes and with them a look of complete despair. " I don't want you to leave..."

"Marilyn, I don't want to leave you." Fighting my own feeling of emptiness even for the thought, I continued. "But I don't want you to go through this again. The next time I might not be by the phone. Don't you see what a close call this was? Don't you see how this must never happen again? We got lucky. That luck might not hold up."

"I don't want you to leave me.." she kept repeating as though not hearing a word I was saying. Finally succumbing to the urge, I reached for her and held her tightly in my arms. She clutched me in an embrace so very tightly as to offer me no choice, if ever there had been one.

With her locked safely in my arms, I whispered into her ear, "I'm not going anywhere. Do you really think I could?

We'll beat this thing. This time you leave the fight to somebody else. You leave it to me. Ok?"

I could feel her shaking her head still nuzzled close to my chest. "Do you think you could go in there and take a shower? We need to get out of here." I suggested, to which she continued to agree with a shake of her head. "Good," I said, helping her from the bed, leaving her one thought before she stepped into the bathroom, and now eye to eye. "You must promise me you will not do this again. "

"I promise," she said, wiping away her own tears with her hand. I gave her one last playful slap on that much publicized fanny, and she was off to the bathroom, leaving me alone with my thoughts. I knew what I had to do, but hadn't a clue as to how to do it. That script thing was as warped as they come, but when a person has something so firmly planted in their minds, there is no way to convince them otherwise.

The sound of the shower gave me renewed hope that the nightmare was over, at least for tonight. My own words then came back to haunt me. What if she hadn't reached me? And, what of the days and nights when I wouldn't be there? Would she have called someone else , and if she had, would that someone else have reacted in the same fashion? Would they have ignored her, or thought this to be just a sympathy ploy? Hoping never to have any of these questions tested, I knew, for now, I would have to get back to Willy.

The dawn of a new day was creeping through the windows of that old hotel and soon the night itself would be over.

It was Friday. It had already been our plan to meet the following Friday and spend some time together. She assured me that plan was still in operation and much anticipated. She also assured me that it would be quite safe for her to return to her apartment now as Miller would have already begun the "flower" campaign. This meant that I had about 5 days to stop Willy and his machine. The decision wasn't a luxury but a necessity. She never asked how I planned to stop this thing, she only trusted that I somehow would.

Before she opened the car door, I left her with instructions that I'd hoped she would follow. "If you have to go anywhere this week, anywhere, you take Paula or someone else you can trust." Paula Strasberg had become a friend of sorts and more reliable than most. "You got a function to go to, she, or someone like her goes with you, or you don't go. What you do or don't do when we're not together is none of my business, but this week you play it by the book."

"There's no one else, Peter," she offered reassuringly.

"Ok," I said, feeling just a twinge of pride for a second, "but, it's more than that. Somebody's watching this thing, and I don't want them to see anything that even remotely feeds anything to them. I mean, not even a flirtation. Keep "Bugs Bunny" in a cage. I need the time to find out "who," and to figure out "how," got it?"

"Got it!" she said, her strength completely recovered.

I watched her walk from the car and immediately started to think. I had lied to her by suggesting I didn't know "who" it was, but the truth of "how" was very real. Threats to any member of the fourth estate would gather the entire profession against the "threator." It was a losing proposition as they would have united, despite what they might have thought of the "threatee" against the common enemy.

Had I been hit in the face with a baseball bat, knocked unconscious, tied behind a truck in that unconscious state, and dragged through the city dump, I would have felt better than I did on that Friday morning. Most of what I had done had been out of reflex. I hadn't had time to consider any of it.

Fortunately I always kept a clean shirt in the desk drawer and the men's washroom was only down the hallway. With a fast growing beard, a razor accompanied that shirt. These tiny amenities permitted me to freshen up after a long day in the city and afforded me the luxury of not having to drive 52 miles round trip to my apartment and back for an evenings activity that might not have been planned. On this particular morning it was all reversed. I had already had the unplanned evening activity.

They say that a sign of love is the amount of worrying you do about a person. On that morning I must have been "madly" in love with Marilyn, or maybe just "mad" period, because that near-death experience was most sobering. Maybe it was because I hadn't yet tasted enough of life, maybe it was because my priorities were different, or lastly, maybe it was because nothing but nothing seemed worth all of this.

Willy's article was in bad taste. No one would dispute that, but even that seemed trivial in the face of it all. How two people, any two people, could live together under such stress and emotional tension went right by me. Their's was a warped, jaded, unrealistic contract which contained an unwritten "revenge" clause. This paragraph, unwritten or not, somehow bound them together.

From Miller's side, he had to see this "script" as a way back to recognition after having survived a five-year drought. He knew that Marilyn's popularity with the fans would assure an audience. He knew his work would be seen. Marilyn, for whatever may or may not have transpired between them, owed him that chance for recovery. Conversely, Marilyn saw the script as an avenue of escape from the screen image that continued to haunt her. Just what it would or wouldn't do for Miller, was the last thing on her mind. What might have begun as a tribute, had now developed into a first-class war.

I know she had never intended us to become part of that battle, and hence her insistence on our keeping the "us" possibility out of the press. The "no camera" soliloquy took on a whole new meaning, and for that interpretation, we would indeed continue to live in, what we at least thought, were the shadows.

In retrospect, I don't honestly think that Miller would have given one single, solitary damn.

If the "flowers" scenario was indeed taking place in the Miller household as Marilyn had described, then it too would only serve as an intermission between bouts. There are just so many flowers one can offer.

Seeing her pale and so very drained of life, so very opposite of any illusion, made her importance to me razor sharp and as clear as glass. There would no longer be any second thoughts or self-induced escape clauses, as she and I were writing our own contract.

If hoping I could give her something that the others hadn't was a delusion, then indeed the Walter Mitty in me had taken over. If it was only a delusion, that fact eluded me on that Friday morning so very long ago by the clock, and only yesterday by the heart. If I could only return her to a "truth," then the sea of contradiction in which she had been swimming would again grow calm. Just what made me think I was equipped to perform such a task, escapes me even in this writing. All I knew was, I had to try.

This thing that Willy had started seemed so infinitesimal against the honest realities of it all, but I had made a promise. Marilyn's life, virtually from its start, had been filled with promises, lies, pledges that were broken seconds after they had been made. This was one promise that would be kept, although at this moment, I hadn't a clue as to how.

"Chock Full Of Nuts" coffee had fostered the claim that "The secret ingredient was money," and whatever that money bought, their's was one hell of a cup of coffee. Including that coffee in the morning ritual of new shirt, new shave, re-awakened my senses and allowed me again, to focus on the issues that had to be addressed. That last night was over, and Marilyn was very much alive. I had been paid in advance for a job I now had to perform. At that moment what was right or wrong, sick or well, sane or insane, had to be placed on the back-burner. Willy had to be stopped for reasons that were important to Marilyn. Whether I agreed with those reasons or not, was superfluous.

As I sat in that restaurant sipping that awakening coffee, thoughts of what couldn't be done flashed in my mind. Inflicting bodily injury was out, as the God I so firmly believed in would have cried for that decision. Threatening the "reporter" in him would have been a waste of time, as Willy ate threats of this sort for breakfast. Somehow I had to get to HIM personally. As I sat and pondered, reaching no decision, that decision was suddenly made for me.

The girls of the than Latin Quarter and Copacabana were built differently then "the girls next door." Like Alaskan King Crabs, their faces took a back seat to their legs. These long legs set them aside from the rest and were a prerequisite for the job. Three of these long-legged lovelies entered the restaurant, obviously on their way to rehearsal. Each of them smiled at me as they passed my table, and it was those smiles that fired a light bulb in my brain that would begin the wildest, nuttiest, craziest campaign I would ever undertake.

My memory has always served me well virtually from the time of my second birthday, and now it would come in mighty handy. In a matter of seconds I finished my coffee and headed out into the street forming a plan that seemed, on the surface, ludicrous at best.

Times Square, Broadway, Manhattan in general was filled with tiny bars and restaurants that would never make the list of the top 20 places to frequent while visiting New York. These places survived on a local trade, and visiting them regularly became habit to many. One such place, we'll call, EDDIE'S BAR, was appropriately named after its owner. Through the depression, the forties and into the fifties, this place had become the "in" joint for members of the fourth estate as well as the jocks of those respective eras. Eight by ten photos, signed by everyone from Jack Dempsey to Joe Louis lined the walls. Trinkets, trophies, and memories of past victories cluttered every corner. Various film personalities enjoyed the atmosphere of this cave, and as a result I had visited it many times by request of whomever it was I had to meet. The one and only Eddie tended his own bar and, as things go, we began to know each other. Being in his sixties, he could forget more than I would ever learn about life, but like Arnold Albinski, he saw something in me that he liked.

Among the stills behind the bar were a few that featured Willy. One, in particular, was the reason for my visit, and my memory had not failed me. It was a medium shot of Willy, arm in arm with several men, including character actor, Fred Clark. It was shot at this very bar, and they were "toasting" each other. I had to borrow that still to make my plan work, and Eddie was more than cooperative. I laid out a line about the company doing a "special" on Clark, and needing all the material we could get. Whether he bought that line or not, didn't matter. I promised to return it within a day. After small talk and a quick cup of coffee more as a courtesy than desire, I left, but not before glancing at the other few photos of Willy that dotted the back wall. It was the subject of these photos that had prompted this craziest of ideas. Willy had considered himself a lady's man which was about as possible as today's own Roseanne being the subject of every man's dream. He would wear expensive cologne, and tubes of Brill Creme on his hair. On the nights he prowled, he would even have his suit pressed. The thought of any woman, this side of a blind and deaf mute even considering him, was delusion in its finest hour. That didn't stop him, however, from surrounding himself with women, at least for the cameras. He would attend premiers and theatrical openings using his press pass to gain entry back stage. As Marilyn had said, cameras do lie, and it was here that statement was proven.

It wouldn't have been as bad as it was sad, this delusion of Willy's, had he not carried it one step too far. No one can ever really blame anyone else for feeling desire or for wanting to be something the mirror tells them they are not. In that, Willy could easily be forgiven. It was the other side of his nature. The side that suggested, for one to succeed, others must fail.

The homosexual life-style was buried in the closets of the world during the 50's. Those who subscribed to this alternate path in life, kept to themselves. What people did behind closed doors was their own business. It was definitely a live and let live situation. Willy seized every opportunity to expose those who followed this alternate life-style. To ridicule and belittle them, and in one case, ruin one man's career.

I suppose, Willy saw these constant exposes' as a further solidification of his masculine "jock" image. THAT was the image I aimed at.

A friend at the film lab created a negative and copy of the picture I had borrowed from Eddie's bar. In a matter of a taxi ride, it was replaced behind that bar before anyone might observe it was missing. Of course, WHAT was replaced was the dupe, which to the naked eye was undetectable. I needed the fine grain of the original for my scheme. The business of motion pictures is a business that thrives on favors. As soon as you are in a position to do something for someone else, they are placed in the same position.

My early rise in the studio system was considered enviable by many, and despite the rumors of my temper and short fuse, there were those who saw me as a way in. As those same rumors were more myth than fact, quite often I would help if I could.

He called himself "Mr Octavio," and his nick-name was "Chip." Unlike those who tried desperately to hide their sexual preferences, Chip would have put it up in lights. Many times he referred to himself as "The Good Fairy." He was a character with a biting, caustic, irreverent sense of humor. His wit could make you laugh in your worst hour. He was also one of the finest choreographers in the business. As dancers are the least appreciated, lowest paid artists in the entertainment business whether on stage or in films, he managed to subsidize his income by operating a school for professionals who needed to keep in shape and ready for that next open call. We had met at a cocktail party, and managed to keep each other awake during the lulls by exchanging jokes and antidotes. He considered the world of the "writer" a fascinating one, and imagined all sorts of adventures one might encounter by even being thought of as one. Pounding a typewriter long into many nights, drinking cold coffee and smoking cigarettes by the carton was not the image he invisioned. Not everyone in the field had a beautiful blonde to occupy their minds.

He painted the picture of Dickens, working by candle light creating the colorful characters of long-ago England, of Poe, fighting the demons of his soul, and perhaps even Hemmingway seated by his precious Kilimanjaro retelling the memories of his conquests and loves. What he could never see, was the plight of a screen writer attempting to make "Junk" believable.

"Every time someone decides to do a musical revue with dancing, they send me all these 'dead bodies' to revive," he said, interrupting his lesson as I made my entrance to his studio. Wiping his face with a towel, which he then placed over his shoulders, he greeted me as the friend I had become. "And just what brings you here, Petey?," he said with a wink, "got a yen to watch some tight asses, or just up to no good as usual."

"I need a favor, Chip," I said in my best business voice. "Oh balls, Petey, you're always so fucking serious. Smile and the world smiles with you, or is that laugh, or cry and you cry alone... Well it's something like that," he went on. "Oh who cares, you know I'll give you anything you want."

"Do you still have those photos you shot on the island last year?" I asked.

"Don't tell me you're finally coming around!" he suggested with a growing mischievous grin.

After offering no comment to that remark, I was ushered into the inner sanctum of his private office, and shown several dozen shots of men frolicking in the sun of a hot August day. "The Island" was exactly that in geographical terms, but in the opinion of a society that had not learned to accept, it was a haven for those who desired to be free of judgement and inquisitive eyes. It took me only a minute to find a still that would work as an integral part of my plan. Three men, dressed in togas, arm in arm, in the front yard of a known hotel on the island. I studied the picture as Chip studied me.

"For God's sake, Petey, what IS going on?"

Offering no explanation, I asked the question: "I need this still, Chip, can I have it?"

"Who are those three men?," he asked, curious of my motives.

"I haven't the foggiest idea," I said.

"Writers are weird people, Peter," he went on, "they are just plain weird! Take it. I've got tons of that stuff, but don't tell anybody where you got it!" Squeezing his arm in gratitude, I offered him a sincere "Thanks," and left him pondering the entire episode.

In late 1958, I had spent 182 hours at The New York Institute Of Photography learning all I could about film, film emulsions, paper and camera technique. It was just another planned step to my knowing as much as possible about an industry that was then quite foreign to me. My first six months of free-lance part time work had me writing resumes and pasting up artwork for non-theatrical catalogs. I had become quite good at it. What I was doing was making one picture out of two and hoping that somehow this creation would scare off a certain little fat man who had already inflicted far too much damage for his own good. It was a gamble of gambles and had to be perfect or no threat would have been possible.

That night I labored in the seclusion of my beach front apartment much as had Victor Frankensteinin in an old abandoned watch tower centuries before. Fiction or not, his monster turned on him. Hopefully mine wouldn't. I blanked everything and everyone from my mind. Even Marilyn whose presence was always with me, was absent that night. Worrying about what she might have been doing, a possible fight at the Miller home, something that could have again gone wrong , was she safe? All thoughts of this and more had to be dismissed as the exacto knife had to be held by steady hands.

At the job's completion, I studied the masterpiece allowing near comic thoughts to re-enter my brain. There was something delightfully outrageous about it all. Within my grasp was the substance dreams are made of...of course, even dreams come with strings attached, but we had broken some of those strings together. In just a few days, I would again be filled with the scent of her, and feel pity for every man who wasn't me. What became nearly comical was the clear and present fact that regardless of all of these unplanned accidents, and superficial delights, my entire life had done a one-eighty in only three weeks. I would have preferred being Robert Mitchum in RIVER OF NO RETURN, throwing her over my shoulder and carrying her off to a quiet wilderness home hoping to have a few great moments in the sack before the indians got us, but instead, I had become Tom Ewell in the SEVEN YEAR ITCH, in the late hour of a Friday night, cutting out paper dolls. Forgetting for the moment the brooding undercurrent to all of this, Robert Benchley would certainly have found the humor in it.

My last thoughts before drifting off to sleep were those of this photographic creation. It had to be the craziest thing I'd ever done.

At 9 am the following day, Saturday, I took my new creation across the street to my beach for the final test. Nothing is capable of revealing the flaws in anything better than the sun. It picks up every blemish and points out any errors not seen by one lamp at midnight. Alright, the sun gave it a B+. So far, so good. In anticipation of the next step, I had called a non-industry friend, Bud Johnson, and asked if I might use his dark room on Saturday if I had to. There was no problem, and now I had to. Bud lived with his wife, Rose, in Baldwin, Long Island, not far from my mother's home in Uniondale. He was a baby photographer by trade, and good at it. His home was equipped with a complete darkroom, and as a friend completely removed from the industry, he would never ask any questions. I had known him since my early teen years. He had been one of the few who hadn't passed judgement on me when I suggested the career I had chosen. Rose had prepared a breakfast big enough to feed the 49'ers, and while indulging in the pursuit of that breakfast we engaged in small talk.

Like so many good, clean, wholesome American couples, they were in quiet awe of the movies. I had become that local kid who managed to scale the walls and who could deliver stories from the "inside." It didn't matter how much I would underplay an issue, to them, their imaginations lifted those issues to greater heights than they deserved. While I never would have given up my career, I envied them for their peaceful, worry-free existence.

After breakfast and chat, Rose went into the kitchen and Bud attacked his lawn, leaving me the run of his studio and darkroom to perform the final phases of my masterpiece. Using a 4x5 Graflex under a time exposure, I photographed the photograph. Grain and texture is the trick when preparing a picture from a picture. It begins with the method in which the picture is taken, carries through the developing of the film solution, and ends with the right paper number in the enlarger. It is not an easy trick, and in this case, it was a dangerous one. Under the yellow light of the darkroom, the final photo looked good. The white light would give it a grade and it had to be "A." Almost hesitantly I flicked it on. After it had finally come off the drying drum, I took it to Bud's worktable and there, under a magnifying glass was proof positive that Marilyn's theories were right. Pictures can lie. There was Willy, the man who spent most of his waking hours proving his masculinity, standing arm in arm with two men outside a hotel well known for its catering to the alternate life-style. I think the toga he was wearing completed the illusion. It was a nice touch. Bud had come in to see my work, and I explained it was an "inside" joke. Already convinced that film people were different, he never questioned it.

Driving through the small but tidy community of Baldwin, Long Island made me remember where so much of it had started. Visiting Bud and Rose reminded me of the joys of the simple life. It was so beautifully real, so unspoiled by needless want, so acceptable....it would have bored the living daylights out of me in a week.

Sunday dragged on as the moment of truth was only hours away. Instead of a peaceful relaxing period of intermission, it became a study in nervous anxiety. This entire preposterous scenario was aimed at only one thing, Willy's ego, a possible "Achilles heel."

The average reporter would have laughed it off. I counted on Willy not being the average reporter. By offering him this created tidbit, I also revealed to him that there was something to his article. No one would have gone through this if there wasn't. If I had been wrong in my appraisal of him, I would have been offering Marilyn and I to him on a silver platter. Had I not remembered the graying pallor of Marilyn's face, returning from that drugged sleep. Had I not felt her desperation. Had I honestly considered all of the possible risks, I would have filed that picture in "13" where it belonged. The importance of it all seems lost in the years, but at that moment in time, it had become my worst nightmare. I could only hope that if it backfired, Marilyn would some how understand. I suppose in these "anything goes" 90's, all of this must seem so very unnecessary. In summation, it would have been unnecessary then, had it not been for that script. Those flimsy sheets of paper that represented freedom to two people. An aging gifted writer who had forgotten how to write, and who had become something he'd never thought he could be, and a beautiful blonde "movie star" who spent her life in pursuit of a dream that would never happen. In many ways I would be performing this trick for Miller as well as Marilyn. It just seemed that both had had enough trouble.

At 9am on Monday, we were on the clock. I had placed an earlier call to Willy telling him that I had something that might interest him. It was GO or GO UNDER time. We had agreed to meet in that same coffee shop at 9:15, and somehow I knew he'd be there. The "hard edge" Marilyn referred to, that part of my nature that seemed so obvious to her, would surely be tested now.

The "plastic" smile was missing from Willy's face on this morning as he moved through the crowd to my table. He'd heard the stories of my temper and believed them. That one important fact gave our team a plus.

Willy was about 5 foot 4, and as wide as he was tall. I was 6 foot 4, and stood as he arrived at my table certain to be able to look down on him. I needed every inch of intimating strength. Outwardly I stood like the Rock of Gibralter. Inwardly, my stomach had the feel of Jello. It was a most uncomfortable antonym. After a moment of eye to eye contact, he sat his flabby frame on the chair opposite my table. His voice was a mixture of curiosity and bitter hostility as this meeting would have been the last one he would have ever invisioned.

"So what's the big deal?," he asked in a whiskey-tone as though he had eaten nails for breakfast.

"You should try the Kaiser rolls in here Willy," I began,"They're great."

"Fuck the Kaiser rolls," he blurted, "You didn't call me to talk about the menu. Let's have it."

"You've been watching too many Humphrey Bogart movies Willy," I said, already reaching for my attache case and withdrawing, from it, an 8x1O manilla envelope.

"I've got something for your rag, Willy, I think you'd call it a scoop." His fat, swollen, stubby hands grabbed the manila envelope and began opening it keeping one eye on me. Watching this swamp creature suddenly reminded me of just how loathsome he really was. The calm anger I had been pretending suddenly became real. The "hard-edge" was no longer a performance, and Marilyn had been right all along. His first reaction on seeing the picture was to immediately hold it below the table. His face went ash-white. "What kinda bullshit is this?" he whispered, and by the fact that he did WHIS-PER, made me instantly aware that we were IN! Had we not have been, he would have laughed, and probably exhibited it to the whole room. He wasn't laughing. As he tried to conceal the photo and simultaneously study it for give away flaws, I added a few verbal stings to help him along.

"Like you said yourself so many times," I chuckled, "You gotta watch those cameras."

Turning the photo upside down on the table, he glared at me, his face turning now a slight reddish color.

"This isn't me!" I could feel my jaw tighten and I allowed my eyes to bore right through him.

"The picture says it is," I said in dead earnest, " and your kind knows that pictures don't lie."

Sealing his fate, Willy ripped the picture into small pieces. His heel had been tapped.

Now in command, I spoke the final lines that would convince him, " I've got the negative in my file." Then something very strange happened, and something very unexpected. To this moment, right, wrong or otherwise, this had been a game of wits. A game of victory and defeat. The odds had been in the other guy's favor. I had expected any number of reactions from anger to laughter, but the eyes that now looked back to me possessed neither. The pathetic look on Willy's face was one I had not been ready for. As a writer, you pride yourself on being able to "read" people, look below the surface. I had missed this one by a mile. The picture, which was clearly a fraud, had uncovered an even bigger one. This had not been part of the plan.

"No one ever has to see this Willy," I said, now feeling for a moment as though from a humanity standpoint this victory might have been a bitter one.

"Yeah, yeah.." he reacted as though trying to bluff his way through something that might have been a moment of honesty even in his world.

"We need to make a trade," I said, using grammatically imperfect street-talk as my lead. He already began shaking his head in affirmation. He knew it the moment he looked at that still. He was slimey, but he wasn't stupid.

"How do I know you'll........" he began

I interrupted him. "No one will see this picture," I said, "You have my word. You already know I'm in a position to make certain everyone in the world sees it..you DO know that.." Again he shook his head.

After a moment of contemplation and a deep sigh, he looked me squarely in the eye. "Tell me, big shot," he began, " Is she really worth all this?" As truth had been our silent partner on this table, perhaps a truth that had surfaced between two enemies being the strongest truth of all, I answered in like fashion.

"Yes, Willy, she is," was all I said before again standing. "Meeting's over."

He fumbled for his briefcase, and rose to his feet. Gone was the bravado. Gone was any trace of a plastic smile. Not being able to resist having the final word, he turned to me and from lips that had gone dry he offered the only parting gesture he could, "I hope she eats you up alive!" With that, he was gone.

We never heard a word from Willy on the matter. The planned series of articles simply dropped into space. No explanations were ever given. By late 1960, Willy himself had disappeared. Just another character in a world that so often makes little, if any, sense.

Chapter Five

Memories of Wisdom

Life is like a rubber band. You select the size you want when you assume your capabilities. As long as you remain within that expandable but controlled area, the band stretches and retracts comfortably. Once you exceed that self-designed limit, it snaps.

Until only a few weeks previous to this day, I felt as though I had my life in regimental order. Things in general were far from perfect, but they had worked for me. From the second our eyes made contact, everything changed. For one thing, I had designed my own rubber band for a youth of my age. Possibly I would have exchanged it later, as time went on, but later came sooner than expected. I believe it snapped on that 2:45am race against time to the city, only a few days earlier. The plan I had so carefully crafted, designed with the brilliance of an architect, met its fate in an unseen garbage can that night.

With Marilyn, there was no such thing as a plan. About the closest we ever came was in prearranging a phone call, or perhaps agreeing on a certain place to meet. Beyond that, she would call often without advance notice. Our relationship was as far away from a plan as anyone could get. Marilyn introduced a new word to my vocabulary, "chaos," defined in the dictionary as "extreme confusion and disorder." She also introduced me to a world that I never dreamed existed. In that world I met pleasures no words can describe, along with disillusionments that would bring tears to the eyes of the Sphinx.

The closer we grew, the more I would see the world through her eyes. All you see is never all you get. People come with shadings, and with those subliminal personal greys and tans, comes an insight about them that no first impression could ever leave. Willy's unspoken confession of being homosexual in the face of all the furor he had outwardly raised against those who shared that preference, was enough contradiction for one day. Through him, Marilyn would score a victory, because nothing would ever be mentioned to upset her plans for that, so very important, script. The weekend had been one big barrel of laughs, beginning with Marilyn's near fatal overdose and climaxing with Willy's revelation. I needed to "take 5" from all of it.

I had one solid good friend, Bob. He would have understood, but was away on a campaign of his own. Of the two other people in the world I could trust, it was only my grandmother I wanted to see. My mother was a wonderful parent, and as a boy I was given everything, with a special accent on love. I suppose, because I was adopted, I may have been more appreciated, but whatever the reason, she was the greatest mom in the world. Something changed in my mid-teens. It had nothing to do with love and devotion. That never changed. There were always girls around, and girls were confusing creatures to my mother who constantly threw her hands in the air in complete bewilderment. My announcement that I was going to be a writer and NOT a concert pianist as had been planned, was probably the final straw. To her dying day my mother was always there for me, but made no secret about the fact that she had long since stopped trying to figure me out. Somewhere around age 15, the second team took over. Whether it was the wisdom of an older age, or just an indescribable sixth-sense, my grandmother always knew exactly what I was doing and why, sometimes better than I. There was no need to keep anything secret from grandma, because what you didn't tell her, she had already guessed. She never offered advice, but in conversation, allowed you to find your own. She left all judgements to you, but would, in her way, silently guide you to those judgements. When my grandfather lost every dime and friend he had in 1929, she stood by him, never wavering for a minute. She used to offer parables in place of lectures. A most efficient device. In describing my ambition, she compared me to a shooting star being careful to remind me of the general path and pattern of such heavenly missiles "They burn brightly," she said, "They blaze across the heavens allowing nothing to stop them, and then, as suddenly as they were formed, they self-destruct in a hail of fire and smoke." That less than comforting thought remained with me as a handy hint to remember, which I did, often.

Mark had agreed to come to my beach apartment that night to wrestle with the script. It was time to finish it, win, lose, or draw. The time between my less than glorious victory over Willy and my night time plans to fight a script that almost refused to be beaten, was about four hours. I could think of no one on this day, climaxing this frenzied, frustrating weekend, that I would have rather spent some of that four hours with than this grand old lady. She and my grandfather now lived with my mother, having had to move from her Richmond Hill apartment when the four flights of stairs became too much for her to climb. My own apartment in Bayville, was only about 12 miles from my mother's home. It was hardly an inconvenience, and a trip I should have taken more often. Whenever I would return home for visits, the place never seemed to change. It had been home to me for 8 years. In the last two years, after having left it, only I had changed. Entering this cleaned and well kept home, with my grandmother's arms to greet me, temporarily closed the gap between my world as it was today and what it had been only a short time ago. The "movies" were something none in that house understood, and although fans, the industry was distant to them. As a result, for the first few minutes of every visit, I must have appeared almost as a stranger. That is, to everyone but my grandmother.

On this particular day, she was alone. My mother was at work, and my grandfather was at the local German delicatessen telling tall tales of the old days. For the many restless moods within me that day, it was just as well she was alone. Whenever I arrived it seemed a strudel had just come out of the oven, and coffee appeared as if by magic. The coffee was a good idea, because I knew I'd need it that night.

Somehow it seemed, by the pictures around the place, that time had stood still for this grand lady. There was her favorite, a shot of her holding me in her arms at the time of my adoption at age 3 weeks. Then my first communion, and finally my graduation from high school. I had changed considerably from age 3 weeks to age 17 years, but not her. As she sliced into the strudel, she began sneaking into conversation, a trick I should have been used to but fell for every time. What an attorney she would have made. She was concerned over my daughter, and just as much over my feelings about her and this new adoption thing. I assured her that I had accepted the arrangement and understood it was the best thing for the child. A smile on her face indicated she liked that answer. Then, as if in control of a crystal ball, she went on, "Everybody thought, well maybe when he gets married he will settle down," she said, "and maybe they were right, but they weren't right for this time and I knew that." She poured some more coffee and, without asking, placed another piece of strudel on my plate. "Someday there will come a girl," she continued, "and that special girl will knock you right off your feet." Her eyes flashed to accent her point. "This girl you will finally love more than yourself. Then, and only then will you know what life is really all about. I hope I am here to see it, but if not, I will be watching from somewhere else, and I will find a way to say 'I told you so'."

"You never know," I said. That was all it took. With that absolutely noncommittal remark, her aged eyes began searching mine, and whatever they saw forced a slight grin to creep onto her face.

"Ah ha!," she exclaimed. "Now we come to it!" She took a sip of coffee to allow me to think about it. "Tell me about her," she whispered.

Using my cup as a prop, I took a sip, but it was no use. Her eyes had already locked onto the target. I could have performed a song and dance and her eyes would have remained fixed. "There really isn't anything to tell," I said, slowly guarding my words, "Not yet at any rate."

"Someone from work?," she went on almost kiddingly and paying no attention to my attempted rebuttal.

"It's a bit involved," I answered.

"And what have you done in the last 10 years that hasn't been," she continued, "Ach! Such going's on!"
Well she was probably right. I continued now even more carefully, "Nothing to rival this."

"Peter" she began, a slight serious tone to her voice, "I understand you better than YOU do, but I don't understand the business you are in. I don't understand the people who work with you in that business. I don't know what they do, how they feel, nothing. But I see a look on your face that confuses me. Why?" She reached her hand to mine, and placed it gently onto it, squeezing it affectionately. As usual, she then completed what I could not. "This is not just someone you work with...this is not someone ordinary, like us, hummmmm?"

My silence answered her question.

"This is someone, maybe, we already know..." I felt my

head agreeing with a slight nod in a nearly unconscious reaction. Her spirit rose to the occasion. "Well then!," she blurted, patting the same hand she had been holding, "When the time is right, maybe soon we will have a movie star in the family."

That thought had never crossed my mind. I knew Marilyn and I were growing closer, but whether we would ever grow this close, was another matter. I smiled at that remark only because I didn't know what else to do. Then, in the most positive manner she could muster, she proudly spoke out, "And just what is wrong with THAT?!" My grandmother had a way of looking everything directly in the face, and in that directness, see its positive merits. She also knew when to stop pushing for an answer. She had what singer Jimmy Jones would have called "Good Timing," and often this knack would leave you considering options that you had overlooked. Again, she never made any decisions for you, more rather helped you make your own.

The remainder of our afternoon visit was filled with the usual dialogue of "How was so and so?" and "Have you heard from Cousin whatchmacallit?" It all ended too soon, but the clock kept running, and Mark would soon appear at my doorstep. A final hug, a final well wish, and I was off, back to a life no one in this house understood.

She left me with a look that said it all- "what has he gotten into now?"- To try and explain it in detail would have been impossible, as, at this moment, I honestly had no answer to that look. Driving through the old neighborhood, I passed houses that used to be on my paper route and spotted parents of former buddies mowing their lawns and washing their cars. It had only been a couple of years, but it seemed much longer. This happy place of my youth was disappearing before my eyes, and there was no way to stop that disappearance. The last house on the block was now occupied by my first real girlfriend, my sweet-sixteen, flute-playing, first partner in the experimenting with sex department. She had married a local boy, and already had one child with another on the way. She was in her back yard hanging clothes on a line as I passed. There was little sense in my beeping the horn or stopping as she, like the rest of it, was now history. Making the left turn from that block used to point me to high school during simpler, less complicated times. Now it was simply the first turn in a series of turns that would lead me out of town. Indeed those few miles could have been a million. Marilyn had had an Aunt Emma, with whom she had lived a short time in her childhood. Her description of this Aunt Emma seemed similar to the grandmother I had just left. She had asked this Aunt Emma if she could call her "momma?" The reply had been "I'm not your mother," a less than polite way to say "no." Under a different set of circumstances, and on a different day, the kind only your dreams permit, "Grandma" would have easily and proudly consented to be "Grandma" to her as well. I didn't know then if she and Marilyn would ever meet. It seemed the wildest of possibilities. Today, so many years later, it doesn't seem as wild. I think, some day, in a place so much better than this we're going to have the coffee clotch to end all coffee clotches. It's going to be something very special.

Sometimes a movie becomes part of a larger memory than itself. Just as a song will remind you of another time and another place, of people who are no longer with you, at least in the physical sense, so too does a film.

It was a rainy night in Brooklyn, the year was 1947. I can remember the huge 24-sheet poster that ran the complete length of the side of the building that housed the Brooklyn Fox Theatre. It was framed by moving lights and exhibited its message unaffected by the rain. The film it advertised was one my mother and I had just seen. It impressed me then, and still does. I would meet its producer, Edward Small, who's offices would be just below mine at Goldwyn Studios many, many, years later but for this moment, I was on my way home to work with one of its writers, Mark. The film had been T-MEN, and it was one of the first to totally impress a then 9-year old boy. He had been right when he said "I was making films when you were in short pants."

Whether right or wrong, warm or cold, depressed or elated, Marilyn had a gift for bringing out the best in me. I think it was an innocence that remained in her, buried deep because of the stark realities she had faced, that again could rise to the surface during our times together. So much had been said of her, and whispered into ears that couldn't really know, and didn't really care, only to be whispered into other ears who knew and cared even less.

I had already heard all of the stories, and was now in a position to see for myself. I kept waiting for the tell-tale signs. I stopped waiting at about 3:15 in the morning of last Friday at the Berkeley Hotel. If I slip on occasion and refer to her as "my Marilyn," forgive me, as it is not meant in the sense of possessiveness. The stories that were whispered then, and continue to be whispered even today, are about someone else. They are not about "My Marilyn." I'm not suggesting that some of them might or might not be true, but rather stating categorically, between us, they never happened. I believe that the privacy she had hoped for was all part of that same thought. A place where two people could just be two people, and where prying eyes could not suggest otherwise. I had become hard, thoughtless, and cruel in my dealings with those who shared my space. First listening to her, then observing what that same kind of cruelty had done to her, and finally being blessed by holding her in my arms, made me aware of that changing image in my mirror. Mark had been as much a target of that thoughtless behavior as anyone. He would then become the first benefactor of the newly formed Monroe-Collins collaboration.

The problems of the script we faced that night were staggering. It was a "dated" piece set in modern times. An impossibility. Had it been set in the period of the 30's, it would have worked beautifully, but it wasn't. With each new generation, comes a whole different bag of worms. Expressions change. Morals change. Dialogues change. You can't make a mystery out of something that is no longer mysterious, and "twenty-three skiddoo" would never be uttered even by your least important character. What was once considered sinful, was now quite common place, and to try and suggest "sinful behavior" in a society that no longer considered it so, was a joke. The movement in the script was stilted, confined. The studio was planning to set and shoot a good portion of this film in London, yet the action of most of it, took place indoors. Common sense would have screamed at you, "If you're going to go to London, shoot London" The original script could just as well have been shot in Davenport, Iowa as no London exteriors were even included.

Sometimes a project that had first been so baffling to so many, just comes together. This one did on that night. For Mark's contribution, England now looked like England. He had successfully moved many of the scenes out-doors. My obligation had been to remove 1947 T-MEN dialogue into 1960, and to change the main character's dialect from New York, the original setting of the piece, to London to suit the English actor who had been selected to play it. Feeling generally proud and accomplished, we wrapped the whole thing up in a tidy package and put the bow on it around 10 pm, much earlier than expected. Completing a script, and then finally a film, gives those who participate a "high" no drugs could ever duplicate. Mark lingered awhile after the finish, savoring the victory that was ours. He also apologized for the seventieth time for suspecting my motives. Now, in the mood set by my blonde angel, I explained that he had had every right to suspect the worst. Almost embarrassingly, I explained my original plan, and how all of that was part of it. To my surprise, he explained how he once concocted a similar plan. It hadn't worked either.

"Something about a writer," he said, sipping some of my instant coffee, "We must always appear to be angry about something, even when we're not. How many 'happy' writers do you know?" He went on, "There must be a sense of the worldly in us that creates its own air of mystery and suspense. A kind-of, unexplained bullshit!" Wisdom is always all around you, if you care to listen. My grandmother had it. Mark had it, and Willy had discovered it in himself. It was a hell of a day. Mark left around midnight knowing his family would now be a bit more secure, that he still possessed what he thought he had lost. Something or someone, below the surface, motivates us all. Thinking, as my last thought of the day, that is was just about 48 hours to Marilyn, clearly expressed mine.

Chapter Six

The First Step To Forever

A war that had begun in the early 50's, fought in living rooms and auditoriums, had nearly reached a truce which seemed to forecast a new age even before our eyes. In the late 40's there seemed only a few hundred television sets in existence. Milton Berle, one of this new "fads" first stars began his Texaco Star Theatre somewhere around 1948, followed by wrestling featuring such canvas stars as Gorgeous George and Antonio Argentina Rocca. Baseball took hold, and on occasion a variety show. On Sunday mornings in New York they ran "The Horn And Hardart Children's Hour." Between these visual bursts, stations would simply run "test" patterns, so at its conception, this new medium was hardly a threat to motion pictures. By the 50's however, only the playing of The Star Spangled Banner, sometime around 2 am would signal a halt to the day's viewing. The test patterns were vanishing and programs were filling in the blanks.

By 1953, there were enough shows offering enough variety for everyone to keep any audience interested. Television manufacturers had reduced the cost of their sets and thereby had made them affordable to the masses. The negatives were that all shows were only in black and white. The positives, they were all FREE. Manufacturers and entrepreneurs experimented with some of the damnedest looking sets and strangest gimmicks in an effort to make their units the best. Some ended up ridiculous, while others remain today. Zenith, one of the earliest to enter the field, developed a "round tube" which they claimed better resembled the human eye. Just what the hell that had to do with anything is still a mystery. Another offered "Halo-light," a dimly lighted frame surrounding the picture portion of the set. The theory, of course, was to prevent eye-strain. Then came the first crude attempts at COLOR, with the first being a "color wheel" that rotated in front of your picture, supposedly creating the illusion of color. What it most often created was a psychedelic headache. Another offered a "color" screen which you would lay over the actual screen. It had been tinted in three layers. Blue on top, red-orange in the middle, and green on the bottom. Sky, people and grass...get it? The general result was not the one promised as neither films or shows prepared for screening had any of this nonsense in mind. What finally happened, sadly and comically, was "blue faces," bodies that look ravaged by Yellow Jaundice and "green clothing." Along with all this P.T. Barnum stuff came the first film packages, and with them, the first real threat to the motion picture theatres. It began with independent productions from "Poverty Row" studios and producers, among them PRC (Producer's Releasing Company), Monogram (later Allied Artists), and United Artists, the latter not so much poverty row as confused. "B" films of the 30's and 40's saw a re-birth in this new medium, which helped one remember, if nothing else, the Saturday matinees of the then recent past. As the East Side Kids never offered Cary Grant any real threat, this sort of film only planted the seeds of what was to come. Along with the films came a barrage of commercials offering everything from nationally known products to "super knives" that could cut through anything from butter to cement. In New York, "lanolin" was discovered and soon appeared in virtually every hair product on the market. Basically sheep oil, this new discovery was hyped as the "end all" of any and all hair problems. After all, how many bald sheep had you seen? The commercials indeed became as entertaining as the films they interrupted.

In an effort to lure people back to the theatres, Hollywood, seeing TV as the enemy, created a barrage of strange films using gimmicks of their own. Horror and science fiction flourished, 3-D came and went, and then CinemaScope arrived with screens five times larger then before, and of course a hundred times larger than TV. By 1959, it seemed an even match. While hundreds of small theatres were closing, Drive-In's became popular as family attractions. Generally you paid one admission per car load and that, in itself, seemed more than fair. You could eat until you burst, burp the baby, or ravage your best girl friend all from the comfort and privacy of your car. If you cared to watch the movie, it was there. TV continued to gain ground, but thanks to a handful of new stars and polished older ones, theatres still had their momentary victories. It was to these theatres that the annual TOA (Theatre Owners Association) convention was aimed. I always made a point to attend, at least for a few hours, as these conventions were exciting, almost "circus-like" and did present advances in technology available to theatres from newly improved lenses to better tasting popcorn. It also helped me determine, personally, just where the films we so labored on were heading.

These conventions were by invitation only. I'd always thought that they should have been open to the public as many had become more interesting than some of the films themselves. Cardboard cut-out "standees" of the stars were placed strategically here and there welcoming the visitor to the various different exhibits. "Elizabeth Taylor" pointed the way to "MGM CAMERA 65," a new sharper lens, "Alfred Hitchcock's" pudgy face stood over Vista-Vision, and, of course, "Marilyn" promised the color and splash of CinemaScope. The camera of choice today, almost an industry staple, PANAVISION, and its then fledgling concept, was seen in a small but intelligent exhibit. My own dear friend, Stanley Cortez, was helping to design the camera that would stand hands above them all in the soon 60's and into the 90's as it became more and more perfected. In the midst of this crowd of glitter and people, a familiar voice rang out. "Heyyyyyy Abbooooottt!," it screamed, and no, it wasn't Lou Costello. Lou had gone to his reward some six months earlier. It was my closest friend, Bob. He and I had gone through high school together. We had shared everything, including the learning experience with girls. As a matter of fact, the young beauty he had once escorted to the roller skating rink had become my first wife. As I said, we shared everything. We would alibi for each other, and defend each other against any enemy including parents and teachers. After graduation, when most young people swear they will stay in touch only to disappear from one another, Bob and I stayed in touch. Along with my grandmother, he was the only one I honestly trusted- a kind of "blood" relationship without all the mess.

Poetically our lives had taken a similar turn as he now pursued a career in broadcast news. If those listening to his "serious" newscasts would have had any idea of the Tom Sawyer character doing the talking, he would have been out of business before he started, Fortunately for him, they had no such idea. The usual hugs and handshakes were shared as we stopped to chat in front of one of the huge displays.

"My station's doing a special on the decay of the modern theatre," he began, which brought a chuckle to me.

"Great" I said, " They're going to love you here for that. These people are spending 70 gizzillian dollars on all this stuff, and you're going to tell a network audience that they're wasting their time."

"No, No," he said, reassuringly, "We're doing a survey..this is not a hanging!" Then with his so typical grin,

"Besides, you've got no problems. TV's gonna need writers too."

Along with the small talk he then said something that would amount to a prophesy come true. "Someday" he said, "all films will go directly into the home- non-stop- and all this will end. You'll even make your own pop-corn." Today, in the ever advancing 90's, Bob's voice may still be heard as anyone can observe the new rising home-entertainment market, the laser disc, the video tape. When matched with the so-called multi-plex theatres offering little more than total discomfort in their "closet-style" presentations, it leaves little question as to what side is winning. Gone are the loge and balcony sections, gone are the massive drapes that would open as a film's proud logo would hit the screen. Gone is the experience in general. In its place, uncomfortable seating, sticky un-kept floors, graying screens and outrageously priced snacks at the make-shift concession stand. Gone, for all time, is the original captivating illusion of film, and much like the dinosaur, only enough of what may tragically be remembered by a select few, will remind us that it was ever really there at all.

In the midst of our talk, the subject of Bob's uncle's boat came up. At an earlier time, he and I had "borrowed it" without permission, for which its further use had been off-limits to him. It was a slick Chris-Craft, and we had gone "joy" riding, or boating if you prefer, on a Sunday afternoon some years back. Unfortunately, Bob had neglected to inform his Uncle George who immediately had reported it stolen. When "Captain Bob" and "First Mate Peter" returned to the dock, they were greeted by three angry men in uniform and a very distraught Uncle George. Things were different now. Bob, in his capacity in the newsroom, had arranged and paid for a weekend in Las Vegas for his uncle and aunt. As gratitude, the "hands-off-the-boat" policy had been lifted. He had tried, unsuccessfully, to reach me for several days, but with my schedule, rescues, and nostalgic visits, I hadn't been home. He had a new girl friend, and wanted me to meet her. A double-date on his boat would be as good a place as any to accomplish that. He knew there were enough women for me to choose from who would gladly come along, perhaps to China, if I asked them, so he saw it as no problem. Of course he was unaware of the "new girl" in my life, and now, in this circus atmosphere, was not the time to bring her up. I wasn't quite certain how it might work, if indeed it was even feasible. I was not in a position to agree to such a suggestion without discussing it with Marilyn, as it put a slight hole in our "private-world" scenario. On the other side of the coin, however, it would have given her an opportunity to meet someone who was very close to me, and who would come with no strings attached, no angles, no hidden, unseen motives.

"Maybe," I said, "It depends on someone else and if she can handle it."

"Handle it?," he exclaimed with a laugh, "A couple of hours on a boat?" As my remark had been more a thinking-out-loud, than a comment, from a purely verbal standpoint, it did sound stupid. Offering no excuse for it, I left him holding mid-air, and an agreement to confirm on Friday night.

That was the best I could do at that time. Once upon a not so long ago time, asking a girl to go for a boat ride did not involve an act of congress. With this particular girl, things were different, and as odd as that may sound, they had to be. A second thought crossed my mind which I assumed could be dealt with if all systems were go. Bob was a professional news caster, and while it was true that ours was a long term friendship, thoughts of dropping this bomb in his lap and asking him to keep quiet, may have been exceeding that friendship. We would see about the whole idea. With all these thoughts on my mind, I swung by the studio to pick up the latest package, an "eastern" that they wanted to do as a "western." It was written as a gangster film, the kind that had made stars of Bogart, Robinson and Cagney in the 30's and 40's. The premise was good but to transfer this piece to a different locale would be a major re-write from page one. One of the studio's biggest western names wanted to do it, so here it was on my car seat heading for my "ranch house" in Bayville. After the nightmare Mark and I had just finished, this script looked like a walk in the park. I began making notes on a per page basis. Time went on. Feeling a bit hungry but not enough to get serious, I popped one of those TV dinners in the oven. Something from Swanson. If you don't remember them, the first ones were pretty awful, but they were convenient. The telephone rang, and not expecting any one in particular, I answered in my "business" voice.

"Yes?" It was a day earlier than I had expected Marilyn to call, but then, as usual, one thing she truly was, was unpredictable.

"Do you miss me?" she began. Had it been anyone but Marilyn, I would have asked, "Who is this," but the sound of her voice, and knowing she was alright and had made it through the week, left no room for humor.

Marilyn could be many things at many times. She could be alluring, sensitive, permissive, on occasion, shy, but what she always was was fragile. The last thing I wanted to do, was test that fragility.

"Only about every hour," I said in place of levity.

"Me too," she countered.

It was at this point in most of our earlier conversations that I waited for the other shoe to drop. It never did.

"We've got three days," she blurted with the excitement

of a child at Christmas "surprising" daddy with his annual bottle of Old Spice. I could feel my blood pressure rising, it was the damnedest sensation.

"Three days?!," I repeated in near shock. For anyone else, this information would have been less than exciting, but for two people who generally only had hours, or perhaps a night at the most, three days sounded like an eternity.

"Yesssssssss!" she replied, as though in control of a major victory.

"Honey, that's super," I said with a kind of sincerity that sometimes surprised even me.

"Can we go to that mountain place you talked about?" she asked.

"I'll call 'em. I'm sure we can. There's something else I'd like to talk to you about."

Her voice dropped, "What did I do now?," she asked. "What's wrong?"

"Baby, there's nothing wrong," I replied quickly, assuring her there wasn't. She had become so used to disappointment, it was dumb of me to begin such a thought. It could have waited until the next day. "It's something I want us to do Saturday, before we go to the mountains," I said.

She then brought "Marilyn Monroe" to the phone,

"I know what I want us to do on Saturday.," she said, breath and all.

What the hell can you say to that. "Besides that , honey," I said trying to remain cool under the circumstances.

"I'll fill you in on Friday"

With that remark, and on a roll, the "naughty Marilyn" took over completely, "and on Saturday, and Sunday and Monday."

Unable to control my laughter, I asked with what ever dignity might have been left, "Marilyn, what's gotten into you?!"

"Nothing yet," she fired back," but you'll fix that."

"Jesus, honey, what have you been eating?" I said.

She suddenly went very serious. "I haven't been eating anything, Peter, I'm just happy. I'm really happy. It's been so long. I'm just so glad you're there. You can't possibly know how glad."

Maybe she was right, but I knew what I felt, and if her feelings were even close to that, no explanation was necessary.

My TV dinner was smoking in the oven. I let it burn away. The hunger I was feeling at this moment, had nothing to do with frozen chicken. If Willy hadn't counted for anything, he had made me aware of "habit." In his stumbling way, he had made his point. Repetitive performance traps most people. At my suggestion, we arranged a different meeting place. After a few more moments of small talk, and with a "good night" wish mutually given, I hung up the receiver. Only the smell of burning mashed potatoes snapped me out of it. They always got the worst of most TV dinners anyway.

Infatuation is a game you play in your mind, sometimes in unconscious reflex. For the game to continue, certain impossible illusions must remain in place. The subject of that infatuation must be guiltless of any human weakness, and must remain untouched by reality. There is no doubt in my mind that on that first chance meeting at the deli, infatuation was clearly the issue. Considering the circumstances, I had no choice. She had literally come out of left field, offering the same surprise had I been struck by lightning on a cloudless, bright, and sunny day. It may have changed a bit when she kept her word about meeting me in the park, but then too, ego was involved. Pouring ego into infatuation might be compared to mixing gasoline with nitroglycerin, and lighting the stove.

The chances are, you're going to create one hell of an explosion.

Infatuation does not pray to see the sparkle return to drugged eyes. It doesn't risk everything to defeat a slander that might have crushed the subject in question. It doesn't remember the scent of her, or hope, against all logic, that there will be other times, good times. "Love" is the alternative. No single word or expression is more misused, abused, or confused than this one. You sign a letter to a distant aunt or uncle you hardly know or remember with "Love from so and so." You can "love" a movie, a book or a song. Poets write of it, giving it a sanctity or condemnation, depending on their mood. It has even become an excuse for murder. It is the single strongest word in any language regardless of how it is spelled or pronounced, and it contains the greatest amount of personal interpretation. When you say to someone, "I Love You," it is only as good as you mean it to be. There are a million reasons why a person "falls in love," none the least is for "love's" sake alone. Perhaps it's the season of the year, or fashion for the moment. There's always the "I love him (or her) but don't like him (or her)" approach. This generally ends when the bed is made up. "Blind love" is another interesting excuse for bad judgement. "I realize he just killed the Pope, but I love him anyway." On rare occasions, parents and children don't always love each other, but feel compelled to say they do. There is "love at first sight" and love that takes years to uncover. It goes on into volumes.

From the very beginning I had great difficulty in determining my feelings for Marilyn. The confusion began with "who" she was, and ended with "who she appeared to be." Considering that she had had 10 years of publicity behind her, should make that easy to understand. Continuing to try and put false labels on it was, clearly, a defense mechanism. Looking back now, these many years later, no longer concerned with opinions in favor of or against, with less years before me than those I have left behind, with nothing to lose or gain by an honest admittance, I can remember the exact moment I fell in love with Marilyn.

It happened on that rainy night in New York, in the Fall of 1959, and the moment, frozen for me in a private time capsule, was the first moment I looked into her eyes. The very first moment.

A slight drizzle was falling at the appointed hour when I pulled my car to the curb, just outside of The Brass Rail, a restaurant on upper Broadway just above Times Square. It was 4:30 in the afternoon, and as usual, she wasn't late. Dodging the rain, she jumped into the car, sat immediately beside me, and kissed me lightly on the cheek, offering a simple "Hi." No cymbals crashed, no background score zoomed up from anywhere, and no choirs were heard. Very simply put, I was whole again.

She carried a larger than normal purse slung over her shoulder which she pitched into the back seat.

To explain it before my question, she said, "Three days worth of stuff!"

"Your luggage," I answered, steering the car off Broadway and into the direction of the Queens Midtown tunnel.

"Of course," she giggled, snuggling close."Things alright now?" , I asked.

"Right now they are," she answered, a slight trace of bitterness building in her voice as if in memory. She began brushing her hair and with each stroke seemed to grow tense. I gave her a light for her cigarette, and after inhaling deeply and blowing the smoke out almost with a vengeance, she began to say what now filled her mind.

"You said you sometimes wondered what I do when

we're not together," she began, "well I'll tell what I've been doing since last Friday."

"It's not important," I said, trying to give her a way out.

"Oh yes it is," she said, her voice filled with fire and spit. "It's damned important, because it's so God-damned typical."

As I could tell she was bound to clear the air, I shook my head to acknowledge the fact that I was listening. Like a poor poker player, Marilyn only swore when things went completely wrong, and thus gave her hand away even before she'd get to the issue.

"I've just spent the entire week FIGHTING!," she continued. "Not arguing, discussing, fighting! You know I've been working on some dance routines for this new film, well, the script hasn't been finished, but I've seen some of the rough drafts. I told them I can't do a film like this, so they've taken it back for re-write. I'm starting to worry that it's going to take more than just that! My lawyer and I got into it first over the phone, and then in person. It was then that I found out that *I* was being unreasonable. Arthur started putting his two-cents into all of it, and, as usual, agreed with everybody else. He called me a spoiled bitch who didn't know her ass from her elbow. SO I THREW HIM OUT! But not before he took a swing at me."

She took another drag from her cigarette.

"Personally, I think Arthur's seeing someone, a secretary or somebody. I wish to hell I could prove that, and we'd be rid of him and could still do his fuckin' script. If I even consider this current thing, it'll make "Sugar Kane" look like Lady MacBeth. The next thing they'll be telling me is that Olivier or Preminger is set to direct. If that happens, the next time we leave town we'll just keep going."

The rain was beginning to subside, unlike the tirade taking place inside the car, which continued to grow.

"Then came the friends," she went on, "a pack of vul-
tures, all of them, reaching for my ass or my wallet, sometimes both."

" You should take it easy Marilyn. You shouldn't get
excited Marilyn. You should act like a fucking dummy,
Marilyn!"

"Honey, take it easy," was all I could think to say as her
face grew angrier in the re-telling. Catching herself, her
mood slowed with the speed of the car which now rounded the bend to the beach.

"I'm sorry," she said, her voice now dropping as if in
guilt. "I just wish we could drive somewhere where none
of them could find me ever again. Where all this would
finally stop!" Her voice softened and returned to the gentle sound, so much more familiar to me. "Maybe I could
begin all over again. Only this time I'd do a lot of things
differently. Am I starting to sound crazy?"

"No," I said surprising her with my directness. "I think
that's a thought we all have every now and then." A slight
smile crept over her face and again she kissed my cheek.

"I know you're asking yourself 'who needs this?', but I
thank you for not saying it."

I slid the car into its parking space, and we walked up
the steps to the door. I had things to say, but that moment
wasn't the time. Her temper display had let the wind out
of her sails, and it was evident she was already sorry for
having said any of it. Upon entering the apartment, I
turned and locked the door behind us. I then took her
hand and walked her to the sofa, literally sitting her
down. For the first time since we had met, I sensed she
was nervous with me, as though not knowing what to
expect. Well, she'd just have to be nervous for a second,
because I wanted her to hear what I had to say and it was
as good a way of getting her attention as any. I knelt
down in front of her so as to be eye-level, and reached for

her hand. Just as in the delicatessen, it was cold.

"Ok, I listened to you, and now it's your turn to listen to me," I said, as her eyes looked right through me as though waiting for some form of chastising, a lecture. "Last week, to the night, I got a call from a friend." I began, "That friend was very sick and made me worry like I've never worried before. As soon as I was certain my friend was alright, I left to take care of the reason for her illness. I succeeded in doing just that." As she listened, the color returned to her cheeks, and her eyes began tearing. It didn't matter. I wasn't finished and had to drive this point home once and for all. "I then went to visit my grandmother," I continued, "and we discussed a very important person without mentioning any names. I finished a script in record time, and then went to the TOA convention where I met the one and only real friend I have in the world." Her hand grew warm, and she held mine tightly now. "And do you know what I said to myself after each meeting, each visit, each chore..?"

She offered a negative shake of her head. "I said to myself, Ok, it's only 96 hours to Marilyn, it's only 72 hours to Marilyn, it's only 48 hours to Marilyn. Am I getting through to you?"

"You said all that?," she replied in almost proud wonder.

"You bet that sweet ass of yours, I did!"

She wiped the forming tears from her face with the free hand.

I concluded, " It was a good week and a bad week as all weeks are, but for me, the worst week in my life won't mean one God damned thing as long as you are there!"

She lurched from the sofa, and grabbed my neck. Hugging me with every ounce of strength in her, she began to cry. It wasn't the gentle tears of distress or frustration over things that suddenly didn't mean anything. It was the years washing away. It was Norma Jeane finally having her day in court. She buried her head deep into my chest and continued to sob. Again I stroked her hair and it began to calm her. I believe the words were as much to myself as to her, because in hearing my grandmother's dialogue resounding off the walls, I found the strength to say them.

"Someday you will love someone more than yourself, and it will be then, and only then, that you understand the real meaning of life, not one second before..."

Still stroking her hair, I looked down to my new reason, and whispered in her ear words I still whisper today, "I love you Marilyn." It was a hell of a way to start a weekend, but sometimes from the worst of situations comes the best.

For the next 96 hours, no one could hurt her. For now, that would have to do.

Chapter Seven

An Intermission From The World

If laughter is good for the soul, then crying is definitely good for the body. Allegorically it is nature's steam valve for the human pressure cooker. The archaic theory that strong people don't cry is riddled with holes. Those who follow the stoical path become prime candidates for nervous disorders and heart attacks. Acknowledged human frailty, stress, anxiety, frustration and all the sisters and brothers of these popular conditions, have to be released somewhere. Just as a volcano must erupt, so too must we. Marilyn was that volcano.

Somewhere between the early days of the idealist Norma Jeane Baker to the then-present time of Marilyn Monroe, simple dreams seemed to disintegrate on a daily schedule. To the observer, Marilyn had accomplished what so many had not. World recognition and fame were held in her tiny hands, but at a cost much greater than she had invisioned. She had graduated from being a lost child that no one wanted, to a lost woman that no one understood. In openly crying in my arms, she paid our relationship its greatest compliment. No pretense existed between us as none was necessary. There were no angles, no hidden motives, nothing in any subtext that would label us anything but what we were. There no longer was any reason to look over our shoulder, as no one was there. During our short time together, the rest of the world simply ceased to exist.

After apologizing unnecessarily for the puffy eyes that remained after the explosion of tears, she felt the need to take a shower. A logical epilog to a rough week, and the best prescription to wash the rest of it away. As she did, I ran down to the Pig N' Whistle and returned with some hamburgers and fries. On entering my apartment I found her waiting, scrubbed, clean and shiny again. She liked wearing my shirts, and I enjoyed seeing her in them. God knows they looked better on her than on me. She was curled up on the sofa reading that masterpiece Mark and I had just finished. It had become my habit to make a copy, to keep, of every script I'd doctored. Often they became a research tool in themselves for future scripts.

Marilyn had an insatiable appetite for everything from sex to hamburgers. She also had an incredible desire to progress, to learn, to improve. She was never willing to lay back and consider the job done. By her own admittance, this same appetite had gotten her into trouble. She spoke openly and adamantly about her past indiscretions, recognizing many of them for what they really were. For some, the memory had been sweet, while for others, bitter. Rather than try to catalog her regrets, she preferred seeing all of them as an additional learning experience.

It appeared everyone wanted a piece of Marilyn, in the strict sense of the word. Whether that piece was physical, emotional, or financial, Marilyn gave whatever she could. Problem was, she was so very seldom repaid for that giving. As the rocket of her success rose higher and higher, there were times when she just seemed to be running amok, as though she suddenly lived only for the hour. Many of those hours would come back to haunt her. It was those hours of promiscuities that now paint an inaccurate picture of her and seem to hold such fascination for writers of scandal. Assuming can be inflammatory, and supposition a million miles from any truth. Had you never looked below the surface, or, if in fact, had you been born on Mars and never heard her name, the writings of the last 30 years would form the following picture:

She was a born neurotic who suffered from schizo

phrenia and paranoia, who ultimately turned to drugs and alcohol to escape the reality of her own delusions. While participating in all of this, she managed to "bed" several hundred men, and generally disrupt the society within her own profession as well as the world at large.

The above portrait comes to you courtesy of many who had the audacity to call themselves friends, and caring associates.

Watching her reading the script, now so comfortably at ease on the sofa, made me acutely aware of the responsibility that was in my hands. The admission that I loved her, and the look in her eyes that returned that feeling to me, put us on the playing field, and the game would certainly not be played on a bed of roses. Both of us had definite personalities. It would have to be give and take in its finest sense, to make it work. The nights may have been filled with untold pleasures, but the days would have to work as well. There was no changing Marilyn, as both DiMaggio and Miller had discovered. Boasting of how lucky she was to have you didn't work either. James Dougherty found that out. The best we could hope for was that each might fine-tune the other. A time to dream and a time to work. Both were good in their places. What would not be good, was confusing them. Marilyn's fire could have seen her conquer worlds even she had not yet dreamed of, but at this point, the flames were darting in opposing directions. They had to be controlled by her and properly channeled. For myself, I was only on the first step and had a great deal to learn. I continued to prove that daily, but like the ram in the story books, my constant beating into the wall would ultimately see it crumble.

We shared the feeling of being an unbeatable duo, and discussed it openly many times. We would alternate between teacher and student, each giving to the other what may have been lacking. It would have been the perfect working scenario, combining and uniting the soft with the hard, had the rest of the world not gotten in the way. It was about 8 pm, and although I really didn't want to disturb her reading of the script as she seemed so intent in that pursuit, I knew Bob would be waiting for my promised phone call and probably with a greater curiosity than usual. I could see, by the pages, that she was near the end.

"When you're through, honey, I want to run something by you," I said, softly enough not to distract, but loudly enough to have her hear.

"Ok," she said, still engrossed. I took this opportunity to pour us each a glass of wine, and by the time I had done so, she closed the script. Handing her the glass, she looked to me and smiled. "It's good!," she said, "It's really good. It had ME goin'."

She took a sip of wine and continued, "No one ever offers me a script like this," she said, "I could do that role, but no one's ever going to ask me to try."

"Well now, you just never know about things like that," I said and meaning it. "Life is full of surprises, just look at us."

"I suppose," she mumbled, "Maybe that script of Arthur's will change some of this...."

"Maybe it will," I answered.

"You think it might?," she bubbled with the thought.

"I don't know, I haven't read it."

"But I have, or at least what he's done so far."

A little voice inside kept nudging me during the conversations about this script. It wasn't just this night, it had been many. At the beginning I had considered keeping that voice quiet, but Marilyn had so counted on this thing, it appeared almost dangerous. I rolled the dice.

"Can I ask you something, I mean, straight ahead?"

I began.

"YOU can ask me anything.," she answered with an accent on our mutual respect for each other.

"Okay, but don't take this the wrong way," I began, before allowing her to consider that statement. "What IS so damned important about that script, what do you see in it, why do you so want to do it?"

"It's a good part for an actress," she returned, " a serious part. It will give me a chance to show them all what I can really do. It will put HER in her place."

I knew all about "HER," and understood, but,...I also understood the public. So many of the script revisions had been because of that public, that massive mob of critics who sat waiting to be entertained with judgement on their minds.

"There's an old actor's story that goes like this," I said, "On his death bed, a famous Shakespearen actor said to the question posed by his best friend on death itself, 'Death is easy, comedy is hard',"
"That story goes right along with the old 'cannon gag', that classic one liner, but in all of these famous stage stories is a hidden truth."

"You don't think I can do it," she said, now ever so much more serious.

"I didn't say that, Marilyn," I answered, wishing to go further.

"When you say 'Marilyn', it's like my mother and my aunt calling me 'Norma Jeane'. That meant that they were mad at me."

"I'm not mad at you," I said, quickly removing that stigma." And it's not that I think you can't do it, it's more than that. You have a gift, and it's a real one. You have a way of making people feel 'happy', a special gift for the human comedy that can not be taught by a thousand Lee Strasbergs. At this point in time, people go to your movies to feel happy. Whatever you do, and however you have learned to do it, you make them identify with you."

"They laugh at me'," she answered wearing a pout.

"They laugh with you'," I said, now finishing. "I know you want them to see you as you are, and I know all about 'her', but I'm not sure they want to see you destroy her that drastically. I've seen Miller's plays, I've read them. They are depressing. No one ever WINS in a Miller scenario. They begin at a low level and manage to go even lower. Now I know he's won praise for his work, and I'm certain that praise was well deserved, but DEATH OF A SALESMAN is hardly the up-lifting experience of the century."

"Lee has told me how to deal with that," she said now proudly, and I know she believed it.

"I'm not getting through," I continued, more than casually frustrated, "This isn't about LEE, this is about YOU." The more I had heard about Lee Strasberg and his magic factory, the more I had begun to dislike certain elements about it. In plain English, her great mentor had spent far too much time blowing smoke up her ass. Somehow, he had convinced her that "drama" was the end of it all. And for her, and for what she had become, he was wrong.

"Now you just said you liked the script you just read," I said.

"Yes," came her timid reply.

"You said you could do that role."

"Yes, I know I could"

"Did you like the ending?"

"Yes, I was glad she made it."

"Okay, suppose, instead of her being 'rescued', she had been killed. Would you still have liked it?"

"Peter, it's a different kind of story."

"Honey, would you still have liked it?"

"No."

Marilyn and those eyes. They said it all, and sometimes there was no fighting them. She was misinterpreting all I was trying to say, and instead of helping, I was hurting. It was time to stop.

"Baby, I wouldn't hurt you for the world," I said, now wrapping it up. "But I don't want anyone else to either. Maybe I'm just not seeing the big picture."

She began to smile, recognizing my intention. "You wait and see," she said, "You'll be proud of me."

On that I shook my head affirmatively. "I'm always proud of you. You never have to worry about that."

She kissed me lightly on the forehead, and moved to the kitchen. We had graduated from wine to Champagne, which she honestly liked better, and she reached into the refrigerator, withdrew a bottle, and popped the cork. Personally, I hated that stuff, but as it made her happy to serve it, had it been gasoline, I would have shared it.

She returned with the two glasses, handed me one, and plunked herself onto the sofa. With glass in hand, I sat on the floor beside her. We toasted, and sipped. "I have to ask you a question," I began," and I need an honest answer."

"Whoops, now what did I do?," she said, half-kiddingly."

"No, it's nothing like that," I said. "As a matter of fact, this is something you might WANT to do, but we need to talk about it." I had her attention. "I'd like to take you somewhere tomorrow, before we leave for the mountains, and have you meet someone."

Looking up to her, I could see the wheels begin turning. "I have one real friend in this world, besides you," I said, "his name is Bob. He and I went through school together. We trust each other. Remember what you said about not mistrusting everybody? Well, here is an example of that."

Her expression went blank, as it so often did, when she had absolutely no idea where the conversation was heading. "I haven't seen him for awhile, but I met him at the TOA Convention last week. During the same time you were probably fighting with your attorney. He asked me to meet his new girl friend, and suggested I bring someone with me for a few hours on his uncle's boat. It's docked only a few miles from here." The blank expression was changing to a slight smile. "I didn't say YES, but I didn't say NO. I said, MAYBE."

Between us there were no secrets, and we could generally tell the other's thoughts before they became verbal. Her smile broadened as I continued. "I know how you feel about privacy, and I know why, but I think we might make a compromise in this case." Marilyn, playfully, took a sip from her wine, allowing those blues to eye me over the rim. I didn't know then had I suggested we go to hell together, she would have asked what time we would leave.

"It doesn't change the Poconos," I continued, now slowing for a reaction, "and it's no big deal if you'd rather not go. Just...."
She interrupted my stammering by placing her hands under my face, peering directly into my eyes.

"Always protecting me," she said in a low, sensuous, caring voice. "You make me ashamed for anything I've ever done wrong." Her spirits lifted. "Of course we can go. We can do anything you want to do, you don't need my approval. I know you would never take me anywhere I could be harmed. I know that." She reached down and kissed me lightly, reassuringly, my head still cupped in her hands. "You call Bob and tell him we'll be there."

"Now you're sure," I countered, giving her one last chance to back out gracefully.

"I'm sure," she said most positively. We both rose from our positions, and as I headed for the telephone, she began to perform stretching exercises after having been seated in one position for such a long time.

As I dialed, I watched her. She was some piece of work. If Bob had waited one more second to pick up his phone, he would have been talking to himself.

"So? Are we doin' it?" he questioned, wondering what new excuse I might invent.

"Under certain conditions," I answered.

"Say what's with you?," he fired back, anxiety and curiosity ringing in his voice.

"I'm going to say this only once, and I need an answer," I continued.

"Ok, Ok!, stop sounding like Lamont Cranston!," he snapped.

"You have to promise to leave your newscaster's hat at home, and if you remember the definition of 'discretion', you have to use it."

"For Christ's sakes Peter, who the hell are you bringin', Marilyn Monroe?"

"Maybe I am," I answered.

"Yeah, right!," he snapped now in complete control of his sarcasm. "I don't know what the joke is, but I hope you let me in on it soon!"

"It's no joke," I said, now to deaf ears. "What time do you want us there?"

"How's eight grab you?"

I turned to a still stretching Marilyn."Is eight too early?" She shook her head, placing me back on the phone. "Eight's fine," I answered, " now get some sleep."

"Ok Lamont!," he concluded, "We're on Slip 12, and, er.." I knew he was fishing for the punch line. He found one.

"Oh, and yes, give my best to Marilyn Monroe will you!"

"Alright," I answered, which just set him into roaring laughter as he hung up the phone.

If the truth were known, I was probably carrying this "cloak and dagger" thing too far, but I still went by the law that rules were made to be followed. If sometimes foolishly.

As though the week finally conceded its defeat, the night of the weekend took hold. It was at times like this, when all that remained was the pleasant sound of two heartbeats. I would forever be grateful to the powers that be for the treasure that lay beside me.

Marilyn had extremely fair skin, and the sun was not her friend, at least not in great doses. She jumped out of the bathroom carrying a tube of sun lotion which I then applied. That maneuver became an extreme endurance test. Among the stuffings in her over-sized purse, she had brought along a pair of short-shorts, which she slipped on. She then grabbed the shirt of mine she had been wearing the night before, slipped it on and tied it into a bow at the waist. We were ready, but I wasn't certain Bob would be.

The parking area was still a short walk to the actual boatslips. I could see Bob and his new girl friend, standing on board the slick Chris-Craft, straining to see just who this "phantom lady" was. The distance was too great. Now near the water's edge, we passed other boats with home-port names like NANTUCKET, MAINE, MARTHA'S VINEYARD. Uncle George had made his money in toys, and had named his boat, appropriately, THE SANTA ONE, below which, in smaller letters was, OYSTER BAY, LONG ISLAND.

Good old Bob was waving and smiling, and waving some more, holding a cup of coffee in his left hand. I knew we were coming into focus, and it became comically obvious the second he recognized Marilyn. His entire face dropped several feet below his waist. Matter-of-factly, I guided Marilyn onto the dock and lifted her gently onto the boat, watching Bob out of the corner of my eye. His features had literally frozen. His lady friend watched as well, but seemed to gain more enjoyment in observing him. She began laughing.

Now, nose to nose, I greeted them. "Gonna be a nice day" I turned to Marilyn who simply smiled, quite used to this sort of reaction.

"Honey," I said, "This is Bob and..." The girl spoke up, "Judy."

"Ok," I continued, Bob and Judy, Bob and Judy, meet Marilyn."

Taking the initiative, Judy immediately reached out to Marilyn and they playfully shook hands. Bob, on the other hand, took a deep sigh.

"I'm very pleased to meet you Miss Monroe," he said, in near broadcast tones. Marilyn shook his hand and in that soft voice ended his agony,

"It's Marilyn, Bob, just Marilyn"

Bob repeated the name, "Marilyn," and then, as if snapping out of his trance, he stumbled to regain control.

"Of course! Marilyn! You must think I'm an idiot"

"Yes she does," I broke in.

"And you!," he fired his mock-angered expression in my direction. "You could have told somebody!!! "

"I did."

"But you didn't expect me to believe you..!" he snapped.

Knowing Bob had a few things on his mind, Judy jumped to the rescue and suggested she and Marilyn explore the boat. Picking up the ball, Marilyn agreed.

Once out of earshot, Bob began: "Exactly what the hell is going on here?," he stammered. "I mean, Pete, you could have said something. She probably thinks I'm a mental retard!"

I found myself grinning in understanding.

"Would you have really believed me if I would have made an issue out of it?"

"No," he replied, " but at least I could have been

warned."

"Don't worry," I assured him, " Marilyn's used to it. I've seen other examples since we've been together."

"Wait! Stop!," he exclaimed, "*since we've been together??* What is all this?," he asked in honest curiosity.

"It's a long story," I said, trying to calm him.

"I'll just bet it is," he concluded.

"That's why I brought up discretion," I said.

"Now I know what you meant by that," he continued, "Yeah, yeah..don't worry" His voice began calming. The initial shock was wearing off. "But Pete, for God's sake..."

"She's a lovely girl, Bob," I said. "And one who's become very special to me"

"Are you telling me this is SERIOUS?," he again screamed in a whisper.

"That's what I'm telling you," I went on, "The situation is kinda mixed up, but we're not. She came into my life purely by accident, and since she has, it's all turned around. Before you make any other judgement calls, I'd like you to get to know her."

"I feel like I already do," he went on, " I've seen all her movies."

"No, not that way," I was quick to jump on that line, "That's not her. Not at all her."

For dramatic purposes, he stepped back a few feet and looked me straight in the eye.

"I'll be a cross-eyed son of a bitch, you are serious. What happened to 'Burn'em Up Barnes'?" He had often used that expression, the title of an old Saturday matinee serial, to describe my plan, my flashing ambitious climb.

"Oh he's still there," I assured him, "He's just found a better reason."

He put his arm over my shoulder. "I gotta admit," he said, "If I hadn't seen it, no one could ever have made me believe it!"

"You mean Marilyn.." I said, looking over my shoulder at Judy and Marilyn who had now advanced to coffee and chit chat.

"Yeah, I suppose, partially," he said with a half-grin on his face. "But no, not just Marilyn, YOU. I guess I mean you. Remember me? I stood up with you on the last go-round. I was the Best Man and I didn't give it 6 months. Can't imagine how anyone else felt. I didn't think I'd ever hear this from you, then, now or ever. I guess it took the champ to knock you down to the rest of us..."

"You have a colorful way of putting things," I said, but then reminding him. "You're the first outside people in on this. Just take a minute to get to know her."

"Under one condition," he said with a grin, "If it goes the distance, which from where I'm sitting it looks like it might, I get to be Best Man again and this time I bring my crew."

"Done," I said, knowing that the road to that possibility would be a long one.

Despite the worlds we had elected to conquer, and the methods by which we had perceived to do so, both Bob and I had been raised by families who considered manners an item of paramount importance. Perhaps in high school, watching us as would a fly on the wall, you might have considered that upbringing forgotten. It wasn't. Bob's initial reaction to Marilyn was no more or less foolish than would have been anyone's, but after our brief talk, and now knowing the truth of it all, he began demonstrating just why he had become my one true friend.

A friend sees you for exactly what you are. If you stumble, he is there to help you regain your footing. If you receive an award, he sits in the first row to applaud. If you lose it all, his couch can become your bed and his loyalty the crutch to lean on to regain whatever it is that has been lost. He is deaf to whatever rumors may be aimed at you, and it is his own opinion that counts and only that. He is there to warn you of impending disaster, and pick you up in the event you fail to heed that warning. If it were possible he would gladly swap his health for your stay in the hospital. Bob was just that kind of friend.

Other than the unnecessary apologies for his first behavior, nothing more was said during the entire 6 hour cruise and stop-over. Aside from a playful "wolf-whistle" if Marilyn would bend or stretch a certain way, Bob had accepted the fact that this was, at least, a very strong friendship and not by any means a weekend fling. Judy, whom I had just met, was a lovely girl, an auburn haired beauty who had chosen as her life's career, the work of a CPA. She was warm, friendly, vivacious and personable. She and Marilyn had already hit it off. No accountant I ever had looked like this, or indeed possessed such charm. By the time the boat actually left the dock, we were, as I had hoped, four friends attending a good time in the warmth of an early Fall day.

There would have been no way for me, even only a few years back, to have ever envisioned this picture. I think Bob had to feel the same, and yet, as we moved lazily down the coast, we had become part of it. Rather than leave the bay area and head out to open sea, we dropped anchor and just floated around for a while engaging in conversation. The girls tolerated the dialogue between Bob and myself about the "good old days" which were then about 2 years before. Bob's reference to my music caught Marilyn's attention and his remarks of how the film industry's gain had been the music world's loss did not go unnoticed. As Marilyn and I were still learning about each other, each new suggestion added to our mutual growing file. Unlike Lauren Bacall who had used a young Andy Williams voice to dub over her songs in TO

HAVE AND HAVE NOT, Marilyn possessed a soft and real voice of her own. Mutual friend Lionel Newman would often comment on that and as he had scored several of her films, he had only compliments in that direction. Judy chipped in with her one and only experience in show-business, where else, but in little theatre.

"My first line was 'Bacon and eggs in the oven mother,'" she said. "But when stepping on stage to observe a full house, it came out 'Bacon and mother in the oven'."

This first performance concluded her career.

Marilyn was quick to rescue her by offering the fact that THIS never changes. She suggested a time when she had rehearsed each line so carefully as to remember every comma and semi-colon, only to have the lights go on to a blank memory. Laughing about it now, she reminisced about having been dropped by both Fox and Columbia in her early career as those then in command saw little in her and felt she wasn't quite what THEY were looking for. Bob jumped in with, "My God, what were they looking for?" to which Marilyn replied, "They're never really sure."

The attention then focused on me, and Bob sounded-off as he had in the beginning of my career regarding my position of anonymity. He never really understood how I could do all this work and not want to be recognized for it. I explained that, in many ways, it was a double-edged sword. If the film hit, I would know I had something to do with it. If it "bombed," it didn't effect my standing. Those on the front line took all the heat. Marilyn was quick to back me up on this point, as two of her films had garnished mixed reviews.

"The public forms an opinion of you even before you do," she began. "When I was given DON'T BOTHER TO KNOCK and NIAGARA, the studio thought they would broaden my image, no pun intended. The audience didn't want to see me as a neurotic baby-sitter or a potential killer plotting her husband's murder. There were some kind notices, and the films broke even, but nothing like the musicals and the comedies."

"Peter and I saw NIAGARA together at the Calderone theatre," Bob chirped in. "I thought you were great!"

"I didn't," she went on, "but not because of the story. I could have made a lot more out of Rose, but I was held back in favor of more shots of my behind. Joe Cotten and I both had some suggestions to give it more meat, but they were shot down in flames."

"It must be rough being part of something you know can be better, and have to settle for a decision made in a tall building somewhere...." Judy commented.

"I don't think I've ever heard it put better," Marilyn concurred.

"I'm only sorry I can't get this all on record," Bob said, the reporter in him itching to get out.

"Don't worry Bob," Marilyn continued, " Nobody wants to hear this stuff anyway, 'least not from me."

"One thing about being a CPA," Judy said, "The only fame I ever receive is around tax time if I can save somebody a bundle."

"And you give such great pencil," Bob added. He aimed his next question at me. "What are you on now? Another mystery, a tale of things that go bump in the night?"

"Far from it," I answered, "It's an eastern-western."

Well that got attention.

"Hopalong Capone!" Bob fired.

"No," I went on, "It's a gangster film that a certain star wants converted to an outlaw film."

"Piece of cake," Bob suggested, "Throw in a few *howdy's* and *partners* and you're in."

"Not really," I said. "It takes a face lift from start to finish."

Whenever I would begin to discuss my work, I could always see Marilyn out of the corner of my eye, smiling and making ready to listen. Something seemed to tickle her about what she referred to as, my "intensity." I think she was proud.

Pictures of myself from that period do not project the image of 22, as I don't think I was ever really 22. I believe I was born 30, and perhaps, on the grand scale, that may have been a contributing factor in leading me to Marilyn, and she to me. As a matter of fact, I know it was. I believe somewhere in this equation, our ages came together.

"One thing about the news," Bob stated, " You can offer opinion but you can't re-write it."

"It has to be fascinating," Marilyn said, "What we do is make-believe, your job concerns history."

"Oh, yeah, it's definitely fascinating," Bob said half serious and half tongue in cheek.

"But we have our big buildings too, those who tell us HOW to.   The news comes in on a ribbon, just facts. We arrange those facts to make news. The interpretation of that news changes every day.   Black and white riots become 'racial unrest', crooked politicians become 'misinterpreted leaders', and social values are masked in clever wordage the likes of 'change' and 'revolution'. It is difficult to report the news without offending someone or some group. Once in a great while, you get to tell the unvarnished truth, or cover a story that has honest merit. So you both can see, especially you Marilyn, why movies are still so popular. Who wants to hear the truth of a failing government when one can rather watch a beautiful girl remind them that there still are such things..?"

It was as good a place as any to pause. The matter of food suddenly reared its head and we all agreed unanimously that breakfast was in order. We piloted the boat into a visitor's slip near a small island town and went ashore. So as not to create a scene or spoil the simple spontaneity of the whole affair, Marilyn slipped on dark glasses and a kerchief, to which Judy remarked: "It must be horrible to be forever hiding from people."

Matter-of-factly, Marilyn answered, "Not horrible, just easier. Saves a lot of fuss all the way around. You get used to it."

This particular town was loaded with curio shops and quaint little personality adornments. We selected a place for breakfast that seemed to take its lead from New England as its decor suggested a time of whalers and sea farers who lived off the bounty of the ocean. It had its own distinct personality as did those who worked there all of whom were dressed for a different period and, indeed, a different era. Conversation continued between us, the why's and wherefore's of it all, talk between friends. When the waitress arrived to hand us the check, which Bob insisted on picking up, she also politely handed Marilyn a piece of paper and a pen, and along with it a great big smile. Marilyn looked up to her, still sporting sunglasses.

"It wasn't the face, Miss Monroe," the waitress beamed. "It was the walk." Our attention then focused to the counter wherein the entire staff stood smiling in unison. Marilyn signed it, "To the gang at Beachers, Love Marilyn." The waitress promised not to exhibit it until we were clearly out of the place. This tactful demonstration brought a singular smile to all our faces, as well as a look of awe from Judy who might have earlier considered the disguise unnecessary. Marilyn thought as did Bob and I. If fans can give that kind of warm respect, they deserve the title of cherished friends in disguise.

After picking up a few six-packs and some Coke, we strolled back to the boat. Bob stepped out of regular position to place his arm around Marilyn for a moment.

"Peter's a lucky guy," he said, "you know I kinda watch out for him, but guess what..?"

Smiling, Marilyn reacted, "What?"

"He's right about you! One hundred percent right!" he answered.

The remainder of that early afternoon was spent in quiet relaxation, mooring once in awhile, moving once in awhile. A great deal of mutual affection was spread over the deck of that boat with each for each other and all for the group. If people in general could only bottle that, how different Bob's newscasts might have been.

Chapter Eight

Promises In A Storm

The city offers lights, excitement, challenge, a place to succeed in ambition, where activity breeds activity, and sleep is regarded as a necessary evil. The city is also a place of foul air, unrest and violence, and of claustrophobic behavior that is both stifling to the human heart, and destructive to the soul. It creates the illusion of being "all," when in fact it very often becomes "nothing" in the grander plan. You can not see the stars from a city, or sniff the fragrance of a flower that has not been touched by carbon monoxide fall-out. If and when you can see it at all, the sky is very rarely blue. It is an ant hill, whose citizen's must keep busy lest they pause and consider the materialistic futility of it all. It is a land of contradiction where only the body can survive, as the spirit and soul withers. It is a place from which one must depart, if only on occasion, to regroup a small portion of life's honest promises.

The drive to the Pocono Mountains took only a few hours, but the change was from day to night. This mountain range bordered the eastern section of Pennsylvania, and contained some of the most beautiful green trees, golden meadows, and clear blue running streams in the world.

Marilyn's head rested on my shoulder for most of the trip, as the excitement of freedom had given her something that had been missing for all too long, peace of mind. This, for us, would be a time to really get away. A time to catch up on dreams, and explore the mysteries of each other. A place where stress found no vacancy.

The Mountain View Lodge was as rustic as its name implied, and sometime around 6pm, we pulled into its tree-lined driveway. Marilyn had awakened a few miles back, in time to observe the full effect of the changing colors of Fall before sunset. It was a sight no mortal artist could paint.

An elderly couple owned and operated the entire place, which included private cabins, the main lodge, a restaurant, and a smaller building set aside for evening dances and private parties. I had stumbled onto this place at one time when the need to get away finally over took me, and had returned when the inner pressure gage read "danger." On one of my former visits I had played the piano for a couple and their friends on the occasion of their 50th Wedding anniversary. As a result, I had a standing invitation to return as often as I had wished. I had never brought anyone here until now, but as Marilyn had changed my life, so too had she changed everything in it. In totally unrealistic terms, I would have had her with me the 24 hours of every day and the 365 days of every year had such a dream been possible.

The owner, we'll call him John, if for no other reason than it seems lots of old-timers are called John, handed me the key to the special cabin. It was special because of the 20 or so cabins on the premises, this one stood isolated from the rest, offered a private patio surrounded by a small well-kept fence, and rested by a running stream.

This particular resort, which had been the private dream of the couple who owned it, catered to whatever your mood might be. For "joiners," there was always activities in progress to keep them busy, but for those who had come to get away, there was no "bubbling camp counselor" to annoy them with planned recreational ideas. With the use of a small cart, they offered what most resorts of this kind didn't, room service. This motorized wagon, an invention of the owner, could have been the prototype to today's elaborate golf carts.

This place had a personality all its own, and could never

be compared to the "cookie cutter" chains of similar resorts that offered only more of the same you had probably just left.

Memories can trick you.

Embellishment is a trap many of us fall into when recalling the past. Stretching the truth to cover up what may have been more mundane than we remember is a common, sometimes subconscious act. While it is both understandable and forgivable, it is still inaccurate. If the memory is that of a very special loved one, the danger of embellishment is even greater. I would enjoy telling you that Marilyn "walked on water," that she was indeed a flawless human being whose radiance dwarfed that of the sun. That the seas parted at her sight, and that the walls of every room she entered sung with her praise.

Marilyn did none of that, and inspired none of that. What Marilyn did do was teach me how to love, to laugh, and to cry. Marilyn was as real as they come, and not at all the poster image that has created the "legend." That same image is a very small fraction of what she was, a one dimensional look at a multi-dimensional person. She may have been a lot of things to a lot of people, but the one thing she never was, was mundane.

It had been a wonderful day, free of stress and worry, and despite the biological sparks between us, we were both tired. We had a light supper on the patio, a chilled bottle of wine, and sat, for a time, on the comfortable couch-like chairs provided by our host. Stars we had never seen filled the sky, and the sounds of crickets and the nearby running stream had, as their underscore, the strains of music originating from the recreation room. For the moment, our mutual treadmills had been switched to "off." The world itself seemed distant.

We lay in bed, facing each other, savoring the memories of the day in small talk. As urgency was not part of this equation, there was no need, for the moment, to stir the coals. In seconds, with my arms about her, she was sleeping. As I had always considered Marilyn a gift, my last word before joining her in that sleep was "thanks," and it was directed to the author of all our lives.

Those of the Jewish faith have a word for it, and sadly it escapes me for the moment, but its translation is "soulmate." It describes a perfection we seldom attain. There is no knack to it, and no amount of practice can create it. It is simply there.

There were private feelings within my heart for Marilyn, that would not normally apply to a relationship. Something inside kept assuring me that when she slept by my side, she was "safe." A thought and word not generally part of any usual equation. There was an overwhelming urge, within me, to protect her, even possibly from herself. With or without her friends, she was very much alone, out on a short limb, and carrying her own saw. She had taken whatever they had thrown her way, and pitched it back to them. The cost had been great. In defense of her actions, she had become venomous, selfish, and spoiled. People are, after all, only people, and they see only that which they wish to see. Above it all, Marilyn had become a victim of misinterpretation and the more she would fight it, the worse it became.

As a child, in one of the many orphanages that she had been forced to call home, out of need, she had invented a father. The subject of that invention had been actor Clark Gable. Her mother had already been locked behind the wall of mental illness, and the need for a solid, recognizable father-figure was a necessity. Lies and truths come in layers. Each day you select one of those layers for what is most important to you. Each become part of the sum total. There is no right and no wrong, only the question "why?" If you can answer that question, then all lies become truths.

Of course Clark Gable was not her father and that secret was revealed in a short time. It would have been as easy to say, "I understand," than "you're a liar," but that is not the way it happened. She was branded. Other kids in the same orphanage teased her about it. Bigger kids again brought it to the surface when her star began to shine.

Then there was James Dougherty, her first husband. She was sixteen, he twenty-one. As Dougherty remembers it, he "rescued her" from still another orphanage by marrying her. When the divorce came, Marilyn again was picked as the rider of the black horse, while poor, unsuspecting James Dougherty was painted as the victim. The fact that their last night together left his immortal words ringing in Marilyn's ears, "I want to fuck you one more time, so you'll know what you'll be missing," seemed unimportant. It was, after all, easier to suspect her motives than to ask the question "why?"

Johnny Hyde had become her first unofficial agent. Hyde, a loving man, many years her senior, had been first to notice that special spark in Marilyn, and had been in a position to bring that notice to the attention of those who could place her before the camera. Unfortunately, he fell helplessly in love with her in the process, divorcing his wife as open testimony to that love.

Hyde had a bad heart. He knew his days were numbered. He proposed marriage to Marilyn, knowing he would soon be gone, and as his widow, she would naturally fall heir to his wealth. The gift of security for her is what he'd designed. Marilyn loved Johnny Hyde, but not in that way. They would share the lover's bed, from her side, out of gratitude. When Johnny died, she was again accused as an ambitious tramp who, knowing of his heart condition, literally "fucked him to death." This thought, of course, never entered her mind, but again, it was easier to see by a world that insists on wearing blinders.

Along came "Joltin' Joe DiMaggio," historically one of the greats of baseball, and deserved of that honor. Marilyn referred to DiMaggio as "My slugger," and for a brief time he was. Their near "story-book" marriage ended after nine short months. That episode crushed Marilyn, but that was soon forgotten by those eager same "bigger kids" who saw it as just another coup in her cap. Her tears were forgotten, but the "legend" lived on. The fact that the "Yankee Clipper" was selfish, and a victim of male chauvinism, honestly expecting Marilyn to give up her own dream to satisfy his, never bubbled to the top. It was Marilyn who was depicted as selfish, basically because she wanted more out of life than an apron. They would remain friends. He would ultimately placate his guilt by coming forth at a much later time but just a little too damned late.

Finally we come to Arthur Miller, who was very much a presence during our time together. Miller clearly swept up the crumbling Marilyn on the re-bound. His only claim to her was that he was there at the right time. She made herself the victim in this warped relationship from day number one. He had always managed to be around and kept popping in on her from the days of GENTLEMEN PREFER BLONDES. She appreciated his friendship and marveled at his use of "big words." Perhaps, she saw him as a father figure. Sex between she and DiMaggio had been good, but it had not worked. Maybe this time she would marry for other reasons. Even she could not remember what those other reasons might have been. Somewhere between James Dougherty and Arthur Miller came the others, a mixture of the known and unknown. Some like Marlon Brando and Frank Sinatra would remain as true friends. Others, not so.

Elsewhere, in this scenario that began on June 1, 1926

Clark Gable was an influence on Marilyn from her childhood.
She adored him as first a father-figure and finally as a friend.
This private snapshot of "The King" on the set of *The Misfits* is one
of the last of him, as he died shortly after the completion of the film.

Marilyn lost in thought enroute to location in Dayton.
It is most difficult to fathom the conflicting thoughts on her
mind at this time. This private snap shot reveals some of that
inner conflict.

Marilyn enroute to make-up call. Even the ice cream cone didn't help much in cooling the 123 degree day.

Marilyn, as she was in 1960, the time of the story.
At its original time of release, *Let's Make Love*, was
received with luke warm reception. It has become
more recognized and better appreciated over the
years.

Author Peter Collins, 1960

The "no photos" clause in our private "contract" was broken by this snap of our final day together. We were photographed by a woman who resided in Dayton, Nevada and who managed, through her grandson, to give the photo to me. Poetically, the snap (which is in Kodachrome) is the only photo memory I have (to date), and as my back is to the camera, the memory is mine alone.

This portrait was purchased by me through a company that offers this kind of thing expressly for magazine and book reproduction. Unfortunately, I do not know the photographer, but whoever he or she was, it captures Marilyn as her fans most remember her. My apologies to that un-named photographer as, in my opinion, this is one of the finest of its kind.

Despite the frustrations connected with the production of
The Misfits, Marilyn always maintained her smile for the fans.

and ended on August 4, 1962, was a man who claimed to have married Marilyn for three days in Mexico. I am in no position to acknowledge this claim or refute it. Throughout all of this, before, during, and after, her side was never heard, or if she tried, never believed. It was for these misinterpretations and contradictions, that the pills and booze scenario was born. From that scenario came the only logical result. People who had once admired her, would no longer work with her. Rumors of her unprofessional behavior on the sets of various films spread like cancer. She had become target for every weak minded, sanctimonious, self-pitying failure to point the finger at, naming her as the reason.

It is for all of this and more, that I felt the only time I knew she was "safe" was when I could literally look her in the eye. It was too late for her to give her side, as it is now too late for me to say what she would have said, but for whatever it is worth, no longer of value to her, "I hope you are all very proud of yourselves."

It was on the first night in the mountains, in what might be called a near "Eden" setting, that I began to feel the twinges of a foreboding I couldn't put my finger on. Whatever it was woke me with a start around 4am. Instinctively I looked to my right to be certain Marilyn was alright. She was sleeping soundly. As the late night, early morning had grown chilly, I covered her with an extra blanket from the foot of the bed. I then rose, made a quick cup of complimentary in-house coffee, slipped on my robe, lighted a cigarette, and stood by the bed for a moment's thought.

When Marilyn slept, she looked at peace, often with the trace of a smile on her face. As I have said, I would often observe her, if only for seconds, a voyeur of her dreams, always hoping they were pleasant ones. It was also a time to study her size, uninterrupted. How very small she was, to have cast such a huge shadow, and how many people had fed off this one human being. I bent over and stroked her hair gently, tucking her in as lightly as I could, to which she offered a quiet sigh of acknowledgement. To me, and perhaps only to me, she would always be the most beautiful girl in the world.

I sat on the patio, sipping my coffee and blowing smoke from the cigarette, staring into the sky observing the stars bidding farewell to the night as traces of a new dawn glowed in the distance.

"I love to dream," she once said, "because dreams have no boundaries." Well, on this particular early morning, in a setting that appeared as right as any could be, it wasn't a dream that had awakened me. It was a feeling that I had to shake before she rose and joined me for the new day.

If it was a premonition, it wasn't a pleasant one. A sudden feeling of sorrow, of loneliness, straight out of left field, with no provocation, had completely engulfed me. Thoughts came to me to remind me of just how fast things had fallen into place, against so many obvious opposing life-styles. How incredible it all had been from the start. It would have been a very easy task to convince anyone in the outside world that this thing between us never really happened at all. Stories like ours only happened in children's books. That kind of logic had become our greatest ally. It would have provided us with a most convenient escape clause, had anyone of the opposing camp gotten wind of it. What had been perceived as something very natural, suddenly seemed impossible, yet here we were. We had found in days what some search a lifetime for, - and all of it appeared to be on a "fast foreword" mode. It was as though Destiny, or Fate, or whatever is responsible, was telling us that we didn't have the time for preliminaries. That time, in fact, was against us, and thereby we were granted the blessing of making every second together worth while.

Her presence had already rearranged my ambitions and channeled them into their proper orbit. By the fact that she was IN my life, had changed it for the better. I began smiling at people I had previously snubbed, thinking about a future beyond that which my work could provide. The normal stress of daily life disappeared with the thoughts of soon holding her. Everything else seemed trivial.

Then came the negatives. What would I do without her? What would I become if she left? Had another man come along, I could have justified that. I might not have liked the idea, but THAT I could have recovered from. It wasn't jealousy. It wasn't ego. It wasn't anything relating to "moon, June, and spoon," it was a shallow feeling of despair that somehow she would be taken from me by a force against which I would be powerless.

Offering myself a million rationalizations only succeeded in giving me a headache. I finally settled on insecurity, and although I didn't feel insecure about anything, I had to give it something to silence the screams.

Her voice startled me, coming from behind.

"You're up early," she said, still in half sleep. She took one look at me, and moved quickly to my side, kneeling to seat level.

"What's the matter?," she asked in genuine concern.

I turned and gazed at her. Those beautiful eyes. I could feel my lips twinge in a gesture that I had always considered a sign of weakness, and damned them for doing so.

"Nothing's the matter," I answered light-heartedly, completely defeating that remark in the next split second by holding her close and whispering, "I just love you so damned much."

Still clasped together, her hand ran up the back of my neck and caressed it.

"It's alright," she whispered, "I'm here, nothing is wrong." I knew then and there, that those were the words I needed to hear. All of the mumbo-jumbo of the "why's" and "what if's" of only a few seconds before had been a waste of time. Gratefully, I began to snap out of it.

"I hope I didn't wake you," I said, now back in control. " I just had a bad dream, and needed to get some air."

"I rolled over and you weren't there," she said, "and that's what woke me up. Then I saw you sitting out here all alone and I said to myself 'Marilyn! Get up', so I did."

She succeeded in bringing a smile to my face. It was a knack she had in the best and worst of times. Well, with the rising sun, came the end of that drama. For the present, all was well again, and the "dream" had passed as had the night.

Spreading jelly onto an English muffin can remove any traces of any unexplainable heart murmurs that might have troubled you only an hour earlier. Watching her parading around the cabin in her birthday suit, primping and preening herself also had a strangely calming effect. Marilyn could inspire more "naughty" thoughts from you than anyone. It was part of her magic, her spell. She could make you glad you were you, and pity anyone who wasn't. She could make you forget that there was even such a word as "problem."

To me, she was a mixed cocktail of Marilyn and Norma Jeane, and it was clear in this atmosphere of peace and freedom, both "girls" could come out into the sunlight. I believe that my age, that same age that had first concerned her, was indeed working in favor of the three of us. There were no barriers between us, and image was something for the posters. She could wade through the stream or run through a field of high grass in her bare feet. There was no world illusion to keep up, no "expected" actions to deliver. She could be whomever she wanted to be. It was a place where she did not have to be "perfect."

We found a tree by the stream that ran by our cabin and sat by it. I leaned on it, and she layed on the grass resting her head on my lap. From that position we watched puffy white clouds drift by. In those clouds, she saw things that, at first, eluded me. We've all seen goats heads and faces in the clouds, sometimes fish, sometimes even giant lizards from a bygone time, but Marilyn saw Castles, the kind only seen in fairy tales. She'd point them out clearly, and soon I would see them too. It was at times like this when words of confession or optimistic hopes would come forth.

Within those words, accurate or not, was the true story of Marilyn Monroe and one that can never honestly be written.

She would speak about her rumored true father, a scoundrel by the name of C. Stanley Gifford. He remained around just long enough to impregnate her mother, Gladys Baker, as both worked at the studio. He would never be there for her, even when she had tried to contact him after the death of Johnny Hyde.

She loved her mother, but had denied her existence until a cold-hearted press discovered her. From that time on she had visited her in the institution. By then, her mother didn't recognize her, and once asked for her autograph. She had re-made contact with a half sister who, while less than famous, lived much of the same life as the early Marilyn.

There was a bond of sorts in that relationship that gave her a touch of happiness. She loved children and animals, and would have had a house filled with both, but to this date it had not happened. She adored the music of Frank Sinatra, and, in fact had had an affair with him early on. At a later time than this, Frank, that rough, tough, offensive man with the vocal strings of gold, would do what he so often did, come through for his friends. He would come through for Marilyn on that level, and as was always his style, no big deal was ever made of it.

Often in the mid-stream of her stories, her confessions, she would veer off in another direction. It would be then that she would talk of Joe with affection, Dougherty, trying to give him credit where she felt credit was due, and Miller with scorn.

The conversations would always return to us.

"What I fear the most," she would say, " is that you will get tired of me. Sooner or later they all seem to."

For that comment I would stroke her hair, as I did again, on that lazy afternoon. As often as I would try to convince her that this was a foolish thought, so often did it return.

I explained some of what I had been feeling in the early morning hours of that day. Unconsciously the re-telling of that premonition, reversed her thoughts on that particular afternoon.

"You'll never get rid of me," she said, "No matter how far away from each other we may be, it will always only be temporary."

I've counted on that, even through the years.

Marilyn would sometimes lose control, for brief periods. Play at being someone she wasn't, and then when the game was over, cry in solitude. Between us, no such game existed, and that, above all, we both had to know.

In a million million unrecorded gestures we would continue to make our mutual affection known, and took nothing for granted. She had been tricked, double-crossed, laughed at, and made part of more than one industry joke. Her awareness of this made her suspicious of everyone and everyone's motives. She had spent much of her life giving, and there were always plenty of people around who would take. No ulterior motive existed between us, and the trust of that, permitted her to give one more time. It also was made clear to her, that not only did I love her , but I also "liked her."

By the weekend in the Pocono's, Marilyn had truly become my Marilyn, and the Marilyn Monroe we spoke of, had finally become Bugs Bunny to us both.

Sometime during the early evening, the white puffy clouds gave way to thunderheads, bringing with them rain. The elements of the storm, however, were clearly outside the cabin, just as the elements of our own personal storms were now, and for a time, beyond the point of harming us. We stood together, gazing at the wind bending the trees, and the rain turning our peaceful stream into a raging rapids, relaxed and at peace knowing that our world would remain warm and secure. We had finally become the observers of a storm rather than the participants.

Soon the rain of that Fall night would give way to the snow of a winter that was yet to come, and the seeds of what appeared to die, would, in fact, only be resting awaiting the next spring. In God's world, after all, nothing ever really dies. It simply sleeps and waits to be re-born in the light of a new time, wherever and whenever that time may be.

The next day would come, and bring us to the return trip, ending this special weekend. Perhaps on that note, a slight trace of sadness filled our hearts, but as with everything, there was always the promise of another time and soon.

"You have a way with words," she often said, "and those words reveal not only who you are but what you are."

Along with the other day dreams of that weekend, came the suggestion of what the years might bring to us, and with that the thoughts of our writing her story together.

She kiddingly promised to keep the "white lies" to a minimum. On this still rainy night, with her now snuggled close to me where she belonged, her final words filled my heart with the thoughts that had started that day.

"Someday you will write about me," she said, "and it will be the truth for everyone to see, and it will make everything right again. I know that you will be the writer in the family, but this one we'll somehow do together. You must promise me this."

Before even answering, she drifted off to sleep. I made the promise with a final squeeze and a light kiss behind her ear. No words were necessary. Sometimes the unspoken word is the strongest after all.

Chapter Nine

Night Does Have A Thousand Eyes

Despite the fact that we had been tucked away in a mountain retreat far from the maddening crowd, didn't seem to upset the city. It never noticed we were gone, and managed to survive without us.

I returned to the "rat race" on Tuesday morning, a day that began just as had 800 or so mornings before it, proving conclusively, that nothing great or small would ever change that.

My schedule called for me to meet with the actor who was to play the lead in the western script I was re-structuring from the eastern gangster movie. Whenever possible, I tried to arrange such a meeting with whomever was to play whatever role was most important, as the inflections in their voice would assist me in writing the dialogue for them. It was a trick I had learned early on, and it worked. Had others done the same, the nightmare of Tony Curtis in Spartacus would never have happened.

Spartacus was an eloquent production, featuring some of the biggest stars around, among them Laurence Olivier, Peter Ustinov and Charles Laughton. Any of these three could have brought tears to your eyes reciting "Three Blind Mice," and their voices fit the biblical period. Jean Simmons, as the leading lady was perfect, as Jean Simmons usually was, and Kirk Douglas as the title lead, swung it with grace, charm and strength. Tony Curtis, the "dead end kid" from Brooklyn stood out like an onion in a rose garden. What was even worse, his role called for him to be a poet, or as the film suggested, "a singer-of sawngs." This bit of casting could be compared to hiring Percy Kilbride to sing The Star Spangled Banner at Yankee Stadium in the opening game of the World Series.

It was ludicrous. Despite Marilyn's opinion of him, Curtis had done some good work in comedies and dramas that called for that tough New York sound. It wasn't fair to Curtis or the film.

 I have no love for Curtis, for reasons that should be obvious, but in this case, I sympathized.

The lunch went off without a hitch, and I found myself very pleased with the actor in question. He knew what he wanted, aggressively pursued the feeling he had for the story, made intelligent suggestions, and listened to objections to some of those suggestions. Personally he had fallen into Hollywood by near accident after having been the most decorated hero of World War II. He had a "baby face," which worked extremely well against type, a slow even speech pattern, and carried with him, an air of authority.   Many disliked him because he knew what he was doing. As a result, most of the westerns in which he appeared were elevated above the norm in that genre. That man was Audie Murphy.

Arnold Albinski's words kept flashing in my mind as upon returning from lunch, I was informed that Mister Rachman had left instructions for me to meet with him in a private session at 2pm. Marvin Rachman was the boss. One of those "work up from mail-room" guys who started with zip and now found himself in total command. No body saw Mr Rachman unless Mr Rachman designed it. Like Claude Rains in THE INVISIBLE MAN, he was always there, at least in presence. It was he who instructed the sun to rise and set, and at what time. It was he who ultimately called the final shots, and whose signature could begin or end a film.....or a career.

Had I been the age of most of my co-workers and associates, I would have probably had the wisdom to tremble at this invitation from "god," but as youth fears little, I looked at it with the indifference of simply another learning experience. As I had been performing my duties in a completely unorthodoxed fashion, I presumed it was time to "pay the piper." I had little time to think about it as it was nearly 2pm, the possible HIGH NOON of my career. What WAS out of the ordinary, he had selected the conference room for this meeting rather than his office. Just what sort of maneuver this represented wasn't clear to me aside from the unwritten LAW of this particular company that this room was OFF LIMITS to anyone during a conference. No one outside of a fireman informing the occupants that the building was ablaze was permitted to interrupt the "conference." It was the most private arena anyone in power could have suggested, the company "confessional" if you like. There were phone jacks in the room, but unless by direct order, no phones, no intercom facilities- no touch with the outside world.

Armed with my "blue blankey," attache case, I pushed the elevator button to "Oz." Well, it had been a good run.

The "Eternal City" of Rome was currently beginning its own restoration, and I knew why it would take longer than expected. All the marble required was here on the 21st floor. The walls echoed every step and had you burped it would have come back at you in stereo. After announcing myself to the cold-blooded secretary in charge, seated at a small but polished desk, I walked the last few feet of what looked like the last mile in the death house to the grand wooden door at the end of the hallway. Upon opening the door to the inner sanctum I was somewhat surprised to find it empty.

The entire room was indirectly lighted and void of the glare of the omni-present florescent world I had just left a few stories down. It was elegant and impressive. Paintings hung on the wall separated by huge red drapes. Portraits of men who had somehow paved the way to the present status of this company itself. Bob had suggested it, Marilyn had known it to be true, and I had referred to it on many occasions. This was where THEY lived. Ominous came to mind.

As no instructions had been given me, I sat myself down near the head of the *60 foot table*, and placed my attache case on its gleaming, overly polished surface and waited. Thoughts of "so this is where it all begins," came to mind, as well as opposing thoughts of "it's not too late to run." My Brooklynese stood fast. "Run from what?", asked myself. "I mean, would this all powerful 'Oz' appear in a Charleton Heston cloud of smoke carrying two stone tablets?"

Before any additional scenarios could be created in my mind, a well-tailored secretary made her entrance from the inner door wearing a plastic smile and carrying a cup of coffee. The fact that it wasn't a styrofoam cup completed the illusion. "Mister Rachman regrets the delay Mister Collins. He will be in shortly," she said, depositing the coffee and tray of sugar before me. "May I bring you something else," she continued as though programmed. A hamburger and fries came to mind, but I passed on it recognizing a lack of that kind of sense of humor.

"This is fine," I said, "thank you."

With that she turned and walked back through the door from whence she had appeared. I observed her retreat and noticed she had no "ass." Her entire body had been encased in girdles and tight-fitting torturous clothing. She was as stiff and as cold as this room. Left with only the echoes of her footsteps I sat alone for a few moments just sipping and staring. It did give me a chance to think as I observed the "stuffed-shirts" glaring down at me from their ornately framed portraits. Places like this had been the responsible arenas for the farewells to an Arnold Albinski, for the construction and destruction of a girl named Marilyn.

For those thoughts I felt like flipping-off the bozo's who stared down at me giving them my honest opinion of the whole thing. I think if I would have had to wait another five minutes, I would have carved my initials in that polished table and left, but before considering that, Mr Rachman made his entrance.

No trumpets accompanied his arrival. Well, he was distinguished, I'll give him that. His graying hair, meticulous clothing, shined Florsheim's and pressed shirt with cuffs that could have cut through plaster, definitely set him aside from the norm. A bit on the heavy side, he wore even THAT with dignity.

A writer isn't a writer if he can't first observe, and by the time he sat down, I had x-rayed him down to his shorts, which I am certain were also pressed. It was immediately evident that one day his portrait would join "the boys" on this wall.

"I'm sorry to have kept you waiting," he began, "overseas phone call. They never seem to get the time changes right" We shook hands. So far, things were fine.

He had been carrying a file folder which he had placed on the table in front of him. In a moment, "Madam Stiff" re-appeared, deposited a cup of coffee before him, handed me another, and turned to depart. It wasn't ambition and greed that kept this business going. It certainly wasn't love and devotion. It was coffee.

"No interruptions," he said to Miss no-ass as she left.

After a well timed beat, he glanced down to the folder before him. "Peter" he said, reading from the top. "Do they call you Pete?"

"Peter," I answered.

"Alright, Peter" he began, slow and deliberate. Then came the "I'm the boss you're nobody" smile. "First off I would like to relieve your mind as to the reason for this somewhat unscheduled meeting. There are some things I prefer doing personally."

"Like pulling the trigger," I thought to myself.

"Peter," he continued, punching the name, "this organization in both its motion picture and recording arms employs approximately 15,000 people on its staff not including technicians, feature players, personalities and craftsmen. At any given time any one of their personnel files can be pulled and reviewed."

"and removed," I thought again to myself.

He sipped his coffee and continued to prolong the getting down to it. I think it was "cat and mouse" time, but what this cat hadn't considered was the short fuse on this mouse. If he didn't spit it out pretty quick, this mouse would have walked leaving him two near empty cups of coffee and a hallow room all to himself. The only patience I'd ever had was for Marilyn and my grandmother, and this guy wasn't either one. "Baby," I thought to myself with her always on my mind, "Don't beat your brains out over something like this..."

"Your name has been coming to the forefront," he began, "in any number of recent conversations within the Board, for the last 16 months or so. As a result, I became curious as to whom this person was. This human dynamo. The bright burning star!"

Whoever wrote his material needed help.

"This person, Peter," he continued with the speed of dripping water, " is you. This person responsible for or directly involved in...," he glanced to his folder, "17 projects, as well as revisionary assignments, film campaigns, and major re-writes. In my humble effort to discover your identity, I naturally called for your file."

His face formed a smile, on cue, and then a frown of bewilderment. Obviously he had been watching too many Louis Calhearn movies. "It seems, Peter," he went on, "that somehow you have accomplished these feats of bravado under the terms of contract labor. An amazing task to say the least. It became obvious to me and some of my constituents that, in a world of payroll and numbers, you do not exist. You simply DO NOT EXIST. For a young man who doesn't exist, you have an amazing feel for this business. How old are you Peter, may I ask?"

"Twenty-two," I answered.

"Twenty-two," he repeated, rolling the thought around in his head. "Incredible," he went on, " almost outrageously so. At that rate, by the time you're thirty-two you'll be seated in this chair. The last person to do that was Irving Thalberg."

"No sir, I won't," I interrupted.

"Oh please," he continued, "don't be modest"

"I'm not being modest," I returned, "I just don't want your chair."

"Oh? And why not?," he questioned raising his bushy but trimmed eyebrows, "You seem to find no difficulty in sharing an office with our in-house writers, sharing their chairs, so to speak. Why not THIS one? Why all the mystery, Peter?"

"No mystery intended, sir," I began, " I find I work more proficiently in a self-disciplined environment" To that jumble, he responded, "What the hell is that, Peter, Greek??!"

I re-stated it, "I work better alone, on my own hours."

"Now THAT I understand" , he said with a sigh and a slight chuckle. "Alright," he continued, "Personally I don't care if you do your writing in the men's room at Madison Square Garden. You might consider, however, when YOU'RE READY, of course, the benefits of a solid insurance plan with a company such as this..as I said, when you're ready. Well, now that we've cleared that up, let's get down to it."

For myself, I would have thought we had just covered

the reason, but apparently we hadn't. The first razzle dazzle was the preliminary sub-plot. His intelligent eyes scanned me with the intensity of a laser beam, accented by the awnings of very expressive eye brows.

"Currently we, the company, have investments all over this globe," he began, " A ton of money Peter, a TON of money. Films we either own or will be distributing for smaller companies are being produced in virtually every corner of the world, each with its own set of problems. It's the coming thing, independent production, and we know that. Of course we receive progress reports, and, in some cases, lack of progress reports. If either myself or those directly under my charge elect to visit these far off locations, most often the problems are swept under the rug. We are too obvious. Because of who we are, we do not receive the accurate picture and therefore can not correct the problem until it is too late. This becomes extremely costly, Peter."

Again he took a calculated beat and a sip of coffee. Lee Strasberg would have been proud. This was a REAL method actor. "I am proposing that we need an extra set of 'eyes' and 'ears', Peter. Someone with the balls to spot a problem and to handle it with a certain degree of discretionary dispatch. I am suggesting that YOU are such a person. "

The wheels started turning. To say the least THIS was totally unexpected. "I'm not sure I'm qualified, sir," was all that came to mind.

A broad smile filled his face. "Peter," there he went again, "Anyone who can finagle his way in and out of this organization, draw a hefty paycheck, and manage to call his own terms against all company policy and at twenty-two years of age, is qualified for anything! You would have 'carte blanche' and report only to this office. Your title would be "Production Representative" and it would be known that you were exactly who you were supposed to be. Now, before your ego takes off, I am not suggesting you personally can *fix* everything. I am, however, convinced that you could SPOT a problem and call it to the attention of someone who could." He sat back in his chair and waited for the wheels in my head to grasp the significance of the offer he had just made.

"Think of it, Peter," he went on, now with a flair, "Had someone made me such an offer 25 years ago, I would have already begun packing my bags!"

He viewed my hesitancy with concern, and suddenly descended from his throne to become very human. "She could go with you, Peter," he said in a near whisper, "all the way, if need be."

Someone hitting me with a sledge hammer would have been less startling than that remark. "Sir?," I quizzed.

Again that broad smile, and this time a bit less starchy. "Put your guard down, son," he smiled, "I'm not the enemy. Let me phrase it so that you can understand WHAT I'm saying and in the spirit in which I am saying it."

It was now my turn to pay strict attention as I honestly was not prepared for what was coming.

"There are about 10 million people on this small island," he began, "which makes for a very crowded place. Most people would find little difficulty in getting LOST in that kind of crowd, but you TWO are NOT most people. What's more, maybe someone like you could help her buy back a few years."

Arnold Albinski's voice now boomed in my head, but I continued to try and figure "how."..

"I'm sorry, Mister Rachman," I said, "This conversation is getting a little strange."

"Maybe I'm just a little jealous, Peter," he said, "maybe we all are ."

The words "jealous" and "all" did it. I could feel my jaw tighten.

"Marilyn, Peter," he said softly, "Marilyn....."

I could feel my throat constrict and gratefully I wasn't drinking coffee at that moment. All sorts of things raced through my head.

"I see," I said, beginning to assemble my attache case in preparation for departure. He placed his hand on mine in a gesture of friendship.

"Oh for Christ's sake Peter, sit down," he said now playing "uncle Marvin." Well, at this moment, he was still the boss, and he did succeed in slowing my exit.

"You're not being objective," he said, "for a minute you're showing your age. Now use your head and take the benefit of mine."

Ok, ..I would listen, but that was probably about all.

"I applaud your code of ethics," he began, " we all do. But they are entirely unworkable in this business. They might work for a farmer in Iowa, but not for a writer in New York. What's more you're partner is hardly 'plain Jane from Spokane.' The moment, the second you set foot into this business, you open your life to the world. This applies most definitely to someone whose image is as recognized as a bottle of Coca-cola. If you honestly think that you can drive through Times Square in a red convertible with Marilyn Monroe by your side and not be noticed, then you are in serious need of psychiatric help. This, however, is not the issue here. It is NO secret, but we have elected to keep it one and I say WE. I have discussed this with men in my position at Fox. I have spoken to columnists, some of whom we own, and hell, I've had lunch with two publicity people from UA who have joined the growing list of your admirers. Now you and she may end up 'the match of the century.' If such a thing happens, I'd be happy to dance at your wedding as would the 50 or so people who have already become your quiet allies."

There was little to say.

"Now I'm sure you both think it's YOU against the world, but you're wrong. Some of us DO CARE, several of whom including myself may have tried to make points with her unsuccessfully. I assume you can understand that. The job offer stands. If you are honestly thinking of her security as well as yours, I suggest you give it some damned serious consideration."

It was his turn to stand and I followed his lead. We shook hands. The twinkle in his eye could have been a well-wish, but it could have cloaked an ultimatum.

"I will," I said with nothing much else to say. As I exited the huge heavily draped, thickly carpeted arena, I felt some honest soul searching was in order. The entire episode had been more than slightly overwhelming.

Chapter Ten

Thoughts

The Impalas recording of "I Ran All The Way Home" seemed a fitting underscore to that day as that is precisely what I did.

The expressway and all of its inhabitants went blurry as my only thoughts were to leave the city for some air. On my subsequent beach stroll that early evening, the former weekend seemed both a zillion miles away and yet only an inch from my mind that then whirred like a buzz saw. Much of what Marvin Rachman had said stuck as would a caramel in a cavity, and I kept trying to replay it in diagnostic fashion. Was it honestly a "golden" opportunity, or did it mask the insinuation of "get out of town before sundown?"

Marilyn was a very hot property in terms of bottom-line at the box office, the only real barometer the industry understands. Had I somehow posed a threat to that same hot property, that "thing" she had come to call it? By Rachman's own words, were those in her home studio, Fox, becoming more than casually interested? Was this sudden job offer a conspiracy within a conspiracy to send me far away from her?

It would not have been the first time the powers at work had performed such a feat and worse. Always remember Sammy Davis Jr's good eye! But then his superficial sincerity....was it just an act, or did he mean it? When he spoke of securing not just myself, but Marilyn as well, he was speaking financially. What better way then to give her the freedom of choice in roles if my career could, indeed, support us both. They would be talking "big bucks." I could give to her what Johnny Hyde had intended, and not die in the process. Of course, as usual, I couldn't run this by her, as we were still operating by the terms of our private agreement. As a matter of fact, it would probably be better if I licked this thing before seeing her again. The final decision came to me as the only one that could. Agree to the offer, play out the hand. Let whoever "them" was, make the first move. If their motives were a bit on the shady side, THEY themselves would reveal that to me in time to turn it around.

As I have always considered this business a "battle ground," it would be necessary to fight fire with fire as I also knew where I could find an extra pair of eyes and ears. Just as Eisenhower and MacArthur would have tabled a strategy, so too would I. It would become necessary to discover just "who" was saying "what," and thereby decipher "why." Had it been real, from the heart, so to speak, it could have meant a lot to Marilyn and I. If not, it had best be done with.

Once anything in my mind made the transition from "problem" to "challenge," it took on a whole different feel. I might have to go against the hierarchy of the business, but their motives would only have been money. There I had them beaten! Mine were two blue eyes looking to me for safety.

Believe me, we would win this one!

Chapter Eleven

The Positives

Everything in life has a balance, and that includes people. For the most despicable among them there are also those who live by a code of ethics and integrity. I can't speak for the 90's, but for the 50's it was a guarantee.

Clarence McDaniels was one of the latter. *I've changed your name, Clarence, but if you're still around to read this, it was a pleasure. Thanks from both of us for being there!* He was a proud Scotsman by birth and carried that proud heritage with him like a badge of honor. In a business that so often turned both men and women into savage beasts, he remained dignified and calm. Clarence was a newspaper reporter from the top shelf, a credit to the fourth estate and one that should have been emulated by the new breed. His daily column entitled something like "BEHIND THE LENS," was the absence of malicious gossip. The direct opposite of Willy who saw everything from the sewer on down.

Lillian Gish had begun her career as the favorite leading lady of D.W. Griffith in silent films and continued to work in active fashion throughout the years to this one. Joyfully, she would continue for many years after. Miss Gish seemed to divide her time away from home by either performing in films or receiving awards for them. This fragile appearing lady had discovered the secret of survival and had made it work, as under that somewhat dainty shell was the heart of a lion.

One of the ingredients of Clarence's column had always been the "upside" of it all. If a celebrity passed on to that next world, he was there to remind the readers of what he or she had accomplished and not belabor what might have been their failures. He was there as the voice of the people themselves in congratulating someone in the public eye on the birth of a baby, a wedding, or an award so richly deserved. If a popular movie figure found "heat" in other columns, if Clarence believed in them, he was quick to come to their defense and offer a sea of comments guaranteed to drown the whispers and accusations. To those reporters of today who find it a rule of thumb to report from the out houses of the world and honestly think the only news that sells is sleaze, get a life. Clarence and men and women like him, proved that was bullshit 36 years ago. He also proved that those who perform in such manner had to, as their abilities and strengths couldn't cut it in the real world of journalism. He was right then, and he's sure as hell right today. By a sheer stroke of luck, and that is all it has ever been, I was privy to an acceptance speech given by Miss Gish on the occasion of this current award. I was asked, so silently, to blue-pencil the remarks that might not be understood as she may have meant them to be. In one of the most exciting moments of my young life, she and I conferred briefly before she rose to the stage. She agreed with the minimum corrections in the short but poignant speech written by several writers, making a comment to me that lives in my memory as one of the finest, most especially considering the source.

"Next time, I'll just call you first," she said. I listened to the speech and applauded louder than anyone upon its completion. She gave me a final wink, and for that moment, I was indeed "star struck!" Clarence had naturally been there covering the event for his column. Having seen Miss Gish and I speaking to one another and then the "wink" in my direction, sparked the newspaper man in him to introduce himself. He had logically assumed I knew her, and was briefly let down when I told him we had met for the first time this evening. We did, however, strike up a conversation, and he appeared to be impressed by whatever I said about the vanishing grace of aging Hollywood. He would have been less impressed had he asked me about the new breed, but then he hadn't. I complimented him on his column and made certain he knew just how important I felt it was. On the same thoughts as the "favor" system, the evening was left with the pledge to assist each other if and when applicable.

As one of his earlier articles had been about Marilyn, from her side, during the DiMaggio break-up, and again following her sympathetically into Miller, it appeared he might be my ally. The situation had become so personal and with my not knowing the reactions of the so-called "friends" we had suddenly acquired, it would have been impossible for me to discover any REAL facts on my own. I needed someone to do just that, and in such a way as to keep Marilyn and I out of it, at least directly. The only risk I would take was the risk of "trust," and I felt Clarence was above that. After my call, he and I agreed to meet for an informal dinner and discuss what I had said was a personal favor. As I suspected, he was cordial and quite willing to help if he could. Scotsman or not, Clarence had a fondness for good Italian food. In a city with better than 40% Italian, you'd think that would have been easy. Well maybe if you ate in a private home it would be, but as far as restaurants were concerned, it wasn't as simple as it should have been. I did know one, however, that put them all to shame. The Red Devil was one of those basement restaurants so popular in the city, and The Red Devil served Italian food the way it should be served.

Before the meeting I had to make certain of just how much I wanted to say, and just what information I hoped to gain. The same ethics that had been his creed could have worked against me if the information looked the slightest bit off color. I decided on the truth, and threw the dice.

To call this restaurant "quaint" would have been an under statement. It was about as large as a good sized living room, had only about 15 tables, each of which was covered by the standard checkered cloth upon which sat the traditional candle in the equally traditional wine bottle. I don't believe the owners gave one hoot, but it seemed the customers expected that sort of "look" so they gave it to them. A small four-stool bar was off to the left, and it was there I waited for Clarence who arrived on the dot of 7pm. He was a big burly man who looked more like a lumber jack than a columnist, but his voice had the ring of truth to it that no ears could escape.

It seemed, with each course, we delved deeper into that which might have been my problem, and he seemed interested and concerned. I discussed Marilyn as simply "a film star" without mentioning her name on the first go-round, but as we got nearer the root of it, I knew I would have to drop the other shoe.

Finally, as if to end the game, he asked me point blank, "Laddie," he said, in the heaviest Scottish accent, "Who ARE we talkin' about?"

I should have waited until he had swallowed, because when I said "Marilyn.." I never got to "Monroe" as he had already choked on his wine in a fitting gesture to the entire scenario. Wiping his mouth and attempting re-composure, he looked at me and apologized for the timely gagging.

"You wouldn't be havin' a bit of fun with me now, would you laddie?," he said probably hoping the answer was yes.

"No," I said. To this day I have not been able to camouflage my reactions when dealing with Marilyn, and I think my serious look ended his thoughts of this being some kind of a joke.

"Now I understand what you've been tryin' to tell me," he said, completely aware.

"I just need to know," I said.

He finished his salad without another word but I could feel the energy of his thoughts racing a mile-a-minute. He kept looking to me, shaking his head, and returning to his salad. Then he sat back, and continued sipping his wine.

"She's a lovely lass Peter," he began, "but a troubled one...and if you'll pardon me for sayin', isn't she a bit old for you?"

"We've been all through that," I snapped, growing weary of that line of questioning. "I didn't realize 'age' had anything to do with it."

"Well then," he continued observing my reaction, "Maybe it doesn't. Come to think of it, I must be getting senile, my own father is ten years younger than my mother. They certainly proved age has nothing to do with it or I wouldn't be sitting here now would I."

His eyes searched mine for any trace of misinterpretation. There wasn't any.

"You know I've covered some of her career, some of her pain," he said now in deadly earnest.

"It's because of HOW you did that that made me think of you," I said.

"I never liked either one of those men, forgive me" he said with a slight chuckle. "But I DO like you, laddie, and I'm damned if I don't like Marilyn too!," he went on now with some bravado. "Give me the details and let me see what I can uncover."

Along with the main course came the story, and my thoughts both of which he savored slowly as not to miss a morsel. Before the evening was done, I felt assured he would do the best job he could on my behalf. I began to observe in Clarence the glimmer of what I may have seen in Marvin Rachman, but then, couldn't be sure. It seemed that when the initial shock wore off, there would be many who would warm to the idea of we two...We honestly had more silent friends than we knew....

I slept little that night. It seemed every sound awakened me. Something was coming, but I didn't know what. We all are possessed of that "sixth sense" that issues us a warning, but we so often ignore it. I have always found it best to give it its due as it had always paid off. Finally about midnight I gave up the effort and poured myself a Coke, deciding to have a go at the new script. It seemed more profitable than bouncing around all night on the sheets of sleeplessness.

Opening my windows wide brought the chilling air of the ocean into my stuffy room, and helped clear the cobwebs from my brain. Staring at a typewriter and hoping for some "magic" does not a script make. The original draft blurred in front of me and attempting to begin re-working it would have been a waste of time, so I elected instead, to sit and observe from my window, the peaceful nothingness that my eyes beheld. The now boarded up "merry-go-round," the quiet barren beach parking lot, the lonely sound of a buoy only added to this feeling of hollow apprehension.

I could have called Bob, but at 2am in the morning, it seemed a lame idea at best. Even your best friend deserves an undisturbed sleep. Flicking on the TV to observe the 500th showing of GHOSTS ON THE LOOSE, wasn't the answer. Wondering what Marilyn might be doing only made things worse. The possible conspiracy within the studio ranks didn't help, and even the Coke tasted flat.

The telephone rang. Now the apprehension would end, or possibly it was a wrong number. Almost reluctantly I picked up the receiver. The cold, clear and authoritative voice of a Sergeant Frazer of the 39th Precinct spoke out.

Just the mention of "police" sent cold chills up my spine as I was almost certain the call pertained to Marilyn. It didn't. After making certain I was who I said I was, he proceeded to tell me that my phone number had been found on the person of one Arnold Albinski, who was currently at the Mid-town Emergency Hospital. He had been listed as a probable attempted suicide.

The obvious concern in my voice, softened his as he then assured me that it "looked like" he would be alright. Then, of course, came the answerless question. "Do you have any idea," he asked, "what might have prompted this?" Personally I had a few, but elected to keep my opinions to myself.

"Can I see him?," I asked instead of answering.

"Can you get down here now?," came the response.

"Give me an hour," I answered.

"Ok," he replied, "we can talk more when you get here."

Unlike just such an early morning drive into town only a few weeks earlier, there was no need to break any laws. Arnold was already in the hospital. The coincidences, however, filled my mind as I made the 26-mile trip.

The "good guys" always seem to get it first, while the guys in the black hats, just breeze along with the breeze. The troubles that Clarence had suggested about Marilyn, had been industry induced. I had already been personal witness to what that could lead to. The "carousel" theory was operating in full form. Arnold, the nicest guy in the world, had watched his whole life flash in front of him and had probably decided he'd seen enough. Buddy Holly, a most treasured friend and gifted musician, had gotten off earlier that year in the only way you really can, and Mark, now low man on the totem pole, would have kissed my ass in Macy's window in gratitude for helping him save his job in a business not worthy of his talents. Whoever said it first, "There's No Business Like Show

Business" was dead on the money. Come to think of it, even Irving Berlin's life came with enough cracks and crevasses to fill more than one volume.

Sergeant Harold Frazer was a strong looking Black police plainclothes man who presented, in person, the same authority his voice transmitted on the phone. After introducing himself, we shook hands and walked over to a bench in the corner of the crowded waiting room. During the course of our conversation, activity filled the place. Bloodied bodies, screaming children, hysterical women, dying men- quite a collection. Doctors and nurses well over-worked and probably underpaid darted from one room to another. No "make-believe" script could have depicted this Dante's Inferno of human suffering.

Frazer wanted to know if I had any idea of what might have prompted Arnold's attempt at suicide. The best I could suggest was the loss of his wife and job.

"People have jumped for less," he remarked, not as much coldly, but rather as someone who had been there many times.

For whatever they are, and whomever they become, policemen are first, human witnesses to human tragedies. This front line position often destroys them as it would anyone in possession of a heart.

"Did he drink?," he asked.

"Only because of the circumstances," I answered.

They had tried to contact his estranged wife who, naturally was unavailable. I had already learned words that describe women like this, but Frazer was probably miles ahead of me. Neither commented. It was better that way. Arnold had claimed it was an accident. The police weren't buying it. New York buys very little until it is proven, and even then, only rarely. In any event, an awning below his 12th story apartment had broken the fall. Without that vestigial structure we would be conducting this interview at the morgue.

"Can I see him?," I asked Frazer, now on my side answered.

"Yeah, sure come on."

A uniformed policeman stood guard outside his door, policy in cases of attempted suicide. On a nod from Frazer, we were allowed in. Arnold lay on a bed wrapped in bandages from head to toe. Again, no movie can duplicate this scene or feeling when it hits so close to home. Frazer courteously remained in the shadows as I approached the bed.

"Don't I have enough problems," I said, looking down to Arnold who attempted an embarrassed smile through 50 yards of surgical bandage.

"It's not what it looks like," he began, hardly able to mouth the words, "Peter, it was an accident."

"If you say so," I said, attempting to remain calm.

"I say so," he went on, " but nobody listens."

The expression on my face must have signaled him that the act was finished. Tears became evident through the bandages. I reached and touched his hand, even under the cast.

"What's the use," he said, "the only accident was, it didn't work!"

I could feel Frazer's movement in the background, but that sensitive "street wise" cop, stayed back.

"What is the point to stick around for pensions, social security, and probably more hospitals," Arnold went on now relieved of his guilt, "What is the point?"

"The point is," I began, "that taking a swan dive from a 12-story window isn't the answer. There are people who give a damn about you, you know."

"Who, Peter?," he asked in a pleading tone, " who gives a damn?"

"I do, for one, you silly son of a bitch!," I answered fighting back a feeling of total inadequacy.

He found a slight chuckle in that approach and asked, suddenly changing the conversation, "Did you take that oversea's job?"

The semi-shocked look on my face, signaled another chuckle. "Don't look so startled," he said, "Everybody knows! I told you this is a very small business."

Having to agree with him on that, I shook my head "yes" for the business, and "no" for the answer. "I'm not sure yet," I answered.

"That's right," he continued, "You make them WAIT. Make them ask again!!"

"It's not a game with me Arnold," I said, "I don't want to make them do anything. I just have some more important things right now to think about..."

"Good!", he responded with gusto. After patting him on the hand and assuring him I'd look in on him tomorrow, I left with Frazer by my side.

"Where does he go from here," I asked Frazer as we side stepped a group of attendants rushing a man in on a stretcher.

"Another kind of hospital," he said, almost matter-of-factly. "There will be at least 6 weeks of observation. He'll be released only when the doctors there think he's rational enough not to try it again."

"Six weeks!," I sighed.

"That's a minimum", Frazer replied, "but since he has no family, it could be a lot longer, probably will be. He'll be here for another couple of days."

Shaking his hand, I thanked him and assured him I'd be back tomorrow.

"Aren't you kinda young to be mixed up in all of this?," he said as we headed for the door.

"Sergeant," I said now almost whimsically, " You don't know the half of it!"

With the sounds of wailing ambulances and police sirens in the background, I was pleased to leave this totally riveting setting. At that moment, I was grateful that I had chosen to race to Marilyn's call rather than to phone the police. To have put her in such a place would have destroyed us both.

Chapter Twelve

The Walls Come Down

The word is oblivious. Literally translated means, forgetful of, unmindful. When it is applied to the constant noise of the city, its reference is sharpened to mean, for all the horns, the screeching brakes, the sirens, the footsteps of a million million people clickity-clacking along the sidewalks, it becomes a dead silence. You are unmindful of it all. When a thousand thoughts race through your head, many of them angered, the sound of a friendly Robin affects you as annoyingly as scraping a blackboard with your fingernails. You lay in wait for someone to wish you a "good morning" so that you can justifiably bite their head off. You are explosive. The only solution is to wear it off quickly enough before damage is done. No, this is not the confession of Norman Bates. It happens to each and every human being, and sometimes quite often.

On that next morning, with the screams and wailing of the emergency room still echoing in my ears, it was happening to me. Jim Carney, the jovial little back-stabber who first introduced me to Arnold Albinski's dilemma during his memorable five-minute speech at the cocktail lounge, was just getting out of his shiny new Ford with some of his associates. I had just passed them heading for a parking spot of my own, and noticed in my rear-view mirror that they were waiting for me. They were laughing. On exiting my car and walking the few hundred feet to the lot entrance, I noticed their laughs were aimed at me. This was NOT a good morning for this. My stomach tightened as did my jaw, and my hand clutching my briefcase near melted the handle. I knew what was coming.

"Hey Pete!," Jim shouted, "Heard about your friend Arnie. Jumped out of a fuckin' window! Didn't you say he was reliable and dependable?!!"

Again, they all laughed. With a steady pace, I moved directly to Jim, who may have thought I would or could have seen the humor in this. He was wrong. I slammed my attache case on the hood of his shiny new Ford, grabbed him by his jacket collar and pinned him against the roof of his car.

"And you think that's funny you perverted bastard?!," I said holding him tight enough to create a breathing problem.

"Get him offa me!," he gurgled to his friends who suddenly stopped laughing, but offered him no assistance in the bargain. They probably didn't wish to get involved, the sign of "true friendship."

Just about the time he began turning blue, I released my grip and allowed him to slide to the cement. Everyone was silent. I could hear some muttering in the background as I walked from the scene. Laughter was not part of that muttering. For me, I felt better. The city could return to oblivion once more.

Mark was first to greet me as I entered the massive labyrinth of offices and headed for our small workable closet. He reached out his hand, a smile on his face, "I never thought I'd be saying this, but congratulations Peter!" I accepted his handshake, but shook my head in uncertainty.

"Thanks Mark," I said, "I know you mean it, but nothing's been settled yet."

"Oh bullshit!," he replied, "it's a chance to really do something in this field. To let 'em all know who you are! To make a difference! You're not going to pass that up! You'd be out of your mind...."

"That's a possibility," I suggested. He followed me into our small office picking up two cups of coffee on the way in and handing me one on our entrance.

"So it came from the big wind himself.." Mark went on in awe.

"Are there any messages for me?," I asked, trying to change the subject. Somewhat confused by my lack of enthusiasm, Mark reached for a paper on the desk.

"Actually there was," he said, handing me a memo, "Clarence McDaniels.. Is that the columnist?"

"Yes," I said.

" He probably wants to do an article on you!" Mark suggested with a gleam in his eye.

"When did he call?," I asked. Mark looked at the memo and thought,

"About a half-hour ago."

"Excuse me a minute," I said as I reached for the telephone. "I'm not trying to ignore you, I need to talk to him..."

"No, no.." Mark waved me on, " I understand! Hey this is big news."

I didn't have time to explain that the phone call had nothing to do with the "big news." He grabbed the local trades and sat down allowing me my call. Clarence answered his own telephone at the newspaper office. His voice was, as always, cheerful.

"Peter, yes laddie," he said, and then with a bit less bravado, "I have some news but would like to tell you personally. This isn't the place. What's your day look like?"

"Say when," I said.

"This morning, say around 11:30," he continued. I agreed, and a place was decided. The sound of his voice gave me the renewed hope for a positive reaction for a change, but not wanting to open the champagne just yet, I held back any thoughts of celebration. It was already 10:45. After hanging up, I began to feel a bit guilty over rejecting Mark's enthusiastic well wishes, so I took a minute to explain what I called a personal situation with out being specific. I made it appear as though I were just nervous about the whole thing. He had also heard of Arnold's brush with eternity and knowing of our friendship attributed that to my poor showing.

"When you see him next, please give him my warmest greetings" was Mark's final comments relating to Arnold.

"Consider it done," I said, proud to shake his hand.

Times Square is, or at least was, riddled with food places from Nedick's Orange Drink stands to coffee shops offering a range of items from a hot dog to a gourmet dinner, and a clientele to match. Clarence and I had selected one somewhere in the middle, almost by need, non-descript. After what I had witnessed the night before, it didn't seem important as to who saw me speaking to Clarence, or in fact, if it even mattered to those who might have put two and two together. This intrigue was becoming a pain in the ass, and based on what Clarence's findings had been I was ready to pitch the whole thing to the industry in large bold letters myself. After the shock and the anger, comes a kind of numbness.

The look on my face prompted him to ask "What's wrong?," and as a result I confided the story of Arnold Albinski. Clarence may have shot from the hip, but that same strong honest logic had little sympathy for quitters. His response was direct.

"Yes it's sad, to be sure," he said, " but it also deserves its own criticism. It's not the way, laddie, it never has been. It's not the way of a man but of a coward. A man stares misfortune in the eye and beats it down. He doesn't jump from a building."

Clarence possessed an incredible sense of fundamentalist logic a kind of cold-shoulder approach to weakness. Much could be learned from this man, if you were willing to listen with both your heart and your head. As neither one of us was ready for lunch, coffee and danish seemed to do it. We got to the issue with no additional fan fare.

"I've found nothing in my search that would indicate any form of conspiracy," he began." Nothing, other than it seems some of those I questioned had, at one time, made an attempt at Marilyn. Maybe even including your boss. What I have found is a mutual dislike for a man named Miller. No one would give specifics, but there was a feel about it. I did speak to several people who are aware of the relationship between you two, and the report is favorable. For the record, I would say there are people, some in high places, who view this with positive interest."

"Who did you speak to?" I asked with justified curiosity.

"Now I don't try to tell you your business, laddie," he answered. "You can't ask me mine. It's part of my job."

"Then there's no threat to her, and the job offer is what it appears to be," I remarked.

"Laddie," he went on, " you're always going to find someone looking for trouble. It's the way of the world. But if you look a bit closer, your also going to find some very good people as well. I think you've allowed your imagination to run away with your own good sense. Now if you were a scoundrel, a n'er do well, they would have the right to stop you, but you're not. I know that."

What could be discovered suddenly boggled my brain. I sipped my coffee in an almost automatic reaction. The "fishbowl" existence suddenly screamed in my head as an undeniable truth.

"Take the job," he said with a positive smile. "If you and Marilyn are really to be, it will only help. Think of how proud she would be. She needs to be proud again, laddie, about something."

"I may need to talk to her about this..," I said, now trying to think of the positives.

"I already have," replied Clarence, startling me with

his candor.

"You already....." I began to react, but was cut short.

"Oh yes," he said, as casually as one pops a potato chip. "I've known her a lot longer than you. I called her."

Seeing the doubt for doubts sake in my eyes, he continued his reasoning.

"No disrespect intended, but I did that first," he went on "and don't you be looking at me as though I'd broken some seal of trust. She has had many would-be suitors, and just as many who have laid claims on her simply because she is who she is. You're not talking about some girl in Yonkers. You're dealing with a commercial institution."

"Did you think I was hallucinating?!" I said, somewhat put out.

"Laddie," he went on rather firmly, "you said you wanted the truth. Well, that truth began the moment you asked me the favor. That's how it works . That's how I work. We don't spray the cabbage with the odor of roses. We call it what it is."

I made a mock-toast to him with my coffee.

"I believed YOU believed what you were saying," he went on, "but even with the likes of her, it takes two to complete the dance. It would not do either of you justice to have a falsity between you. There's far too much of that these days. I would not have gone a step further had it been only a solo reaction."

"Ok, the defense rests," I said.

"Remember this for anything that comes up," he said, "you can not solve the puzzle until you have all the pieces. She was alone when I called, I asked that first. Please give me credit for that. I've known her for ten years, so understand we trust each other..."

"It's just something I didn't expect," I said now nearly defeated in this barrage of calculating logic.

"You've been associatin' with the wrong people," he said, and so wisely, "and you've gotten a whole lot of wrong impressions. When you want the answers, go to the source, not around it."

As though saving the finale, he sat back, sipped his coffee, stared at me for a moment almost as though a "beat" in a script. Then his finely chiseled "sword of truth" attitude softened.

"She's going to be a handful, laddie," he continued, "a very large order for a very young man. But I can tell you, if you treat her fairly, she would gladly go to hell for you. She's that loyal."

"Did she...," I began, his hand in my face to stop.

"I'm not finished," he said, "give me that chance. Now you had better feel everything you say you feel, mean every word you say you mean, because she's been terribly used, and I would take it as a personal slap if you would continue in that fashion."

"I think you know better," I answered, containing a bit of resentment in my voice.

"I believe I do," he said, now lifting his stern epistle to a higher level. A smile now crept onto his face. "I even think I understand the studio's position. After all, what ever you two do for each other, makes their job easier. It is to their benefit that they allow you to continue to do it."

"Good business," I said, now understanding the "romance" from their side. "Practical, even." I concluded.

"Very," Clarence echoed. With a sip from his coffee, he continued. "From a personal side, forgetting business for the moment, she substantiated every word with a warmth I've never heard from her. I believe she knows her own mind, and her decision is a great deal more difficult than yours. Understand that, Peter. Understand its responsibility. Never take it lightly. She gave me a message to give to you, and wanted to be sure I knew it too.

Simply put, she told me to tell you that she loves you, to stop worrying so much about her, and that she would see you as soon as she could. I think that about sums it up for all of us, and with that, I include the studio's position."

"Thanks, Clarence," I said, assuring myself that things might be better served if less intrigued accompanied them.

"It was a pleasure," he concluded, taking a final sip of coffee. "Now you go out there and get the job done it's now two lives to be built."

With the immediate question of the studio's reasonings put to rest, and the petty thoughts of a conspiracy deposited in the waste basket, the overwhelming grandness of what had transpired suddenly took hold. It had been easier to see it on a day by day, one thing at a time, basis. Marilyn's words of commitment to a third party made it solidly real.

As real as she and WE had become I would see Clarence again, from time to time, during the good times and the bad. His memories of truth would remain with me, and help see me through periods that seemed lacking in that element. He would forever be remembered as the bearer of information, unclouded, unedited. A silent witness to the fact that the world was, indeed, mine.

Chapter Thirteen

As Time Goes By

Christmas comes to New York earlier every year. The pumpkins lead the way, followed by the march of the turkeys, and finally Santa himself. Somehow, through it all, we manage to remember the birth of a very important man. The city gears up with one series of mass decorations after another, and then there's the parade to end all parades, climaxing at Macy's department store. The skies become a bit more cloudy, but the human spirit shines brighter than it does the rest of the year long.

Clarence had also been the name of George Bailey's "guardian angel" in Frank Capra's magnificent film dedicated to life, love and that same human spirit. Later in my life my production manager would appropriately be named Clarence Eurist, with an accent on "Clarence." He too would be among the few I could honestly trust. The name, therefore, seemed to lift me when even mentioned, and it was an absolute certainty that Clarence McDaniels had put a new whistle into my tune that year. I had accepted the offer and been congratulated for doing so by more people than I knew existed. My current Clarence had been right about there being far more friends than I had realized. The city itself seemed to bow to a victory of one of their own. I recall even getting a free pastrami sandwich at The Stage.

The one I waited most to hear from, however, had been absent during this time of personal glory, and it was she who deserved the accolades as much, if not more, than myself. Her spark had ignited the brush fire by giving me the reasons. The woman in your life can do that. If you think the Almighty put them here to help you run up bills, then you haven't lived long enough to understand at all what I'm saying. Oh I dated other girls, as yet I had not resigned myself to permanent phone duty. There were lovely girls, one from the local front in Glen Cove. A brown-eyed Italian with deep rich dark hair. In knowing her, I had come to know her family which included the usual 3 older brothers and one older sister. We had been receptive to one another, and had fun together, sometimes as an entire family. Then there were the girls who just happened to be there from the studio or the acting lab. Dinner, a show, the usual. Pleasant warm memories.

None, however, shared my bed or, for that matter, me. Looking back I believe it was just a way of proving I was still alive, if possibly only half so. Maybe I missed something wonderful, a new experience if nothing else. This abstinence was not born out of any false suggestions of ethics. The Queen simply remained in my heart, and apparently strongly enough. There was no reason to look for the Joker.

Under these possibly unrealistic terms, I was at once surrounded by the adventure of an incredible career boost, the already insinuated thoughts of Christmas, and the darkest and loneliest of nights that felt, quite often, as though they would never end. Willy, in his own way, had already proven that whether in success or failure, you DO get into habits. Those near robotic things you do daily, that are, at the very least, automatic. They require no thought. One of those "automatic" gestures was my picking up the mail before ascending my outside staircase. The small amount I received was generally as stimulating as a stale cup of coffee. Once in awhile, a letter from my mother or grandmother, or some distant relative who would be visiting New York and just "had" to get together. Those were particularly "interesting" as most of these distant relatives had vanished from my life at childhood. Ditto with the birthday and Christmas cards I would receive from aunts and uncles, cousins, second cousins twice removed, great aunts, great uncles- NONE OF WHOM I REMEMBERED with any special fondness. The rest of the mail was either bills or an occasional invitation to some function that I could have taken or left.

On this particular evening, one envelope stuck out by its obvious size, and contained no return address. Well, if it was an "ad," it achieved its purpose as I opened it first. It was a blank, all white greeting card except for words on the bottom spelled in "typewriter" lettering: "WRITER'S BLOCK" Inside, a personal note, "Macy's- 2 o' clock Friday- Toys- Love M." Nothing else needed to be said.

In the 50's, Macy's greatest claim of being "The largest Store in the World" was a truism. Perhaps today, when you consider the malls and expansive co-mingling of major chains it no longer can be considered thus, but then..oh yes. You could literally get lost in Macy's. Memory does not accurately record to me just how many floors there were, but as I remember, there had to be at least ten, with the top one reserved for the corporate offices. Elevators were available on two sides of the four corners. It was a labyrinth that would have confused The Phantom Of The Opera. A city within a city, and jammed with about every conceivable item for sale this side of an automobile. As the season grew nearer, beginning in mid-October, decorations blossomed at Macy's. The sights, sounds, and smells were all carefully orchestrated to get you to "buy." Had you indeed gone in to use the bathroom, you would have left with a purchase. As I had been a visitor many times as a boy, I knew instinctively where the toy department was. A place of magic. At this point, Santa had not yet arrived, but his "house" was under construction. What HAD already been made operational, however, was the huge and cleverly constructed Lionel Electric Train display. These miniature marvels had long been as much a part of Christmas as egg-nog, and it was at this time of the year that every man became a boy again. If you were fortunate enough to have a son, you could use him as an excuse. If not, you would have to throw adult dignity out of the window, and admit you simply enjoyed them yourself.

Marilyn loved children and indeed had always prayed for one or more. That prayer was never to be answered. Again, with us, so many things might have been different. With memories still of an orphanage or two, she would enjoy being around them and the radiance of her smile would translate to them that this lady was special in more ways than one. You see, they never got to read the gossip columns, never got to listen to the black fairy tales of those who had to chip away. All they felt was what they saw, and in that vision, they saw Marilyn as she was, not as some had painted her to be. They saw the truth before it was re-arranged for them by many oh so much "wiser" adults. It was more than logical to me that she would have selected the toy department as our rendezvous point, as the girl who sadly never had a childhood did attempt a bit of catching up at times like this.

Lionel trains were constantly improving their effects. By this year, you could drop pellets into the small smoke stacks of the "O" gage models that circled the tracks, and in a moment or two, smoke would billow out in neat smoke rings. A recording of train sounds and conductor "calls" was built into the tiny station, along with a little man who would wave his lantern as the train passed. In these days of super electric hi-speed trains, and diesel engines, powerful but coldly impersonal, it is probably difficult to imagine the thrill of watching a real steam locomotive chugging into a station rocking the very ground on which you stood with its weight and power. Trust me, it was some experience. With Lionel and, in all fairness, American Flyer, you could relive that experience, if only in your mind. As was so often the case, I had already become hypnotized by the engines, transfixed by the trains and the memories. Suddenly, a pair of soft hands covered my eyes, a whisper and a breath tickled my ear, and the overwhelming scent of lilac snapped me out of my trance.

"Chugga,chugga,chugga," she whispered. I turned to behold the reason for my sleepless nights. It is most difficult to translate into words that which only your heart can feel. Nothing in this life has ever frightened me. Wiser men than I have suggested that fear is a sign of caring, and now, what finally did frighten me, was losing her. She stood there, not the image the world had come to know, but the girl I had come to love, with all my heart. Where anyone else was concerned, there really wasn't any contest.

Along with her smile had come a surprise, and indeed it caught me unawares. She wore a pair of slacks, a Pendelton jacket, minimum make-up, and no kerchief. I believe it was, for that moment, her way of saying that our secret had lost its significance that perhaps soon, we could shout it to the world. I had made an earlier remark during one of our long conversations, that I would someday like us to parade openly through Macy's department store to show the world. That remark had been born partly out of ego and partly out of pride. The ego I no longer needed. She had remembered that chance remark and this was an early Christmas present, a "Marilynism." "What are you doing?," I asked referring to her exposed hair."

"Watching the trains go round and round", she said.

"No, no," I blurted, " Honey, the hair...!"

"Oh let them look!," she replied casually. Well, they were. The crowd had begun to assemble as they so often did. I suppose my physical size suggested that I might have been a bodyguard, and I let them go on thinking that. They kept their distance. Marilyn, of course, fell right into the program by turning toward them and waving.

"It's early, but Merry Christmas everybody" she proclaimed.

The crowd applauded, and wished her the same in as many voices as there were people. This was all very nice, but the size of that crowd was growing. A security guard had no difficulty in finding us, and also being aware of what could transpire, he began to separate the crowd. Maybe it was an early Christmas spirit, or just a way for them to behave, but no instances of desperation took place. No hostility or frantic hands reaching for her.

As soon as I spotted an opening, I put my arm around her and escorted her away from this heading for the nearest elevator. Marilyn found fun in all of this. As I raised the collar on her jacket and continued to shield her from eyes that obviously followed us, her giggling didn't make it easy.

"Didn't you say you wanted to walk hand in hand through Macy's?", she laughed now on the elevator down to the lower floor.

Well I knew that was coming, and *yes* I had said that, but at this moment, and despite the underlying well wishes from certain people, I still felt something could have back fired.

The music department was considerably more private than toys, and as the elevator deposited us on that floor, Marilyn pulled me towards a display on pianos. There it sat in the middle of the floor all decorated in holly and tinsel. A magnificent white Baby Grand.

"I remember you said you played," she said, sparkling brighter than the lights and tinsel that surrounded us.

"Only for friends," I replied, touching the keys lightly out of habit.

"Would you play for me?," she asked.

"Here?," I questioned already knowing what THAT would do.

"No!," she laughed, and continuing with a twinkle to her eyes, "I know a special place," she said suddenly pulling me toward the elevator.

I could feel those wheels turning again, and with Marilyn, you could never be sure of where THAT was taking you. I am sure we passed hundreds of people on our way from the store. People who probably glanced at us as we whizzed by. People who perhaps thought later, "did they see who they thought they saw?" Then there would be those from the toy department. Their ordinary, otherwise normal lives, had been interrupted by a vision, and one they would repeat to their friends and family alike. Marilyn had that affect on people. You didn't forget her so easily. She was the direct opposite to many of the film personalities I had already come to know. Many of them would get lost in a crowd, and if you did notice them, their off screen attitudes might disappoint you. They were strictly illusions, and the realities of those illusions were so often not favorable.

Marilyn was the absolute contradiction to all of that. The in-person Marilyn dwarfed the on-screen Marilyn. With the possible exception of Boris Karloff, that's right, I don't know of anyone in the field who was so exceptionally different in what some call "real life" as she. And that difference was richer, deeper, and lovelier. Miller once referred to her as having a "cupie doll" personality. Well, perhaps that's how he saw her. Poor Arthur. He was so wrong about everything. A quick taxi ride and an autograph substituting for a fare, saw us now before an old theatre on 53rd street, as near as I can remember. It was in a row of legitimate stage houses, and yet, because of its age, it stood out. The building itself was from another era. Still anxiously pulling my hand, she led me through the alley next to the theatre to the stage door entrance in the back. Here was a set right out of the movies, replete with bare bulb and sign, STAGE DOOR-DELIVERIES- NO ONE PERMITTED WITHOUT A PASS. Marilyn eagerly pushed the bell which rang even through the heavy old door like an alarm.

"I hope he's here," she said anxiously walking in place. As usual, during moments like this, I hadn't a clue as to who "he" was, or for that matter just what we were doing here. I wouldn't have long to wait. After a few moments, the old door creaked open, and an elderly stage-hand stared at me from inside.

"What can I do for ya bub?" he asked.

Marilyn stepped in front of me. "Marty!," she blurted.

His old eyes lighted up. "Well Marilyn....."

"This is Peter, Marty," she went on, "Can we come in?"

"Well sure, honey, sure..," he said simultaneously opening the still creaking door.

Once inside, Marilyn continued to lead the way as Marty closed the old door behind us. The giant, ancient, vintage stage with only its bare work light stood before us. Marilyn continued to forge onward with me following and Marty following behind then curious about my part in all of this.

About all that was missing from this place was Ruby Keeler and Dick Powell.

The huge drapes, a bit on the dusty side, hung as they probably had during their hay-day somewhere around the 20's. The blue velour color, now a bit faded, seemed gentle in texture and fairly glowed with the memories they must have held in their strong fabric. Marilyn walked behind one of the "legs" (drapes) and returned rolling out a black baby grand piano. Seeing her persistence, Marty and I lent a hand. As she pushed and pulled she spoke of it all:

"We did some improv's here about 4 years ago, didn't we Marty," she said, arranging the piano center stage.

"Yes 'mm", Marty answered, still looking at me and not certain how I fit into this.

"Now I come here to study, sometimes," she went on, "and Marty watches out for me."

On that remark, Marty shook his head in affirmation. At this point, Marty was STILL watching out for her with me as his target.

"Can't you just feel the ghosts of the greats who played here?," Marilyn continued, "They're all around us."

She then directed the obvious toward the still suspicious Marty.

"Peter plays the piano."

"Oh really.." Marty replied now ready for the showdown.

"Well then, you're in luck," he went on leading the condemned to the gallows, "it's just been tuned. We're doing a revival here these days."

I didn't blame him, not really. In fact, I was pleased to discover the likes of him. Those who DID care about her, and DID watch after her. It seemed she could have used an "army" of Marty's. To him, at least at that moment, I was just another "hot shot" trying to get my mits on her, and using the piano as my particular gag. The piano sat before me, an old friend, a Baldwin, which, for my money, is the best you can get. At least those of that vintage. The years had not been kind to the finish, as chips of wear were evident, but you didn't play a Baldwin for the image not on your life.

Marilyn stood poised, waiting as I sat down and began "chop sticks."

Her face drooped and Marty's lit up. I don't believe I could have kept that going for a second longer as I could not stand the disappointment on her face. It was a cruel tease, a let-down. It wasn't very funny. Without further deception, I began playing a few chords and asked her for a selection..something she would like to hear. Almost reluctantly, she requested " My Foolish Heart," not knowing just what that would bring and prepared for the worst. I had begun playing piano at age 3, given my first concert at 6. The piano had been the truest of my childhood friends, and would now permit me my most personal concert. I gave her what she wanted, including all the trimmings. The total production. Liberace would have been proud. More importantly, Marilyn's face beamed! In the background, Marty chalked off "round one." Seeing her reaction, he walked to stage left, the light board, switched off the bare stage work light, and cranked up the mighty blue and amber lights of this old place, a much better mood setter. Marilyn needed so desperately to believe in me, almost as a last symbol. It would have been in the worst possible taste to treat that lightly. The music helped that need. She stood by the piano, leaning on it and looking toward me as I played. She began humming and then finally singing the song. We had finally come full circle. If ever a moment needed to be frozen in a time capsule, this was the one. With that old grand piano, shining again as it undoubtedly had for decades, the magnificence of that equally grand old stage, the powerful lights that had probably shined on the greatest of them, reflected off her golden hair like just so many rays of sun, I would have, for all time, my Marilyn. There was no doubt about it. Nothing would remain in my life as such a powerful reminder as to just how very very blessed I had become. There are some images time simply can not erase.

Finishing the song got me a really big hug, and I could see Marty stepping from the shadows.

"You kids want some coffee to go with your concert?" he asked.

"Sure Marty," I answered.

"You don't look like no piano player," he said as he stepped back to get the coffee from a small off stage table, "but you're damn good on those ivories."

"That ain't all he's damn good at!," Marilyn said with a naughty laugh. With that she puckered up and threw me a "Marilyn" kiss.

I believe the fact that we both could poke fun at the "Bugs Bunny" character, helped make US real. By playing at it, the sting was removed. On private occasions, she would perform a complete show number in a bed room or a living room, and once a kitchen. "Diamonds Are A Girl's Best Friend" was often rehashed just for the hell of it. The end result was always a laugh, and with it a sea of hugs. We had put "Marilyn" in her place. She was kinda nice to know as a friend, and one from whom we could depart with a simple kiss.

Marty returned with the coffee.

"Do you know 'I Wonder Who's Kissing Her Now?'", he asked, timidly. I played it and won a fan. At its completion, Marty seemed transfixed.

"I'd a thought that was too old for you." he said. Having some more fun, Marilyn answered that with:

"Don't you know Peter's the oldest Young man in the business...?"

I then began to play a tune I had remembered was among my grandmother's favorites, and one that I had played surely hundreds of times. It had an old-fashioned ring to it, but the melody was pretty and the lyrics said more of the subject than many of the songs that promised the same but didn't quite deliver. As far as the piano went, I could hold my own against most, but as to my singing ability it was strictly from the shower. As I began "Have I Told You Lately That I Love You," I chose to speak the lyrics rather than even attempt to sing them. Marilyn began to hum along, and indeed everything was going along just fine until I reached the refrain- the "bridge." It was then that the damndest thing happened.

On "*My world would end if ever you'd refuse me, I'm no good without you anyhow...*," my voice cracked. Unexplainable tears suddenly filled my eyes. It had to be one of the dumbest things that had ever happened to me. It caught me completely off guard. Marilyn, recognizing my plight, placed her hands on my shoulders and finished the song with my then feeble piano background.

"*Have I told you lately that I love you, well darlin' I'm tellin' you now...*"

"I'm sorry," I said, "that was dumb. I don't know what happened. It's a corny old song I've played a hundred times."

She reached down and kissed me lightly. "That's why I love you," she said, "You're just a corny old guy."

It wasn't the song, damn it. I had played it the same way many times. Like its age, it was sincere, and its lyrics just pushed one of those invisible buttons. Those same lyrics had never applied before. Then the most damnable thought came to me....no one would ever see her as I did. That would be the most deplorable sin of them all.

It was just about 5:30 in the PM when the "concert" came to an end, as Marty had to ready the old theatre for its nightly revival. It had been a most enjoyable afternoon for all. Marty had been on still another level of "show business," and managed to slip in some antidotes of his last 60 years in between songs and idle chatter. As with most of his breed, he could have forgotten more than Marilyn and I would ever know, and in that I found the same kind of enrichment as I would later find from some of the truly greats I would meet along the way. Marty had also seen enough behind the scenes to ignore it all. I was still new to him, but on first impression, it appeared as if I would pass the test. He adored Marilyn. Not because of her curvaceous rear-end, or her blossoming bust-line, but because of her, the girl beneath it all. He was an insignificant little man whose loyalty and friendship dwarfed those in high places who claimed both and delivered neither. Marty was as real as they come, and his affection for Marilyn the equal to that reality.

The sun had already bid farewell to the day when we strolled the beach that evening. The chill of the Fall had granted us even more privacy than usual, but we enjoyed the walk regardless of the cold. It had been a very special day. It wasn't only the season that was changing, but our lives as well. Some might call it life's honest progression. I suppose, on the surface, that is honestly what we all want, to move forward, to attain more, to see an ambition realized. The job offer was something you couldn't buy, something any one at any age, would gladly have considered a major coup. The kid from Brooklyn was beginning to get even more than he'd hoped, and it was coming faster than even he could have dreamed, but another dream had suddenly stepped into the frame and was blocking this picture of rapid success. It would have been foolish to think we could just stay this way. That we simply continue doing what we had been doing, remain in a state of limbo.

Originally I had seen the world as a challenge. I wanted to be in the "business," well, OK, I was in the business. So what. Why didn't they just leave me the hell alone. Who asked for this promotion? Who wanted to be more important? Who gave a shit? I had what I wanted. Everything. Why do you work anyway? You work to get the things you want, the things you can buy, a better car than the next guy, a larger house. Big fuckin' deal. When it's all over, what have you got? I already had more than all of that right here beside me on this beach. Things had changed. I wasn't that 9-year old lusting after Virginia Mayo anymore. I had screwed up by growing up. But then too, look at what had happened to Arthur Miller. He had put his life in limbo and had chosen to stay and keep things "nice," and where had that gotten both of them? His career was in the toilet, and Marilyn had come to despise him. It was a crossroad and I was frightened.

"I spoke to Mr McDaniels," Marilyn said, picking up a piece of naturally-crafted driftwood. "He's a genuine person, don't you think?"

I agreed with a nod, still privately considering the entire event.

"He told me what you said, and what you're doing," she went on, a twinkle in her eye, " I think it's wonderful."

"Yeah," was an automatic answer that came from my throat more as a reaction. Inwardly I still felt it might be considered "too wonderful." This business was not known for gift-giving. And yet, there she was, bright eyed, ever-believing, despite the fact that most promises made to her had been broken, most dreams had been smashed. Her vulnerability projected from her eyes, those same eyes that could embrace you. Eyes that had already tried so many, many times, to take from a charade or masquerade, and make it a truth. It was something that came from way deep down inside of her. It was beyond me to squash that positive feeling with any negative fly-swatter. We paused by a rock and leaned on it. I pulled her gently toward me, buttoning her jacket against the increasing chill. Had I been able, I would have built a protective wall around her penetrable only by invitation. No such structure was possible.

"It's a watch-dog kind of thing." I said, preparing some explanation of sorts. "I don't think there's even a guild classification for it."

"And you're afraid it's a trick," she said, again in words of wisdom that erupted from this physically unlikely source.

"I thought about it," I said, attempting to remove my true concern. "What made me really think about it, was the fact that *you and I* suddenly came into the conversation. It seems we're not the best kept secret after all. As a matter- of fact, according to my boss, the 'big-cigar smokers' know all about us. I'm sure that's what did it. I know how important this is to you, this 'keeping it quiet' business, and apparently it's not quiet at all."

I might have expected a "shocked" look, or even one of concern, but, instead, she smiled ever so slightly.

"Oh," she said, as though possessed of a knowledge foreign to me. "It comes down to worrying about me again, doesn't it?"

"Honey," I began, almost thinking out loud, " I just don't want to lose you through all of this, and I don't want to be sent off to some Christ knows where country, in case you need me. I also don't want either of us to become part of some elaborate chess game. The whole thing stinks."

Once in awhile, for effect, Marilyn would call upon her age and wisdom to bring a point home. It was deliberate, carefully thought-out, and concise. She would call herself "Mama," meant as an expression of that age and experience.

"Sugar," she began, "you listen to Mama now." I could hear it coming. She took my hands, and together we slid from that rock to the sand. The fact that the sand was cold, and a chill could be felt from the water had little to do with that maneuver. It wasn't as much staged as necessary. Eye to eye contact was required at times like this.

For all the joys Marilyn brought to me, for all the physical, emotional, and even spiritual pleasure I felt by her presence, once in awhile, truth got in the way. It was our relationship's strongest ally.

"From the time I was a little girl," she began, "everybody has been taking a chunk out of me one way or the other. Hardly anyone has ever given any thought to what I want. I used to tell them, but I stopped a long time ago because all it did was make them laugh. I used to say to myself, "Norma Jeane, you're gonna have to do this thing by yourself,' and I have. Then 'Marilyn' would say, 'Ok, we're going to beat them at their own game.' She was right. Marilyn could always understand things that Norma Jeane couldn't. Marilyn came to trust nobody, and sometimes she was wrong." As she spoke, her hands never left mine, and she would squeeze them with certain words to make a point. Her eyes locked into mine, and she went on, determined to have it out." When I first met you, Norma Jeane said 'Here's something special', but Marilyn said 'only for the moment.' Things happened, Peter, that made even Marilyn a believer. Nobody can change that now, can't you see that? You don't have to keep coming to my rescue. Not anymore. I know you're there, I really know you're there. That's all that's necessary. Sugar, they can't do anything now to hurt me. You made that possible." I knew she meant every word , and I suppose I should have taken pride in the fact that she so openly called a spade a spade, but something inside me still lingered. Something, maybe the sound of my own thoughts, that kept saying, "you can't leave her alone, not on such a short limb."

"I'm no good at this," she went on, "and I know there are days when I don't know which end is up. I get confused to the point when I don't know what's a lie and what's the truth. I don't know what I dreamed and what really happened. But I do know this, you and I are not a dream. I know that because it has lasted too long for a dream. I'll tell you about a dream I had the other night. Want to hear it?"

I nodded in affirmation.

"Good, because I'm going to tell it to you anyway," she said, lifting her head triumphantly. "I dreamed we were 'presenters' at the Awards. A big booming voice announced us as Mr and Mrs Collins, and out we came. I wore that 'Itch' dress that you like so much, and you were so very handsome in a tux. I dreamed they all stood and applauded. I dreamed we'd won. When I woke up, I looked in the mirror. I had this kinda rosey glow on my face. That school-girl blush stayed with me all day long. Then Clarence called. He told me all that was happening, told me all about you and your promotion, and I knew it fit into that dream."

The sand wasn't cold anymore. The chill was now a blast of heat. The more she spoke of seeing all of this as a positive, the more I felt the coming of a great loneliness. My thoughts had been fraudulent. The plain simple truth, so cleverly camouflaged in the guise of protector, was really a coward's trick to mask the cold reality of needing her so very desperately. I didn't know and could not have comprehended one person being so empty without the other. I sometimes wished, secretly, that none of this had ever happened. That I had not gone to that deli that night, or if I had, that she would have found another table to sit at. That I would have kept my nose in the copy of Variety where it belonged. Then I'd go further. Ok, maybe it should have ended after that first night between the sheets. Maybe that's what it should have been all about. The conquest of a great body! Memories for the steam bath. But, oh no. It had to keep going. It had to grow, and grow, and she had to be so damned real! Why couldn't she just have been Marilyn Monroe, why did she have to become a real person? Why did I have to love her so much? Who the hell needed all of this? Why did Grandma always have to be right?

I lifted her from the sand, and brushed off its traces from her slacks. We began to walk toward my apartment, my arm securely around her. There really wasn't a whole lot to say. She'd said it all. We'd both made vows on that beach that night. Vows that would bind us more strongly than any on the written page.

"There's going to come a time and a place where we can just be," she said, " and wherever and whenever that is, we'll find it."

"I just miss the hell out of you when you're not here," I said, answering it all. The conversation grew lighter by design.

"You should learn to do what I do," she said, nuzzling against me as we walked. "Close your eyes, take a minute, pass everything from your mind, and then 'poof', there I'll be."

"Right." I answered, not ready to enter that world of fantasy just yet.

"Ohhhhhhh," she said with a mock scorn, "you have to work on it. Takes practice. You have to know I'm there, and I will be. Honest. Distance doesn't mean anything. We can be together no matter where we are. When does this job start?"

"I'm supposed to go to England in 10 days," I said, nearly gagging with the idea.

"Ok!," she said so very positively, "you go to England. You won't have Olivier there to tell you to be 'sexy', so you'll have a great time. You get that job done. Make me proud. Hey, this old broad hasn't got many bumps left in her caboose. We may need that job!"

It was the "WE" that did it. Rachman and Clarence had

suggested it, and Marilyn had said it. That was good enough.

"And one more thing," she said, " While you're gone, don't you DARE believe everything you read! It'll just fog up your head and give you more to worry about. You don't have to do that anymore. Who cares who knows what. If they were going to say anything, they already would have. Remember, when I make a movie, there is always some gossip to help sell tickets. Remember, first, it's not ME, it's Bugs Bunny, and second, it'll be over when the film is."

"Ok," I said, honestly understanding. She had a most convincing way about her. My only hope was to remember those words of wisdom from 6000 miles away. The first thing I did upon entering my apartment was to give her Bob's station's number, just in case some of this positive bravado wore off. An insurance policy in the event... Time then graciously slowed for us. I would savor every inch of her, pull her tightly to me and endlessly in possession of an endurance far and above even my own capability. It was a storing up of her that I knew I would need. Outside the door winter may have been approaching. Inside a melting hot bed of coals. Words cannot describe it. As our roads would truly separate from this night, with thousands of miles between us, I wanted all of her to linger. I drank deep of the smell of her, and counted every pore on her body. I knew I would need this when closing my eyes would, indeed, be all I had. Thoughts of separation disappeared. There would be none of that from this moment. In its simplest term, we two had become one. It is that same "one" that remains today. It is finally, proudly, an unchallenged truth.

Chapter Fourteen

Unknown Factors

As I prepared for England, Marilyn prepared for hell. As though both knowing the distance would soon be much greater between us, the phone calls occurred with greater frequency. It was through them that I learned what had been transpiring during some of those days when we were not together, and what the results began to resemble. Fox had begun by introducing her to the idea of doing a film entitled, THE STORY ON PAGE ONE. For any number of reasons, this property was not to her liking, none the least that she had seen it somewhat as a reflection of her own life. Historically, Rita Hayworth would get the role, and it would be among the finest of her last period. Then along came a script called, originally, THE BILLIONAIRE. The concept was good, but the script was yet unfinished. As this idea appealed to Marilyn, she agreed to do it almost sight unseen. As her final film in her existing contract with Fox, and one in which she had a financial interest, it was beyond her to think it would be anything but good.

To this date, in late 1959, it seemed as though her feelings were right. In October she had begun working up dance routines for the film with seasoned choreographer and trusted ally, Jack Cole. All seemed fine. Preproduction meetings appeared to be laced only with the usual guess work, but essentially, nothing seemed too terribly unworkable. Nothing much had changed with Miller, but even that could not dampen her enthusiasm for a new film. She had begun to look at things optimistically, and I know the time we spent together helped. For whatever the reasons superficially or below the surface, Marilyn had begun to feel like her old self.

At this point in time, our relationship had been good for us. I had gained a dynamic raise in career, and financially, if all else failed, I could support us both. Through my eyes, she could again look into her own mirror, and see what I saw.

The nightmare of SOME LIKE IT HOT was behind her, and only the success of it lingered. Fox had begun to submit the co-star idea to various names, and each would have been more than solid. Gregory Peck, Rock Hudson, etc. Her work with Lee Strasberg had proven her own ability to her, and although he did go somewhat overboard in his appraisal, the lillie had not been completely gilded. She had undergone some minor therapy as a means of getting in touch with herself, and no harm was coming from it. It was somebody to talk to, away from anyone personal, and as she said, "I just tell him what he wants to hear and we get along just fine."

The little bells that kept ringing in my head were not necessarily inspired by Marilyn's touch. She was all that mattered to me, and the sound of her voice both excited my senses as well as lulled them into a false sense of security that, somehow, I knew wasn't going to last. Everything was just too damned "ducky," too wonderful, and too smooth. I had long stopped believing in the tooth fairy and Santa Claus. Had everything worked as it appeared, we would have been in reel number 3 of SNOW WHITE AND THE SEVEN DWARFS. Unfortunately, had I been the one to suggest any kind of disaster, proposed or real, would have created "rain" for her parade. I could not bring myself to offer a storm on such a sunny day. All that was left for me was to fulfill my end of the bargain, go to England, and cross my fingers. A few prayers were thrown in for extra good measure. My last few nights before departure were far from restful. Marilyn had already left for the coast, on further preliminary obligations, and contact ceased for the time. Her constant reassurances of "being alright" weren't that convincing, but nothing is more irritating than having someone repeatedly asking "are you sure?" Writing my fears off to unnecessary concern, and not wishing to smother either myself or she in, what might have been, needless worry, I decided on the course of least resistance. For most people the statement "she did very well before you came into her life" might have applied. For Marilyn, it didn't. On occasions like this, I always had the guilty feeling of a physician deserting his patient. It was dumb, and outwardly, presumptuous. Unfortunately, it always came back as the truth, and generally after the fact.

Chapter Fifteen

England

There is something final and foreboding about leaving the ground in an airplane knowing it will not again touch down until thousands of miles have passed, most especially when you know the most important ingredient in your life has been left behind. The great skyline, the people, the noise, along with Macy's, The Stage Delicatessen, Bayville, my beach, an old vintage theatre and tree lined babbling brooks, all disappeared beneath me as I rode this magic carpet into a clouded sky of uncertainties and emptiness. By the time she would accomplish anything on this day, I would be well over an endless ocean heading even further into a new world. The send-off had been nice. The office had prepared a little tribute and Rachman himself had come down from his throne to grace the festivities. It was one of those rare moments when warmth over comes tension. It is difficult to transmit thoughts of such mixed emotions and under such contradictory terms. Had she been seated by my side on that airplane, all would have been perfect. This, of course, was not the case, and yet, I was flying off to the kind of position for which people in this profession would gladly hock their souls.

It had been just about 10 days since we had made the silent vows and unwritten plans, along with the moments of daydreams on that untroubled beach. She had placed the "WE" into it, and that thought seemed to help. If, under all of this razzle-dazzle, the big pay check, the unlimited credit card, the fanfare and balloons, could come a solid trace of security for the future, this otherwise worthless misdirected glory would become worthwhile. I was never one to wear "gloom" on my shirt sleeve, and I have never subscribed to the cocktail of love and depression as being one substance. Had I been a victim of such a concoction my life would have ended by my own hand on August 5, 1962. Gratefully I saw other alternatives. Suspended in a fancy aluminum foil-wrapped cigar box over what seems like an endless black ocean on one side and an even more indefinite endless sky on the other makes you realize the fragility of it all. I have always seen moments like this as lessons in humility. A sharp focusing of how truly unimportant we all really are unto ourselves, and how, by ourselves, we stand for nothing. How necessary that second half truly is. Our accomplishments and ambitions toward those accomplishments all are based only on society directed goals. Totally worthless when compared to the universe, totally small and insignificant against the tapestry of infinity. Damned near comical.

Of course my work had improved, of course I was on this plane moving silently through the heavens toward even greater "glory" for lack of a better term, and of course my life had far larger responsibilities than even I could have predicted. What was the big mystery ? There wasn't one. The word "WE" had firmly entered my life. Marilyn was the more important partner to that expression. Had it been chiseled into cement and dropped onto my head from a 50 story building it couldn't have been more clear. As others slept on the flight, dimming the lights of that suspended cabin, I found myself gazing upward from that tiny window to the stars which shined so brightly without the interruption of lights from below. The churning black waters of the Atlantic offer no trace of neon and allow the heavens their spectacular due. Aside from a blinking light on the wing of this artificial bird, the stars and moon were the all of it. They would continue to be that same "'all of it" long after my short visit became history. What I had considered "an accident" in the hubbub of living on the ground whether one of noise and confusion, or of peace and tranquility, took on a different appearance when viewed from a higher level, this temporary position of suspension granted me by this manmade invention. It was no accident. The very word seemed to accompany others the likes of "surprise," "glorious mistakes," alibis we all make when our limited intelligence can't determine an answer. No, the speed of our encounter, the openness of our dialogue and understanding of each other with little preamble, the knowledge of each others thoughts and needs was no accident. We had simply done it all before. Just "how" and "when" was the only mystery. The question remained as to "when" would we get it right?

The word "religion" is defined as a belief in God, or of gods, with a secondary definition being, "a code of ethics." It is a word that is misused almost as much as "love," and misunderstood with the same intensity. The term is manmade for the audience of the same. One of the greatest minds of the century, Albert Einstein, admitted to the unseen power of a larger force than even he could comprehend. Yet, in everything we do, in all of our clawing and scratching to reach the top of our individual ant hills, we fail to see it. Those who DID see it, Jesus, Moses, Buddha, are revered for having done so. We follow their teachings and praise their glories never realizing that their strongest messages are that we have within us the same attributes as they. Along with their honest answers to it all, we add our own sociological mumbo-jumbo and create additions to their words which are strictly the interpretations of man. We create punishments that we can identify, and methods of redemption that are self-indulgent excuses for not understanding the simple truths in the first place. The bodies we wear are coats, chemically worth about 75¢ in U.S. currency. Those coats get old and are finally discarded. They are buried or burned, and, in some cases, remembered. We go on. We continue to go on. Those we love go on with us, in some cases, even those we dream of in one lifetime, rejoin us in another. We are to each other, a link. Heaven, then, is a time when all the broken links are finally repaired. Hell is what we create within ourselves during our lifetimes that we build on the blocks of misdirected ideals. No, Marilyn was no accident. My continued reference to that is merely as a form of expression for the immediate and one that is more easily identified. The toughest among us fear "death" as though the very word was, in itself, frightening. Somehow we define it as "an end," which in truth is really " a beginning." Another chance to try and get it right.

The constant hum of the plane's engines as the only underscore to these revelations seemed to add a degree of solemnity to my thoughts on that lonely night. Utilizing the simplest of human emotions, it became irreversibly focused that I missed her more than even I could have prophesied. When loneliness becomes more an ache than an expression, it becomes non-translatable. However, the game goes on, and the hope of victory remains. The importance of making every current moment count becomes equal to that of whatever a thousand futures might promise. It is the successes of each minute that determine each individual's path to eternity. Waiting for that "better world" is a sin against this one and a defeating of the very concept of that same place. We each create that "better world" and its promise...daily. Looking for that "silver lining" is nowhere as exciting as building it. Somewhere over the Atlantic, on that night so long ago, that is exactly what I was doing.

The British are a different race, and to acquaint you with that fact, they begin on your trip to their country. The smiling attractive flight attendants with their equally attractive accents offer you a prevue of what is to come. British ladies just seem to bristle with charm and suggestion, crossing the line only by decision and leaving the rest to your own active imagination. The men all seem a bit stuffy and possessed of a dry sense of humor, all of which is a contradiction to their honest personalities. Prim and proper in the workplace so easily give way to outrageous adventure when the work day is done. These things I had learned on my last go-round with them, a most stimulating period to be sure. I had been to this very same film company a year or so back, under the assignment to assist in a film campaign for the first film released under our company banner. It had been an eleven week blast. During that time my education had benefited from both their extremely desirable women who were eager to teach this young buck a few tricks, to the devoted craftsmen who found that same youth a worthwhile student. It was a rounded education, to say the least.

From the production side I had been astounded at the results achieved on screen with a budget of less than a quarter of those I had been part of in the states. "Acting" to those in Great Britain was not something treated lightly. It was considered an honorable profession and one that required dedication. The "star" system did not apply. They pursued their craft with reverence for the whole picture rather than for the buck, and it showed with most of the money actually finding its way to the screen. I sincerely doubt those who worked with such fervor would have tolerated the antics of a prima-donna of either sex.

Because of Marilyn's on-set problems with Laurence Olivier, and with Arthur Miller along to drive her personally up the wall, her experience in this country of wonders had been less than wonderful. Perhaps through my current efforts we might, on some later day, return together and have her see these people in action. To have her work among them would have been better than a room filled with Lee Strasbergs. As we reached what pilots call "the point of no return," wherein it is the same distance to return as it is to go on, I began to think of the entire thing in a more positive light. A pioneering effort for the Monroe-Collins corporation. As always, my "dumb blonde" wasn't as dumb after all. When she said "Go for it!," she spoke for us both, and that same "both" could easily benefit now. To mope around wouldn't get the job done and would have done more to disgrace not only we two, but the company who had laid this out for me. It was not their intention to sponsor and grant carte blanche to a love-sick puppy, but more to tap the talents I had proven to them did exist.

"Ok Baby," I said to myself as the plane began its descent into Heathrow Airport, "bring 'em on!"

So many of them I had known from before, and that made my job now easy. The shock of my youth had worn off on the last go-round, and the greetings came in groups. It became obvious within a few short days that I was taking money under false pretenses. This finely tuned production company had no concept of "skimming," didn't even know the word. They had used every tiny corner of their equally tiny studio to create sets that on screen looked three times their size. The actors and actresses worked tirelessly around the clock, and no talks of "meal penalties" and "golden time" ever came up. They were creating a film in the genre of gothic horror, and yet, before they would finish, it wore the stamp of "classic." What these people could do with a few miles of film would make me wonder just what the hell we were doing back home.

The only pressures on the set were the self-induced variety, to get the job done. If a cast call was set for 7 am, they were there at 7 am, not 7:05. The Director had only to move them around as each member of the cast from the leading players to the walk-ons had studied their lines, knew their characters, and had come prepared. On rare occasion, their version of a production manager would suggest that they were running a bit behind. To them "behind" meant in minutes or possibly an hour. In the U.S., it might have meant a week or a month, or Christ only knows.

On the homefront, via the trade papers, I read of new problems in Marilyn's life, other than Arthur Miller who had become an old one. There was some discord at Fox over that script in the informal stages, and Marilyn, as always, was in the middle. Marilyn, as always, was being blamed. Remembering that she had said, "I can handle it," I tried to clear my mind of that old worry that kept edging its way in.

I had again made friends in London, and reacquainted myself with some former ones. It seemed Marilyn and I were suddenly in two different professions. In her life, for the moment, discord had again begun. In mine, total harmony. None of those I worked with could have begun to identify with the shananigans taking place back home. It simply wasn't within them. During the course of filming, I had made a special friend of the leading lady whom we'll call Yvette as that is as close as I'm going to get. She was a delightful girl possessed of both beauty and intelligence. We had had a few dinners, and a stroll or two through the streets. Having lived here all her life, she had become a most attractive guide. Anyone would have been proud to have her on their arm. Unfortunately or fortunately as ever you wish, on a particularly lonely night for me, we shared a bed. It was comfortable and indeed gratifying. Under normal circumstances it would have been entirely exciting, quite real and lovely. Sadly, for me, it evoked all the wrong feelings. She would never know because she had done nothing to deserve those feelings. She too was a bit older than me, but then so was everybody. With her, it was about three years. She had blossomed into full vibrant womanhood, and offered all that you might ever think to want. Problem was, there were three of us in that bed and that made it impossible.

Love, sometimes cruelly, offers you no intermission. Then, the worst of it, maybe it was my cologne, she began making noises which indicated the possibilities of home and hearth, that sort of thing, which only scared the hell out of me. This enchanting human being did not deserve this mental trip through the garden of fantasy, she deserved so much better. With only a week left to wrap, I did what I could to avoid her, but even that had become a cruel game. The look on her face was a constant reminder that an explanation was in order, and this selfish bastard had just better give her one. I had attempted to call Marilyn once on the private number she had given me. With no answer, I had decided to wait and finish the job rather than wonder and worry. At this point I was 6,000 miles away and nothing could have been changed if, indeed, it had to be. Throughout the 6 weeks or so, I had kept in touch with Bob, and to this final week, nothing had been said of any phone calls. I also remembered her words."Pay no attention to what you may read," so I didn't.

On the eve of the last day of shooting, with all reports already packaged for the studio, I had arranged a quiet dinner for my British lady and myself. Arriving at her home, I observed a picture of loveliness. She was truly a dazzler. Little, if anything, was said enroute to the dinner. It began shortly after a cocktail, and SHE began it.

"There is someone else here," she said. "We can't see her, but she's here all the same."

"It's all kinda mixed up," I said. "I don't think I can explain it." With that her big brown eyes searched my face.

"I don't believe you have to," she remarked with the kind of tenderness that comes from deep inside and can not be manufactured.

"Well," she continued, " You know what I think? I think she is very fortunate and must be very special."

Without clouding the issue and designing a dozen clever, if even true, sentimental expressions aimed to and about her, I simply shook my head.

Every woman either superficially or way down deep comes equipped with a natural maternal instinct. It is part of the package, and to those who wear it honestly, it shines as brightly as a beacon. It is generally aimed at the children of the species, but once in awhile, it points to the partner, that macho, brave and fearless warrior who crumbles under its touch. It is always the lioness who dominates the lion.

"Don't look so sad, Peter," she began. "It's not a reason for an excuse, it is a gift. To be cherished is every woman's dream. Oh how truly lucky she is." She raised her glass. "Well then," she said, "let's drink to her, whoever she is, and to you for providing me a very special and warm page for my diary."

In her wisdom, she had granted me a graceful exit. And for that, her memory would last. I am certain, or at least it was my hope, that she went on to marry someone worthy of her. He too would have been truly lucky.

On the final day, and after the "cut and print it," the film was over. It had come in under budget, a rarity in this profession. It would take me weeks down the road to convince my home base that it was through no genius of mine. All involved just knew what they were doing. The Brits will always hold a reserved place in my heart. They were, all of them, a class act.

Chapter Sixteen

Let's Make Garbage

Winter had come to New York and the light snow falling witnessed from the descending plane, changed the look of the city to something from Courier and Ives. 1959 was history. The new decade was before us. The changes that had begun in the rebellious 50's would soon manifest themselves into proper chaos, for the generation to come would indeed destroy a good deal of the heart and soul of the world. The 60's naturally would have their moments, but they would be few and far between. For me, more than an age would die.

I was somewhat shocked to discover Bob waiting for me at the deboarding gate. His smile looked just a bit put-on, and for him, that wasn't easy. His outstretched hand greeted me with the familiar arm around the shoulder. As we headed for the baggage section, he remarked, "How WAS Jolly Old England?"

"Jolly Old England was fine," I said, "but what's the reason for the cab service?"

"Got your letter last week saying you'd be back. Studio told me when...," he went on.

"Ok," I interrupted, "and.....????"

Receiving my letter didn't call for curb service. Something was up, and knowing me, he knew he'd better get on with it. Hail fellow well met lasted for about 2 seconds with me when I smelled a problem.

"And...," he paused. We both stopped walking.

"What is it?," I asked with new urgency.

"Marilyn called the station last night," he blurted. Seeing the look on my face he quickly added, "She's alright..she's alright!" He then reached into his pocket and withdrew a folded piece of paper. Handed it to me.

"She left a number," he went on, " I called TWA and found out what flight you'd be on and called her back. I told her I'd meet the plane."

"Ok, Ok," I stammered still trying to get to the point. "Where is she?"

"It's an L.A. number," he said, "She's expecting your call at 9 Eastern. We've got plenty of time. Hey, she sounded Ok."

I glanced at the number, placed it into my pocket, and continued the walk to the baggage claim.

Few words were spoken on our trip to the beach, which took longer, complicated by icy road conditions. It was around 8 when Bob slid into my driveway. Another quality of a good friend, is to know when to disappear, which he did with my gratitude for being there. 9 my time would have been 6 her time, and I had to assume that was part of the pre-arrangement. As I waited, thumbing through a ton of mail, bills, circulars, and Christmas cards, I called the studio. Naturally no one was there. I did manage to leave a message with the night switchboard informing them I had arrived safely and would see them in the morning.

Suddenly the peace and order of England seemed to gain my envy. For the weeks I had been there, all that had surrounded me was warmth, comradeship and professional and personal courtesy. One second off the plane, and the treadmill had already been turned on. Then came the haunting truth that perhaps I had lulled myself into thinking otherwise. It had most likely been cranking all the time. I then remembered Clarence's words of wisdom only a few weeks back, "She'll be a handful..." Well, Clarence, you were on the money with that one. My blonde bombshell was probably up to her pretty little ass in something.

At 9pm straight up, I dialed. Waited. As usual, with

Marilyn, I never had a clue as to what to expect. I didn't have long to wait. Her voice trembled with apprehension, "Hello," she said in only half expectancy.

"Baby?," was all I could get out.

"Oh God," she blurted, "I'm so glad to hear your voice." Her apprehension dissolved into anxiety. "Bob gave me your message," I said. "What's wrong?"

"Everything!," she blurted. "Everything you can imagine!" She began to speak in 90 mile-per-hour patter. "The script is awful! It's just another 'dumb blonde.' It's worse than anything I've ever done! It's like punishment! Why, Peter, Why!???"

"Whoa, whoa," I said, trying to calm her. "Honey slow-down. Easy...What kind of a film is it?"

"A bad one!," she replied, attempting to regain some composure. "It's supposed to be a musical comedy, but it's not funny, it's stupid! It's like my worst nightmare."

"Okay, okay," I interrupted, trying to get a fix on the whole thing, and more than slightly overwhelmed by the frenzy in her voice.

"Slow down, honey. What about director and script approval? This isn't GENTLEMEN PREFER BLONDES, I thought they've re-written your contract."

"Oh, yeah, that!" she went on, a slight sadistic quality to her voice ebbing from down deep. "We've got George Cukor, a nice old man with one foot in the grave and the other on a banana peel." It became obvious this line was getting no where.

"Are you alone?," I asked.

"Right now I am, but Arthur's with me ," she blurted, as though that fact should mean something.

"Good!," I answered. "No matter what you think, he's not going to let them screw around with you." If I ever had any doubts about the state of the Miller household, they were all put to rest with the next angered reply.

"Are you kidding?!," she slapped back in disgust. "He's worse than the rest of them! He just stands around making lewd noises and telling me to behave myself. Fox slipped him a check to write some 'jokes' for this film, Can you believe that? Is the entire world crazy? Arthur Miller writing jokes??!" Her breathing became harder as she plunged further into it, "This isn't DEATH OF A SALESMAN! Arthur's about as funny as the Black Plaque. Fox insisted I do this picture, and now we're only days away from principal shooting. They've blackmailed me into either doing it or not releasing me for Arthur's, and even though I hate the son of a bitch, that script is GOOD! It's all the reasons we've been sneaking in and out of back alleys, and now they hold this piece of shit over my head."

"Honey, Marilyn, STOP!, ..just stop," I said, already thinking of my schedule and knowing what HAD to come next. "Let me think...."

"Can you come?," she asked almost pleadingly as though that was necessary. I had already begun working out the details in my head.

"You know I'm coming," I said, reassuringly, "I have to arrange some of the fine points...give me a minute..."

I could hear her breathing on the other end, and after a short time, she had waited long enough.

"Was England good for you?" she asked knowing my mind was now on the arrangement of that schedule.

"England was fine, and it was good for US," I answered.

"Did you miss me?" she asked, as if necessary.

"Only every hour, honey, only every minute" I said, and the schedule popped into my brain.

"Ok, here's where we sink or swim," I began, "I have to give my report to my boss in the morning, and then I'll hop a plane. I can be there by tomorrow night, but you'll have to tell me where."

"You're coming...you're really coming..." she said with a new uplift to her voice.

"Did you think I wouldn't?" I said.

She began a kind of relieved laugh, a quiet kind of welcomed hysteria. "No Peter," she began, "I just...Never mind. It's not important at all. I love you, I love you, I love you" she kept repeating, the needle on a broken record.

It was a record she could have played for as long as she wanted even under these more than casually strained circumstances. I am living testimony to the axiom, "when you're in you're in." Yvette saw it, Clarence knew it, Rachman suspected it, and my grandmother felt it. Never would there ever be someone who could so stir my blood, who could lift my spirit to such heights...Had the music been permitted to go on, what songs we would have sung.

Gazing at my image in the mirror, these days, reminds me of where those bags under my eyes began. One small thing I kept overlooking back then, was sleep. I suppose that goes right along with youth. At least I'd like to think it does. They're like badges of honor now. Testimonial medals to the burning of a candle at both ends and in the middle. She helped put those bags there, along with the greying hair that now requires some assistance from Clairol. To gaze at the basset is to remember the greyhound. The problem seems to be, I'd do it all over again in a second, and now at 57, no one could blame it on youth!

The early morning meeting was basically a re-hashing of the last few weeks in London. The figures substantiated my glowing report. On a budget just slightly higher than the coffee and donut allotment for THE TEN COMMANDMENTS, this little company in England had created a magnificent film, in 3-strip Technicolor no less. The film boasted a literate script, superb performances, excellent camera work, and spawned a "creature" with whom you could sympathize. All the necessary ingredients for a worthwhile terror film. After all, from the dawn of movies, how many people do YOU know who didn't feel pity for Kong when he took the big dive off the top of the 1931 Empire State Building? I would return to England again, and re-meet my new found friends as the studio had now guaranteed to distribute for them world-wide. In that and to that end, I had done my job. It would make sense to the big boss that I now needed some time to rest or so I said.

Chapter Seventeen

Los Angeles

When God created California he had reached perfection in the land. Pioneers and early missionaries continued in that spirit by harvesting crops and souls in equal proportions. The majestic mountains gave shelter to the lush green valleys, and all was at peace. The crystal waters that surrounded this land of plenty were as clear as the finest cut diamond, and the sky was a rich and pure blue.

Sometime in the early 20's, "the movies" discovered California for its year round near perfect climate. People began flocking to this "promised land" of dreams and hopes.....arriving by the hundreds, then thousands. In a matter of a few years they managed to screw up the works. Los Angeles, so named by the Spanish missionaries meaning "The City Of The Angels," in a time where that might have applied, became the mecca of fools, and thereby could have been re-named "Los Locos," "The City Of The Crazies." The early film pioneers saw only the good of it, but what had transpired by 1960, was an indescribable bag of nuts, all of whom had forgotten the original plan.

Los Angeles, and the industry, hand in hand, had become almost a caricature of itself. It was a land of artificial props, artificial sets, and artificial people. While rain was still conspicuously absent for a good portion of the time, in other ways, it "snowed all year in Hollywood." The chief industry might still have been "the movies," but the resulting major by-product had become "bullshit." There were always people "pitching" other people. Ideas that would never see the light of day, preposterous un-earned titles, and ludicrous concepts that could be and would be fed to a starving world anxious to swallow them. Everyone saw themselves as "important," and most were quick to tell you about it. Writers who couldn't write became movie critics. Actors who couldn't act, became drama coaches. The few truly great people often got lost in the shuffle of a hype that suggested they weren't.

Television had already begun to create its own brand of new stars, many of whom could be easily forgotten when a particular series got the axe. A new breed of independent film makers would begin their reign in this year. Some would show honest promise. Others would hit and run. The studios would soon lose their control of the industry, and many would be sold off as real estate. Because of unrealistic rising costs, many film makers would go elsewhere to shoot their films, and many would do so non-union. In truth, with the silliness of it all, the industry was pricing itself out of its own business. The remaining studio properties were being rushed through for distribution to return the invested buck more quickly. Grainy, out of focus films were released as "art," which of course they weren't. They were grainy, out of focus films. "Statement" films would soon emerge, which weren't statements of anything.

Some films, in their attempt at realism, became "so real" that they lost their audience. In the "golden days'" of movies, they had provided an "escape" from trouble, from reality, but as the 60's rolled on, they began to focus sharply on subjects that most people were trying to over- look. Now you could see close-up on giant 50 foot screens, violence, unrest, and mass murder. The ratings system began. What this meant was now you could study close-up things that had been better left to the imagina- tion. Those studios that did remain in operation made deals with certain stars in co-production mingling. This was constructed to "guarantee" success, and of course, it didn't. There is no such animal as the "guaranteed" picture in the industry. Never has been, never will be. Flying at 25,000 feet can sometimes help to clear your brain. It literally takes you above it all, and just as in an ocean voyage, makes you aware of just how insignificant it and we really are. 20th Century Fox Film Studios had created a background of movies in the 40's and 50's that could easily have been rated excellent. When that proud logo appeared on the screen, with that so well identified fanfare music, it meant you were in for something special. Whatever may or may not have been transpiring behind the scenes, Fox turned out winners.

Marilyn had been one of those winners, the nearest thing to a "guarantee." To them, her "Bugs Bunny" character had continued to put bread on the table, and the thought of placing her into a dramatic vehicle never entered their mind. Oh they could say they tried, but considering the few feeble stabs at it, perhaps not hard enough. At the beginning, they had seen her as a "fluke," a passing "freak" who might bump and grind her way in and out of a few films, then disappear as had so many. They had also treated her that way. No one ever took Marilyn seriously. She had a natural gift of comedy, and a lilting, easy to listen to voice, all of which were incased in a dynamite body. All they saw was the body. I never suggested to her that she should attempt ANNA KARENNINA, but there were featured roles for women that would have suited her as well if not better than those who got to play them.

As the announcement of the final descent of our plane came officially booming through the overhead speaker, I had already decided I knew what the immediate problems were. I knew nothing about the script, but I didn't have to. Her frustration said it all. Marilyn had scored big in films like BUS STOP and THE SEVEN YEAR

ITCH for Fox, as well as her recent triumph in the comedy on screen, tragedy off screen, SOME LIKE IT HOT for UA. She had every right to expect a continued escalation of her talent, not a slide back to her walk-on in LOVE HAPPY ten years before. Her unspoken words and the desperate sound of her voice was a clear indication that they again were aiming at their quintessential "dumb blonde."

Later in my life, I would meet and come to know other screen blonde bombshells. Jayne Mansfield, for one. Jayney may have begun as a "Marilyn clone," but she was developing her own following rather successfully. She enjoyed playing the role, and it showed. THE GIRL CAN'T HELP IT, WILL SUCCESS SPOIL ROCK HUNTER, KISS THEM FOR ME , this was pure Jayne. Then there was the lovely Joi Lansing whom I would meet through a commercial artist friend. Joi would become a personal friend with no back street suggestions. Just a nice lady. She would even visit me in a hospital and give the nurses something to talk about.   There was Sheree North, exploding her image onto the screen very reminiscent of the earlier Betty Hutton. The world was filled with blondes, or, at least the movie world was.

Aside from these dynamite ladies, there were others standing in the wings waiting for their moment.

As far as Fox was concerned, the Marilyn era would soon be relegated to history. It was too late for her side to be heard, and as I said, no one would have listened anyway. To them, there was one more film and the contract would be over. Co-production deal or not, Marilyn and Fox would part company....at least for awhile. Her reputation, both personally and professionally, had preempted any thoughts, at that moment, of a continuing relationship between star and studio. She had made them bundles of money, and poetically had seen little of that money herself. Aside from the financial "points" she would have from SOME LIKE IT HOT, this current thing, and the nightmare film to come, Marilyn, one of the biggest stars in the history of films, would never make more than $1500 per week. It was the lousiest contract in the industry. I was making that amount at age 22, and nobody in the world even knew who the hell I was.

Not knowing all of the above, and returning to the moment, all that mattered to me was that my girl was in trouble. Whether I could or couldn't help was a mystery, but I had not come to Los Angeles for the scenery. My room at The Beverly Hilton was there as arranged, and upon stepping into it, I immediately hit the phone. The private number she had given me was at the neighboring Beverly Hills Hotel a few miles away. Along with the number had come the instructions. It was her private number and if no one answered, I was to call back until she did. Technically only she would answer that number, BUT, if someone else did, I was to hang up. I suddenly had this vision of dialing and hanging up on a continuing basis. If we honestly were trying to look inconspicuous, this wouldn't have been the way to do it. Along with this vision came another, that of my sitting in this room all night staring at the mass produced prints on the wall waiting...waiting. What we had done in New York seemed right and justifiably motivated. The reasons seemed clear enough, and the results had been wonderful, but here in Los Angeles, it began to take a different road.

A feeling of "cheap" began creeping into my thoughts, and I didn't like it. Gratefully she had been as anxious as myself and immediately answered the phone, and thereby silenced the growing feelings of guilt. The first "Hello" sounded less than exciting but when I returned with "Hi honey," her tone lifted. She did have a way of making you forget any thoughts that might have been ebbing into your mind along the lines of my first feelings of apprehension. Her voice and immediate enthusiasm smothered any mental signals of guilt.

After the usual "how was the flight," "is it a nice room" chit chat, mutual anticipation took over as it always had, and it was left that she would be here in about an hour. I showered, shaved and grabbed some coffee from room service. Sipping the over priced brew, I managed to step to my window from where I could observe the flickering lights of the city. The Beverly Hilton is on the corner of Wilshire Blvd and Santa Monica Blvd, and from my window I was able to look out over the immediate Beverly Hills area and into Hollywood only a few miles up the road. I could watch the stream of cars, many of them limos arriving and departing from the hotel. I began to think in near comical terms. All that glitters in Los Angeles is definitely not gold, in fact, in most cases, it is rented. There was something glaringly contrived about the whole thing. It wasn't real. This "thing" we had become involved in wasn't right. The feelings certainly were, but the method in which we had followed the lines of this play had to be changed. When Marilyn and I were together, it seemed the rest of the world simply didn't exist. Realistically, it DID. Constructing an "island" on which to hide makes for good stories, but life doesn't permit such hideaways, at least not on an ongoing basis. Such dreams are as artificial as the city below this window. One single thought kept pounding in my ears, "With the truth you have little hope, with a lie you have none." This wasn't a good time to get philosophical. And yet, poetically, now in this city of so much falsity this might have been the best time.

I had never prepared myself for Marilyn. She had literally come to me out of the rain, and from that glorious night had developed something as magnificent as life itself. From that first moment, I was never sure what she was going to do and when, and for just as many reasons, I had begun to fall into that pattern of taking for the moment, and damning the consequences. Marilyn was a doer and a dreamer, and quite often got the two mixed up. She had been poked, punched, and pillaged by an army of allies and adversaries alike. Wherever she went someone waited to screw her in one way or another. However, despite her personal demons, somewhere, someplace at all times her name and picture flashed in front of someone's eyes. Clarence had been right when referring to her as an "institution." And now this same "institution" whose image once stood 4-stories high on a billboard in Times Square, was coming to my room. Somehow in New York I had been able to disassociate her image from her reality. Whether that would hold true here in La La land, remained to be seen.

Before I could drive myself completely crazy with the onslaught of thoughts that stormed the castle of my mind, a gentle knock on the door snapped me out of it. My opening of the door was a "fade-in" to a new scene. She stood there wearing a coy look and sporting sunglasses. Her now trademark kerchief obviously necessary as the "enemy" lurked only a few miles down the road. She carried a script under her arm and in that split second, I supposed it was this latest epic. Maybe she was bringing the patient to the doctor, I didn't know, and frankly, at this moment, I didn't care. All I saw was what I had so prayed to see, what I had so missed. The subject who had given me guilt in London, who had been with me across the ocean, in my heart. Philosophy would have to wait. Thoughts of what might be socially accepted, the rights and wrongs of it, would have to be put on that back-burner for a time. She stepped into the room and closed the door behind her. No words were spoken as no words were required. She removed her kerchief and threw her arms around me. We remained frozen for those first few seconds, in an embrace that dynamite could not have separated. To the industry, she meant trouble, to the world, excitement, sex, an image of beauty, something you dream about but cannot attain. To me, she meant "home," the reasons for it all.

From that quiet, pensive, moment, erupted, what could have been, a scene from a 1930's screwball comedy. She began kissing me, and, at the same time, pushing me toward the bed. She did not stop kissing me long enough to say "hello." It continued in near frenzy. After the initial shock of such a welcome, the shower of kisses came to rest on one very long one, and so it began again. The near savage sexual encounter that followed, immediately indicated very strongly, that we most assuredly had missed each other. Once again, the world disappeared.

After the "storm," came the "eye" of the hurricane, that moment to rest. We were clearly back where we had belonged.

"I should go away more often," I said, now just gazing at her. With that, she snuggled closer. I remember the caresses, the joys of, again, stroking her hair, her fragrance, her touch. Once again, translation escapes me. On a path to that translation, perhaps I may be able to offer a few thoughts that may assist you in a better understanding. The first thing you have to do, is not separate us from you. Don't see this picture as larger than life, and don't, please don't visualize it in CinemaScope and Technicolor. That is not what it was. If you can look to the left or to the right, and see that person who now shares your life, and either know or remember the feelings that exist between only you two, then the image that you read on this page, will only be a reflection of your own. Whether your partner is known to the world or only to you, makes very little difference.

After the extremely warm greeting, we flicked on the dimmest lights we could find. By her suggestion, I ordered some sandwiches and wine from room service. As we waited for delivery, she jumped into the shower, returned, grabbed one of my shirts, and put it on. It was her way of telling me, things were exactly as they had been. Tragically, they were not.

The entire episode had been so overwhelming, that now and only now, would I look closely into her eyes. Room service had come and gone, and we were alone. Those eyes had haunted me across two continents. I had seen them in my sleep. Their memory had been enough to get me through. Now, those same eyes, those same beautiful eyes, had changed. A glazed look covered them. One that had not been there before. Something was very different, and that difference wasn't good. There was a helplessness about them, almost as though they couldn't see. It had been easy to stroll and sit on a lonely beach in Bayville Long Island and dream of victory, of days in the sun and of projections for a future. Here, the reality of what had already begun to tear apart those dreams, stared at me through vacant defeated beacons. What were they doing to my Marilyn...........

The current script was a farce, and it did reduce her to her worst fears.

"It's only a script," I said, "Get through it."

With that, her look changed. Anger crept in that had not been there before. A bit of venom came my way. "You too?," she said now putting me into the category of the rest, "Have they gotten to you too?"

"Nobody's gotten to me," I said now a bit on the defensive.

"Oh yes they have," she went on suddenly slightly hysterical. "Of course you can't see it, because you're still YOUNG! YOUNG PEOPLE don't care about this kind of thing...Nobody gives a fuck! Throw the old broad a bone! She'll dance for you, and maybe if you get lucky, she'll even fuck you!"

Now I was young and she was old. Now that same youth that she had allowed herself to become part of, was a threat. For that moment, I had been transported to the enemy camp. In favor of defending, I elected to remain quiet and permitted her this necessary tirade, realizing in that moment where DiMaggio and Miller had gone wrong. "When she was good she was very very good, but when she was bad she was horrid..." She could turn on a dime when pressed, and aim her venom at the nearest body. What would transpire would be your decision, not hers.

She continued: "This script is a piece of crap! And what's really the biggest joke of all, I have nothing to say about it. All that bullshit about director choice, script choice, just that, bullshit! And now YOU sit there and tell me 'I'll get through it.' How the fuck do YOU know that?! You sit on your young pompous ass, and judge..your idealistic air of superiority!"

Ok, I'd sat there long enough. Her voice and blood pressure were beginning to rise. I stood up. I was still a whole lot bigger and taller than she was, and right now I felt I'd better be a whole lot stronger. She stood, raving, about 3 feet from me. I reached for her and pulled her close. I could feel the tension in her body. At that moment she was ready for a fight. My arms did not "grab" her, but instead slowly pulled her to me. I then put them around her and held her more tightly than I had ever done. I would not let her go until I actually felt the tension leave her.

She began to cry, and with the tears, "I'm sorry," she said,

"I didn't mean...."

I held her tear filled face in my hands, and kissed her. She returned the kiss which lasted far longer then perhaps intended. We then moved to the edge of the bed and sat together. I grabbed a kleenex from the bedstand. Dabbed her face lightly. We had to get over this thing right then...or lose it all right here in Plastic town.

"You're right, I don't understand," I said, "I don't understand why you worry as much about so little."

She looked as though she was making ready for a second assault. I put my finger on her lips.

"Wait, honey, wait..," I said, " but just because I don't understand doesn't mean your problem isn't a real one. Consider it my inexperience, my pompous idealistic hangup. What I really meant to say was that you can get through it because you're bigger than it is. You didn't give me a chance to finish."

"I don't think you're pompous," she said now trying to calm.

"Of course I'm pompous," I returned, " and I'm also idealistic. But there's nothing wrong with being that way."

"I'm the one who's fucked up not you," she continued. "Look at me! No, don't! I can't see how you'd even want to. I'm falling apart. Peter, they've won! Who the hell do you know who wants to pay to look at this...? eh? Would you pay to watch this..this physical wreck?"

"Now you listen to me," I began, " Marilyn, Marilyn Monroe, Norma Jeane, all of you listen up. I love you..all of you. I don't give a rats ass what the world thinks. That love is stronger today than it was yesterday, and then it was stronger than the day before..Not even you can defeat it. Now you want to get angry? Good! Get angry."

Her expression softened some. She was always a good listener. I went on having to make a point or go down trying. "Get angry at the world, Fox, Miller...pick one or all, but leave yourself out of it. And don't be calling yourself names. Not to me! Something inside this YOUNG man tells me what I should do right now is get you dressed, take you back to your hotel, help you pack, and get you out of this whole God-damned thing, and leave them all holding their peckers wondering what the hell happened......"

A slight smile finally returned to her face. She shook her head with that smile."You would really do that wouldn't you," she said now gratefully through a smile.

"You bet that sweet ass of yours I would!" I continued, "but don't worry, I won't. I know what you think that other script means to you, and I'll bend to that right now. It's just something else I don't understand."

"Could you imagine their faces," she said with a small chuckle.

"Marilyn," I continued now most seriously, "You are the only thing in this whole world that counts to me. The ONLY thing. If you haven't figured that out by now, you'd better realize it this very minute. The *young/old* thing won't work. Nice try. Age hasn't been an issue for us since second one. It's not one now."

I finally reached her. She reached out for me and I was there. She cradled my head in her hands and kissed me lightly, tenderly, honestly. The anger directed at me for so many other reasons, vanished. She was my Marilyn again.

"Ok," I said, "Now that we've gotten that out of the way, here's what you have to do."

She took a couple of deep breaths, pushed her now disheveled hair away from her face, and regained her composure.

"What kind of a character is it?" I asked. She picked up the script. "She's a girl working in little theatre, a dancer..." she said.

"Ok," I went on, " What happens?"

" Well," she went on trying to allow her professional side to take over. "She meets this millionaire, he falls for her but doesn't want to tell her who he is afraid that she will love him only for his money....it's so stupid.."

"Wait a minute" I said, "No it's not..so far it's entirely possible, then what?"

"Well, then he decides to join this little theatre and try to woo her as an equal," she went on. "He hires teachers to show him how to be funny, how to sing, how to dance, how to make her fall in love with him on those terms. Honestly Peter, it's so lame."

"Just a minute," I said, "just finish."

Biting her lips, she continued. "True love wins, she finds out who he is and loves him anyway..ta daaa!"

"Ok," I said. "I've seen worse, remember me? That's what I do..take the awful and make it acceptable. This isn't so awful, a little corny, but not awful. Awful is your friend Tony Curtis playing in Spartacus."

That got the laugh it was aimed at.

"To get YOU through this," I went on,"Here's what YOU have to do. You have to rise above the material. This thing..do you sing? dance? what?"

"Both" she said.

"Ok, well in that you need no help. Wiggle this," I suggested by patting her on her rear end, "and give them what they want.. Be Marilyn..the Marilyn they think you are. Ok, now, with the character...Find something that YOU want to put into that character. Do it all by yourself."

"My motivation," she answered sounding like a Strasberg alumni.

"Yes, if you like," I continued. "Give the girl a background. Make her real. She's from a broken home..this is something she's always wanted to do. Let Norma Jeane help you. She will if you let her. Give this girl some of her dreams. Try to remember when it all started. I know you remember because you've told me enough about it. The character YOU create will help you through this. You do not have to make her a 'dumb blonde'. Before they know it, you'll pull that out from under them."

"You know, you might be right," she said, now thinking for a moment.

"Doctor Greenson has been trying to help me do the same thing."

"Who's Doctor Greenson?" I asked, a bit concerned as this was a new name to me.

"He's my analyst. He's been trying to get me to think back to my childhood and find out where my problems started. I'm not sure he's helping me that much, but he's fun to talk to."

"FUN TO TALK TO?," I reacted.

"Well, he was at the beginning," she said, as though now analyzing the analyst. "He's got some different ideas about therapy, in fact he lectures on them."

I have never been against therapy, as a matter of principal, but the more she spoke of this Doctor Greenson, the more it sounded like he was only doing what so many had already done, confusing her. That is the one thing she didn't need at this juncture.

"He gives me valium to relax and then asks me all sorts of things. Sometimes the answers even surprise me."

This guy was sounding better every minute. Now he was giving her pills.

"Where did you find this guy?," I finally asked, cutting to the chase.

"Oh, he does a lot of people in our industry. He's getting quite a name for himself."

"I'll bet he is," I said, almost under my breath.

"Please don't be mad at me," she said, honest tears in her voice. "I started seeing him because of Arthur and our problems. I thought he could help me work my way through this."

"Honey, I'm not mad at you," I said, " It seems that...." I decided to stop. "Oh hell, what do I know. Maybe this Doctor Greenson's the best thing since canned tuna, I just don't want you to get all jumbled up in your head right now. You need your wits about you." It seemed the more I said, the more blank her look became. This time, retreat was in order.

"Honey, I don't know this guy," I began," and that's not being fair to him. Just use your head, and let's get back to the script."

"You don't have to worry, Sugar, I can stop seeing him anytime I want to. If it gets too much, I will, honest."

The subject was dropped, at least outwardly, and the chore of dissecting the script took over. It was the first time in our relationship when I could actually help her in the field I knew best. I believe, by her reactions, that this new dimension gave her a bit of security. We had often talked of this, for some future time. It was only logical that a writer and an actress could have easily combined talents, and not have the result be the epic being created by Miller. Had they worked together rather than apart, a whole bundle of "good" could come from it. This was our first preview of what that could have been, and it was most satisfying. Marilyn, indeed, possessed an incredible gift to learn and absorb. Had life been different, more than one award would have found her name on it. Her blowing off steam was also a victory for both of us, as the tensions of the profession were indeed defeated by our much stronger feelings. It was good. It was a lesson and an example of love under fire. And we had passed. Had this only happened, somehow, a few years before, a physical impossibility, I am certain it would have changed history.

Responsibilities I then thought so important, would call

me back to New York that next day but with a promise to be only a phone call away. After one more tender hour on the bed that had so often carried us away to other worlds, she stepped back out into the night. An early rehearsal the next morning required her to rest.

It was all so very logical. The larger problem, of course, was that I had no knowledge of what was transpiring behind the scenes. I believe Marilyn knew that if I did, I would have, in fact, taken her away that night, under screams and kicking if need be. I believe she wanted to show me that she could do it. I think she wanted to make me proud of her, not that for a second, I hadn't been. When do you really know "what to do?" When does your brain connect the facts that something more than a film had become a problem? When do you say "that's enough, we're leaving." The scenario I had concocted about "the packing bags" and so on, should have been the climax to that evening. That other script should not have prevented my doing what I honestly thought I should do. But it had. Marilyn was a hell of a salesperson. She had me convinced that she was now back on track, and continued to offer unnecessary apologies for her behavior. None of those apologies were required, but she felt compelled to offer them. She also assured me that Doctor Greenson would be good for her, if for no reason other than an impartial ear to speak to. If he really worried me that much, she would dismiss him the next day. It was not my decision to make, so no such statement was uttered. I had been placed in the less than enviable position of judging a man I knew nothing about, and possibly doing irreparable harm in such a judgement. It was a no-win situation, and one I honestly hoped she could deal with, using the common sense I knew she possessed.

As a result of England, there were many things I had to complete back at home. Despite her constant reminders of the importance of my career for both of us, as the plane left the runway, those suggestions and plans all blurred under the heavy weight of the truth that I should have stayed. Leaving her, even by her own guarantees, might not have been the biggest mistake of my life, but certainly among the top two. The biggest would occur several months later. I had the unique distinction of making the same mistake twice. There would be no third chance to correct it.

Chapter Eighteen
The Barber Shop

Remember, we never said "Goodbye." As each moment, be it a day or several, came to an end, we chose instead to say "Until next time." It was lighter, un-final, and gave hope for the words it suggested. It helped cement the lonely days and weeks, bridged them and made them bearable creating an anticipation of their own. It gave permanency to it all.

Never feel envy for those of us either under the lights or behind them. To extract even a few precious moments, is to pay the heaviest dues. Each moment in the sun is either borrowed or stolen from as many, if not more, in the dark.

Every town has a barber shop. Population is unimportant. Within the confines of that barber shop, decisions are made, thoughts expressed, and verdicts given. It is a meeting place for opinion and a seeding place for gossip. The friendly barber is the judge, and his customers, the prosecution, defense and the jury. On the face of it, it seems harmless- a place to exchange ideas. Below its surface lies the roots of destruction. On a small town level, thoughts and insinuations formed at the barber shop can destroy lives.

The media is that same barber shop, on a much larger scale. The facts come in and are reported. Then come the opinions of those who are paid to make them. Hearsay becomes fact,and supposition reality, simply by the constant re-telling. Each new ear hears what it wants to hear, and each new mouth translates its version. The old parlor game. Tell one person a story, and pass it on to ten. By the time the tenth person repeats it, none of the original story remains. It's fun at parties, but not so in life. Marilyn's life had been one big parlor game for the media, and what was currently transpiring, during this particular period, was to demonstrate the barber shop in its finest hour.

Life is always just slightly comedic under the most severe of circumstances. It is that balance, given us by our Maker, that permits us to survive. Her final words to me on the beach had been "Don't you dare believe everything you read." The media was about to have a field day. What read to most people like a tragedy, was in fact, the comedy of the year. It was a plot within a plot, and that same media fed off it as was expected, too gullible to realize they had swallowed the bait, hook, line and sinker.

As I labored in the wee small hours of each day, doing what I did best, now complicating it with budgets, production woes, and handy suggestions, Marilyn had again moved to center stage. She might not have been in charge of the film, but she now would be in charge of the behind-the-scenes show. She would give them everything they wanted. She would also completely hoodwink her so-called friends with a performance that would rival Helen Hayes' finest hour on stage. She would also prove both triumphantly and sadly, that those who called themselves friends, didn't know her at all.

Yves Montand had paid his dues in France, his native country, and had for years appeared in a number of dramatic films all bearing sub-titles. He had a face that resembled half-Bogart, half-basset hound, but below or beyond that mask, was an actor of intensity. Fox had first chosen Gregory Peck as the lead in this new film, but Peck had declined for reasons of his own.

It is a performer's privilege to do so when not threatened by a so-called contract obligation as in Marilyn's case. As Montand had expressed interest in finding an "American" audience, Fox and his representatives saw this as the possible flagship of that interest. Because of a girl named Marilyn, the Montand "camp" knew the film would be seen by the numbers. If that same film became less than GONE WITH THE WIND, it would, nevertheless, gain exposure. It all seemed quite workable for this French basset hound. Yves would also give it a continental flavor, and after having read that draft presented to me by Marilyn, "any" flavor would have helped.

Miller, of course, lurked in the background, selfishly brooding, mumbling "Hemmingway" farewell speeches to his own career, bemoaning his ever-slipping status. He had become the president of the "Poor Arthur" fan club. He would commute between Los Angeles and Connecticut, and occasionally Ireland. While in Los Angeles, he would be the subject of Marilyn's scorn, a paid servant to administer coffee, pills and booze when asked. Away from Los Angeles, he would continue to write, undisturbed, that "great" script we'd all been hearing about. The one that so possessed Marilyn's mind. In writing this epic, he would use the tools of a writer and expose his own misery, and in the character he had written specifically for Marilyn, originally in tribute, vindicate his own deflated ego. Whatever were his private reasons, will have to remain just that. Whatever truce they may have agreed upon, only related to that script.

Miller had abused Marilyn, emotionally and even physically. Just what they did and didn't do must remain a mystery, but I had seen on her legs and thighs black and blue marks that didn't come from bumping into chairs as she once tried to suggest. Their verbal contests had become legendary. By the time of this current film, LET'S MAKE LOVE, their own version had been re-titled, LET'S MAKE WAR, and that they did. Whether Miller cried into his beer or into the bosom of a new paramour was his own secret , and one that didn't interest Marilyn in the least. Their's had become a warped contest of getting even, and as Miller would use his typewriter, Marilyn would use Yves Montand, just vain and self-impressed enough to buy it himself. It was a great hype for Montand, always the Frenchman, always the consummate lover. The very sound of their accent seems to indicate romance, although, behind that accent is so often laughter aimed at you. The French, for whatever self-imposed reasons, have always felt superior to the Americans. They make no bones about it. They will laugh with you, love with you, and stick it to you whenever they get the chance. They are indeed victims of an overly imaginative press agent. To their credit, they will admit it. Just as you must constantly remind the British that "we won," so too must you enlighten the French with the fact that you already know all of this. Once they know YOU know, they are among the best friends you will ever have. Just one of life's nuttier scenarios.

Just as I had shared a bed with my British Yvette, and not brought it home for dissection, would I not have required the same from Marilyn. The media barber shop had already begun to perform. A romance was blossoming on the set of LET'S MAKE LOVE. It was a torrid thing to be sure. In the "Willy" tabloids of that period, Montand was King, and with a snap of his fingers, he could control Monroe! His power had been proven by his statements to the effect, "She will do whatever I demand." He had demanded that she never be late on the set and that she give the director no static. Well, she was never late on the set and she never even spoke to the director, a much befuddled George Cukor.

Marilyn would call me on the average of twice a week, and keep me appraised of the situation, sometimes indicating the next adventure before it happened. Miller was getting his due, as the world saw what she had wanted it to see, Montand getting her to do things Miller couldn't. Fox loved it, because to them, whatever the reason, the film was coming in on schedule. A Writer's Guild strike, linked to a Screen Actor's Guild strike at the time of key production scenes, didn't help anything, but the film survived even under that. Miller was actually paid to write some "extra dialogue." He had considered that a prostituting of his "art," while Fox saw it as a small price to pay to keep him quiet and out of Marilyn's way. George Cukor, often considered a "woman's director," shared in the film schedule coming in damn near on the money, if only by innocent fall-out. Marilyn was giving the performance of a lifetime, and nobody knew it.

For years, most researchers and writers of this sort of thing, would give great importance to the Montand-Monroe affair, reading into it a significance that never existed. Whether they ever shared a bed or didn't wasn't important. If they had, which is entirely likely, it would have been for the pure joy of it all. No eternal pledges were given or accepted. Montand's French actress wife, the very talented Simon Signoret, would burst onto the set offering her own jealous tirades, which were real. To Marilyn, in her explanation of these wild and crazy moments, they couldn't have been better timed had they been staged and rehearsed. Montand would soon be able to calm his furious wife with his own pledges of love and support.

The circus continued....Certainly his ego was boosted, the press saw to that, but above it all, Marilyn was the sole possessor of a private victory. She had convinced her friends and co-workers that this romance was real. She had followed Lee Strasberg's guidelines to the hilt. If tears were required, she would shed them, if panic was needed, she would throw in a bit of that. Chekhov would have been proud. Rumors would abound from the set to the world. Montand would gloat over the rumors, and Marilyn would accept a private Oscar as a result of them.

The film finished, on time, and on budget.

The producers of the film, and indeed the studio itself would proclaim "the new Monroe," which, had they stopped to give even a moments thoughts to, was really the only Monroe. Montand would return to his wife making statements to the press that Marilyn was a child and now I will return to the real woman in my life. An actor can get carried away by his own importance, and a French actor...well, we've already covered that. Marilyn would try to call him, try to stop him from returning to his wife..but, alas, true love won out, and Montand would fade out into the sunset. She would be "crushed," discarded, abandoned. Her friends would run to her aid. Some she would tell, others not. To Miller she would say "It was heaven."

On the night of her greatest "heartbreak," she called me and whispered lovingly on the phone, "It's over!" and along with that, "I need you very much right now this has been difficult. I will be coming back east very shortly. Please have those arms waiting." They would be, gratefully.

LET'S MAKE LOVE would breeze through with moderate acceptance. Even in this less than exciting film, reviews of Marilyn had been favorable. "Marilyn proves she still has it even when the film doesn't.," "Marilyn, always a joy to watch," words to that effect. Montand would not benefit from it all, other than the fact that the world would now see him. If the game had provided him with a false ego, the reviews would certainly take care of that. As a Frenchman, he would heal the wounds with a million tiny excuses. As an unseen friend, I would be forever grateful to Yves Montand, for whatever they did or didn't do, his presence kept Marilyn alive and well.

On her way back to Connecticut, Marilyn stopped off at "home." It was a most glorious homecoming. Whatever was suggested of she and Montand, was showered on me. I remember it was one of the few times I called in sick to work. She had given me two months in two days. I believe that says it all. My original forebodings had been proven wrong, and for that I was grateful. We had managed a bit of borrowed time. The mistake I had been certain I had made, was premature. She had, again, pulled it off.

For all outward signs, she appeared to be, indeed, indestructible. Then too, so had the Titanic. With the completion of LET'S MAKE LOVE, the contract was finished. The drama loomed ahead. Had I only been the possessor of a crystal ball, I would have seen LET'S MAKE LOVE as only the prelude to disaster, and not one of its own. A warning, of sorts.

Wisdom has always found it difficult to rear its head in moments of ecstasy. Thoughts of doom simply do not come forth when all you live for is in your arms. It is a damnable camouflage.

Chapter Nineteen

All The Marbles

By the time the smoke had cleared, we were looking at a few short moments in late spring, early summer. There were more calls, and an isolated visit, serving as a reminder to us both of what might lay ahead. We knew, even months before, that when this thing happened, it would be all consuming. She knew I would not try and reach her, as this is what all of it had been about from day one. As a writer, I also tried to understand Miller's position, despite my growing dislike for him. It would be the end of a five-year drought, an awakening from a coma. For whatever he was, and for whatever had been his sins, this was the moment of his return. I believe even Marilyn subconsciously wished this to be her farewell gift to him for whatever her part in their fiasco had been. It is never, after all, completely a one-way street.

The advance publicity and glowing critique on the yet unfilmed script, placed everyone in center stage. For this period, it would first appear that Marilyn and Arthur had declared a temporary cease-fire. On the surface, it looked as though the impossible would actually occur, and under the world's worst conditions, a victory might be claimed...But then....that was on the surface.

There is a time to stand your ground, and also a time to back off in favor of common sense. For me, this was that time. It was best I watch from a distance, as both their relationship and this project had more than their share of problems. What I didn't know then, but would discover much later, was that the intermission between LET'S MAKE LOVE, and this new "thing," which someone finally titled THE MISFITS, had taken its toll on Marilyn.

In an effort to silence Marilyn, who continually reminded him of the Montand fiasco, Miller had become her pusher, getting pills from whatever source he could. The drugs were damaging her body as well as her mind. She would call me and tell me she was sick again. What this had come to mean, in a coded message of sorts, was that her normal menstrual cycles were tearing her apart. She would be bed-ridden, unable to function, unable to sleep. When sleep came, she was unable to wake. When she did wake, the sight of Miller would set her to rage. Violent cramps would only add to the hot water which was set to boil over at any second. She needed to talk to me, but we both had already considered a visit dangerously inappropriate. With every call, I died a little, hoping that this film would somehow just go away, or, at least, they'd get the damned thing over with.

In June of that year, a call came in that sounded like that prayer would finally be answered.

"I have a fitting date for wardrobe," she said. "It looks like everything is settled. I hope it's true, because another week of this, and you can come and pick me up in a basket."

"Keep the number handy," I told her, having little else to offer. I would have given her that old tried and true show business wish, "Break a leg," but decided against it. The way her luck was running, she might have.

There were insurmountable, below the surface, problems with this production that nearly doomed it weekly. United Artists, its producers, had become a company whose policies and officers changed as frequently as diapers on a 5 month-old. A deal on Tuesday did not necessarily mean you would still have that deal on Thursday. This company may have been founded by Chaplin, Fairbanks and their like, but what had happened to it over the years was an industry joke. Through it all, by accident or luck, they had made some winners. They had become known for taking chances, and quite often, those chances paid off. They did not have the pumping oil wells of a 20th Century Fox, or the real-estate holdings of a Universal to back them up. Their's was a roll of the dice. One roll of craps, and they would have been relegated to history.

Clark Gable had been Box-office King for 30 years. Since the time of his ill-fated voyage on "The Bounty," he had set hearts a flutter. Now it was his heart that was fluttering. In an industry that spends money like they had it, there are a select few high-risk insurance companies who will bond a film. For a high fee, they will guarantee the film's completion or repay the money to the investors. They will insure the director and the stars in their special "key-man" clauses. Because of his health, Gable was considered too high a risk, and they wouldn't touch him. UA (United Artists) had to provide their own guarantees. As the locale of this piece was the hot desert of Nevada, they prayed he wouldn't drop dead in the middle of it. Montgomery Clift, considered by many to have been one of the finest actors of his day, was now known for his breakfasts of grapefruit juice and vodka. He was bondable, but with restrictions. Marilyn's reputation preceded her. The late calls, the nightmare of SOME LIKE IT HOT, also a UA film, the booze and the pills. In the eyes of the producers, if ever there were three people who should not be allowed on a set, much less to star in one film, these were the three.

It finally came down to the director. Since Jesus, Moses and Buddha were busy that week, the man who had been mentally and physically on the script since its inception, John Huston, was given the official green light. It was assumed by Miller that Huston would give it the necessary touch required. Possessed of a Hemmingway personality, Huston could drink with the best of them, and tear up a place faster than a Kansas tornado, but under it all, he had a reputation for bringing a film in against all odds. In truth, he was wilder than all of them put together, but he had a gift. I assume UA counted on that gift. Below the fire and reckless frivolity, was a dedicated film maker. Never having met the man, I can only assume that producer Frank Taylor, spent a good deal of time lighting as many candles as he could in as many churches as he could find.

The film, which had been so much a part of our lives, began filming in July. Marilyn called me from a phone booth in Reno, Nevada on the eve of the first day of shooting.

"I'm afraid, Peter" she said. "After all this time, I'm afraid."

"You're an actress," I said, just as frightened as she but for different reasons. "Now you go out there and tear up the sprockets of that film. I love you, honey. Keep the number handy."

My stomach was filled with rocks. After hanging up the phone I just sat there, numb. This wasn't the way to make a film. This wasn't what it was all about. Nobody needed this kind of stress.

On my home front, my ever caring boss, the man most people feared and hated, knew what had to be on my mind. The workload decreased. Script changes and re-writes were of the simple variety. Our loyal friend, cigar and all, was watching out for us, the best way he could. I walked a deep path in the sands of my beach on a nightly basis, my ear always close to the phone. I never stayed away from it for longer than 15 minutes, and slept on and off only two or three hours a night. Even from that short sleep, I would often awaken with a rock in my stomach. There had been no calls.

One night, around 7 pm, Bob suddenly appeared at my

door. Something I had said in a phone conversation earlier that day hadn't sat right with him. Making some pretense for having been in the area, was his excuse for the visit. He didn't just happen to be in the area. He was a dear friend. You might lie to a world, but never to a friend. There's no need to, as a friend takes you just the way you are. Over coffee and some stale donuts, I relayed the events of the past two months.

"I'm sorry for any joke I have ever made to you about this," he said. "I can see now they were all in the worst of taste."

"No," I assured him. "What I need right now *is* a good joke. When she calls, and she will, I can't speak to her in this condition. She doesn't need another moral cripple."

Bob stayed that night, long into the early hours of morning. We talked, reminisced about high-school, laughed about how simple it all had been. When our biggest problems had been Mr. Fish's American History course, or staying awake during Biology 2.

Without meaning to, we drifted back to the Calderone Theatre and NIAGARA. Who the hell would ever have dreamed what that would lead to? Who could have conceived it?

"I don't think I ever want to love this much," he said. "It's too big a headache."

"Yeah, I know," I began, " but you wanna know something? It doesn't matter. Nothing matters when she's not there, so, I guess I better keep the aspirins handy."

"I must be as crazy as you," he said with a silent chuckle. "In a way I envy you."

"Don't," I said. "Go back to your accountant, take her in your arms, and be grateful for her. Let her know it. That's all any of them need, you know..."

"Are you going to be ok?," he asked.

"I'm gonna be fine," I assured him, and meant it.

Sometime around 4:30 am he left. His visit had been on a Friday evening, and it left me the weekend to remember other weekends. Sneaking in and out of a 42nd Street theatre watching a double bill of her films, eating popcorn with the rest of the patrons. Listening to them whistle and stomp their feet, never realizing the subject of this adoration, sat only a few feet behind them. Taking a ride to Montauk Point to see an ocean we could have seen from my window. Playfully rough-housing in the sand. A million, million memories you're never going to read in this diary.

I had begun to rationalize that this morbid vigil was getting me nowhere, but I had no answer as to what to do. Mark had called as I had been noticeably absent from the studio. I laid the old "flu" story on him. If everything else fails, you can always catch the flu. It's good for a few days anyway. Just about the time I had run out of excuses to friends, co-workers and myself, the call came. It was 2:30 am, and I don't remember on what day of the week it came, only that it finally did come.

"Peter," she said in a voice echoing of sadness and desperation, "Please come."

"Where honey, where?," was all I could think to say in this mid-night stupor of half sleep.

"I just need you here," she repeated.

"Baby, where's HERE?," I stammered, trying to get a fix. I wrote it all down, not trusting my foggy senses to remember.

"Are you alright?," I asked. A stupid question, based on the sound of her voice.

"I think so," she said, which was less than gratifying.

"What about Miller?," I asked.

"I don't care anymore, Peter," she said. "Please, I don't care anymore."

"I'll be there," I said, dropping the entire issue. "I'll clear it tomorrow, and be on the red-eye tomorrow night."

"You will?" she exclaimed, her voice lightening a bit.

"Did you think I wouldn't be?" I asked now a bit giddy myself. "Don't you know I've been waiting for this call?"

"You have?"

I could feel her smile through the line.

"Well hell yes I have," I said, now almost into a small laugh, that nervous thing you do when something pulls you back from the edge.

"I'll be there tomorrow," I said. "Don't look for me, I'll find you! Until next time, honey. I'll see you soon."

"Now you be careful," she said. " Cross with the lights, drive carefully. Please be careful. I love you."

Sometimes on occasions of the worst stress, can come the simplest concerns. Driving into town on the next morning found me arranging my thoughts, my schedules even in the midst of all of this mayhem. My assignments had been small, but important, nevertheless. My sudden announcement that I was leaving for Reno, Nevada, without a look back, would have been in the worst pro-fessional taste. "By the way, I have to get on my white horse now, and rescue the fair maiden. See you later,"- not quite. The only one I could trust to act as relief pitcher was Mark. Whether he would be free to jump in, was another story.

The moment I entered the maze of desks and typists, I placed a call to my immediate supervisor, hoping he'd have licked his weekend hangover by now. As though he had been instructed to wait for my call, he plugged me immediately into Marvin Rachman's office. It all hap-pened so fast. Rachman then insisted I come to his office immediately. All of this began sounding just a little bit weird, but then, what wasn't in this business. I followed his instructions. When I arrived at his office, the girl in front offered me an immediate cup of coffee with just the right amount of cream and sugar. Along with that coffee, her face wore the biggest smile. Executive secretaries are not supposed to smile. It's against their religion. Three important "suits" were in Rachman's office, and they were immediately asked to leave. I was either getting the V.I.P. treatment, or the axe. I didn't know which.

Now in his private office, he closed the door, and moved to his big over-stuffed chair, bidding me to sit as well. I preferred to stand, moving toward the window.

"When are you leaving?," he began, shocking me out of five year's growth. I had no answer for that second as the situation had somehow become reversed.

"Call from Reno come in did it?," he went on. I could feel my head shaking affirmatively in a near subconscious answer.

"Good!," he continued, "About time, eh?"

"Yes sir," I answered, still in a semi-daze.

"When are you going?" he asked, almost matter-of-factly.

"I'd like to leave tonight, If I can arrange my script schedule. I'm pretty sure I can."

"Peter," he began, "fuck the script schedule! Get out there boy! That shoot's in trouble. Go to her! Don't screw around here!"

I remember thinking out loud, "the grapevine," to which he replied,

"Grapevine my ass. UA has been on the phone to me daily!"

I suppose the look of surprise, or stupidity, lead him into the next lines.

"You haven't figured it out yet, have you son? It hasn't sunk in. Well we don't have time to talk about it now."

He rose from his chair, and approached me at the window.

"Go home and clean up, take a shower, you look like hell!" he demanded, seeming almost more in a hurry than I.

"You got enough money?"

"I'm fine," I answered. He put his arm around my shoulder and literally walked me to the door.

"If you get delayed, need anything, call me direct, got it?" he said, just before opening the door and throwing me out. He reached his hand to mine. I accepted it, gratefully.

"And one last thing," he began, now in possession of a smile seldom seen by anyone. "Give her my best, will you?"

"Yes sir, I will," I said.

"Now go, already! Get out of here!"

The man I've called Marvin Rachman, for reasons of privacy, was a very special man. What he possessed could never be found in books.

Chapter Twenty

The Biggest Little Mess In The World

I never liked Reno. Maybe today it's different, more modern, cleaned-up. Maybe it has a different look. In 1960, the only word that comes to mind is seedy, and that is an understatement. A well known comedian once described it as The Bowery with bigger hotels. The desolation of this part of the state of Nevada, seemed to complete the pictures that swam in my head as the plane descended into Reno Airport. Flying over this no-man's land made you wonder how the pioneers ever got through it to discover California. Then too, at this moment, I wasn't being fair to the State or the town, as my current frame of mind would have made me angry about anything.

I had made reservations at Harold's Club, and although I didn't know whether I'd be staying there or not, it was as good a place to start as any. The cab ride from the airport rekindled the few memories I'd had about this place, having visited it only once, a year or so earlier for a convention. The flashing lights, the "WIN" signs over huge jackpot numbers, seemed a sad contradiction to the bums who sat in doorways or who layed on benches just below those signs. The tiny store-front type operations that advertised weddings and divorces for $39.95. You could take your choice. When Omar Khayyam said, "Live fast and reckon not the cost," he must have had Reno in mind.

After checking in and walking through rows and rows of clanging slot machines, I found the elevator that would take me to my room. At least there it was quiet. I washed, shaved, changed my clothes, and left for the car rental booth. The 39 mile drive from Reno to the small desert town of Dayton, now being used as the location for this epic, began taking on its own ominous undertones. Considering Miller's forte had been writing of the doom and gloom of mankind, this setting seemed extremely appropriate.

The road itself was good, but all around it seemed to echo "trail's end." A couple of steer skulls, one dead coyote, a few squashed rabbits, and a flattened rattle snake set the stage. It was a long way from Manhattan, and just what the hell Roy and Gene were singing about in their westerns, escaped me. I'm sure there are those who find all this quaint and charming, but for me, it was driving through a huge kitty-litter box. The little town itself was all decked out for the occasion, and as an added attraction, a rodeo was taking place. It's tiny dust-covered streets were jammed with people, many hoping to catch a glimpse of one of the Hollywood elite who now mingled with them.

I parked by an old restaurant, and began to filter into the crowd hoping to discover where everyone was on that bright sun-scorched 123 degree day. The current day's shooting was a ways out of town as one of the local's put it. Following the direction of his finger, I departed quickly. Drawing nearer to the location, it became obvious that most involved had been spoken for. Only a few onlookers stood back behind roped-off sections. Feeling that no one there, other than Marilyn, would know me , I simply stood in that small crowd and watched. The scene in progress had something to do with the taming of wild horses, and by guild rules, this involved the presence of special animal handlers called "wranglers." They were there for the horses, not the people. In some cases they would assist an actor onto a horse and try to give him a 30-second course on how to ride. It had been a wrangler who first put Bill Boyd on a horse. Not only had he possessed no knowledge of how to ride, he cared even less about it. As a matter-of-fact, about the only thing he cared less about than horses, was kids. So much for the legend of Hopalong Cassidy.

As luck would have it, or perhaps it's an invisible badge we all wear that can spot us in a crowd, one of the wranglers approached me and began talking about the shoot. He hadn't gone near any of the other dozen or so onlookers. No, he had to call attention to me, and the more I tried to ignore him, the more he kept talking. He had to give me a blow by blow account of how many times they had tried to shoot this scene, and along with the numbers, the reasons why it hadn't yet worked.

Marilyn, of course, was one of those reasons. I had seen Marilyn, and watched enough of the scene with Clift, Gable, and Eli Wallach, to know where the problems were. It was unnecessary for this cowboy standing next to me to provide narration. I didn't know whether they finished the scene or not, but Huston called "cut," and everything stopped. He and Miller went into a huddle, the cast into a small make-shift dressing room, and the wranglers went for the horses. Script people, camera operators, grips, second-assistants, all seemed busy in their jobs.

My final decision to leave came when I recognized one particular crew member. Before the recognizing became mutual, I thought it best to head back to Dayton. This was not the time to renew old friendships. I didn't know his name, but we'd seen each other on previous films. Most of the cast and crew were based either in Dayton or Reno. Sooner or later they would all have to, at least, come through this place. I'd have to wait.

It was late afternoon and the town was all ablaze with excitement for the rodeo. The first element in writing has to be curiosity, and in that curiosity, I decided to explore the town, meet the people. This became a most pleasant trip through the norm. I found the locals extremely nice, down-home people. Friendly. I'd been around pretense for so long, I'd forgotten what real could be.There were those who had come to see Gable, both men and women, many of them now graying. Whether they had fantasized him as a lover or a friend, he had become part of their family. The Clift school of fans were young girls and not-so young women who wanted to baby him, to cradle him in their arms and tell him everything was going to be alright.

Monty Clift always wore the look of a man torn between two worlds, as though every sentence he uttered could have had any number of interpretations. Whether that brooding was caused by his own private sexual revolution or not, outwardly he remained that little lost boy. Male fans saw him as intense, female fans saw so many other things.

Everyone knew Marilyn. Most everyone loved her. Her appraisal of her public was accurate, but in that statement, was the truth of it all. Oh they said it in different ways, with different accents, but the general feeling was unanimous. No one there seemed to know just what she was doing here, as, to a fault, none felt this movie was her! One old timer, a gas jockey at the small filling station summed it up perfectly.

"I'd rather see her sing and dance. What's she doin' here anyway. This ain't her kind of movie. Why in blazes would she want to do such a thing?"

My answer to him was simple, "Beats the hell outta me!"

I should have sent UA a bill for my services that day, because in only a few hours, I knew where that film was going and why. Since they had made such an effort to become part of our lives, turnabout would have been fair play. The ticket buying public may be fickle, but they KNOW what they want. For all the affection they had poured onto John Wayne and Gary Cooper, they never bought them as Genghis Khan or Marco Polo.

Marilyn had become the stuff dreams are made of, and her character of Roslyn in this dusty western epic of people on the edge, was not the way they wanted to see her. She had been right to want to improve her craft, and there could have been many roles for her. It was the subject of many of our conversations. It would have been very easy to write for Marilyn, as she was extremely flexible. In that condition, she would have grown gradually into heavier roles, keeping in touch, at all times, with the natural flair she already possessed. This plunge from glitter to the gutter was too drastic. Poetically, she gave a stunning performance in the film, and Miller's lines were as good as they had ever been. As far as the average public was concerned, it just didn't work.

The "Millers" had been registered at the Mapes Hotel in Reno, but for obvious reasons, hardly ever stayed there. As the sun began to disappear below the mountains, I found myself a table in the small Dayton restaurant from where I could observe the street and those who would have to pass by. Unlike in New York or even Los Angeles, no formal plans had been made. The entire thing had to be based on instinct.

With all the possible alternatives running through my mind, I grabbed a turkey sandwich and a cup of coffee. As it was nearing the dinner hour, the place became crowded. I spotted the script girl (today called script person), and I knew, by her appearance, the shoot was finished for the day. No one was paying attention to anything or anyone else. Appetite seemed the only motivating force for the moment.

Before I had a chance to react, I heard the chair next to mine, slide across the hardwood floor, and turned to greet my lady. I am certain she was spotted by some of the crew, but by the end of a hard day's shoot, no one really cares. The kerchief and sunglasses really weren't fooling anybody.

"I'm so glad to see you," she whispered.

"Just happened to be in the neighborhood," I said, straining inwardly to touch her.

"I saw you today, at the location," she said, " but didn't know what to do."

"What could you have done?," I asked, now giving her a smile. "I thought you handled it beautifully."

"There's a cabin not far from here that belongs to a very nice lady who lets me stay there sometimes, to get away." She continued. "I'm going to call her..."

"Careful honey, this isn't New York," I cautioned.

She was scribbling an address on a paper napkin, and handed it to me.

"I know what I'm doing," she said. "I'll meet you there at 8 o'clock. She's a good lady. I'll explain it to her on the phone."

The thought of *explain what* crossed my mind, but there was no time for the question. I nodded my head in affirmation, and then read the address to be certain I could.

"We're getting some new pages and I've got to get cleaned up," she went on. "But wait for me. I'll be there."

Then came her signature approval for the entire scenario, that smile.

"Oh, I'm so happy to see you," she said again.

I could feel my one hand clinched around my coffee cup, and the other made into a fist. I could smell her, see her, talk to her, but couldn't touch her. It was a totally nerve-wracking experience. With one final eye contact saying silently all that I too wanted to say, she rose, and walked from the place. My final glimpse of her was that special walk. Returning from that last look to a turkey sandwich was most difficult.

The little house with the nice lady wasn't far, by her

directions, and there was a matter of some three hours to kill. Just what I did for those three hours seems a blur, as they seemed like three years. I do remember browsing in stores, and mingling, but now with a purpose, the relaxation part of it was over. Each time I looked at my watch, it seemed only a minute or so had been gained. By 8 pm, I knew I would qualify as a candidate for a strait-jacket. All I kept repeating to myself was a question I have not answered to this day, "What the hell are we doing here, either of us ?"

Somehow time passed. The quaint little house whose address Marilyn had listed on the napkin, was actually walking distance from the center of town. The building was old, but well kept. As it was out of the main stream, I hoped that Marilyn would have been close to on-time, as I don't know what I would have said to the occupant of the bigger house in terms of explaining what I was doing here. Worse than that, I didn't know what Marilyn had told her. This little place had obviously been a guest house attached to the larger house by a yard. It was private, but to get to it, you'd have to pass a window.

I was certain that nice little lady would have been at that window, so in deference to that, I waited across the street. The town was still celebrating the rodeo, but here the lights and activity ceased. At 8:10, just a few minutes after the arranged time, a nondescript dark blue four-door sedan pulled up in the front of the place. Marilyn stepped out of the back door carrying her dress for the next day's shoot. She thanked the driver, and off he went in a cloud of sand and dust. So as not to look as sneaky as I then felt, I waited for the car to turn off the street before moving the short distance to her.

Seeing me coming, and realizing that I had literally been waiting in the shadows, she smiled. On our way up the path that led to the door of the tiny house, she explained that the studio driver who had brought her, had done so many times. This was the place she would come to relax. It was not out of the ordinary. Finally inside, we left the lights off and found our way to a necessary embrace. No words were spoken as words were never really needed. From the embrace, we sat on the bed in the room still lighted only by the fragments of an outside world. She closed the drapes. I reached for the small bedside lamp. She grabbed for my hand in an effort to stop me, but it was too late. It was clear, even in this dimly lighted room, that the soft features of her face had changed to a mask of lines and physical wear.

I contained the shock within my heart so as not to ruin the moment, but it was painfully obvious that the last few months had not been restful to her in body or in spirit. The drugs had left those beautiful eyes, glazed, unaware and near sightless. The whites of those eyes, blood-shot and spotted. What the hell had they all done to my girl?

She reached into her purse for a tissue and blew her nose, now staring at me as though to give me the full treatment.

"You were never supposed to see me like this," she said, in a soft voice filled with regret. "I just wanted to be with you so much, I guess I wasn't thinking."

In her mind, in that flashed second, I suppose she saw this as my moment of awakening. A time for me to observe just how severely an illusion can be smashed. Without an answer to her comment, I lifted her feet from the floor, and layed her on the bed, quickly sliding beside her. I placed my arms around her, and held her tightly. She softly began to cry, her head resting against my chest, in a position that had become entirely familiar to us both. Again, in a purposeful gesture, I stroked her hair as I had done a thousand times before. I was hoping she would get the message that nothing would ever be different between us.

"How long does this go on?," I asked, still holding her tightly. "How much of this will it take?"

She said nothing, but shook her head slightly as if not having the answer to that question. I then spoke to someone who wasn't even there, a presence I had hoped was listening,

"When do we all stop beating her to death?"

Finally she spoke through the tears, " I'm sorry I look so bad," she said, "It's not a very good welcome."

Lifting her head from my chest, I kissed her. I could feel with her mouth the very core of her desperation. Laying her head again against my chest, I finally found the words.

"Baby, what the hell are you doing to yourself?"

"I just want to finish this picture," she whispered.

Thoughts raced through my mind, this time silently. "Picture?!, who the hell gives a fuck about this picture??!!" Thinking it wise to refrain from such thoughts openly, I elected to nod my head instead. She rose from the bed, and moved to the small table on which she had placed the "new pages" of tomorrow's shoot. Taking her lead, I now sat beside her, wiping the final trace of tears from her eyes.

"John says we have a picture," she began, holding the pages as proof of that. "Arthur is re-writing every day, changing moods and characters," she went on, "He says he's trying to establish the focal point. If UA doesn't shut us down, we should be finished in a couple of weeks." Her voice grew cold and through clinched teeth, she continued, "I just want to finish it!"

"Shut you down?" I asked, as she had quickly breezed through that statement and I saw it as more important than Miller changing his words, or Huston claiming to have a picture.

"Yes." She nodded and continued, "We're behind schedule. I can't seem to get into it until later each day. I know it's driving Clark crazy. And John, well, he's going a little crazy himself."

Her jaw tightened in defense. "I know I'm making them all mad at me, but I can't get any sleep! By the time I get up, the day's half over. Peter, I don't know whether I'm killing this picture or this picture is killing me."

"What about the others?" I asked, remembering Tony Curtis, Jack Lemmon and Billy Wilder.

"Clark's been wonderful, patient and understanding. Monty's more fucked up than I am, and can't tell the difference."

"And Huston?" I asked.

"John's been gambling every night. He's under pressure, but he's been staying out to all hours. He's so tired, sometimes he falls asleep during a take. He's also losing money left and right, which is making him disagreeable as hell! I don't think he gives a damn anymore. Everybody's blaming me for all of it. If I could just get some damned sleep!"

"Jesus Christ, what a scenario." I said. "And where is Arthur during all of this?"

A look of distaste filled her face.

"He's got some new doctor giving me a stronger prescription." She went on. "But it doesn't work unless I take a handful. After that everything just goes fuzzy. I feel like a zombie. I don't even know where the hell I am half the time. When I finally figure it out, the first thing Arthur does is yell at me with words I've never heard before."

"Marilyn." I looked her straight in the eyes. "This is no way to make a film! No one can work like this. Honey, not even you."

The determination was still written all over her face. This appeal was being made to deaf ears. It was time to turn it around.

I sat back in my chair, moving away from her, trying to see this nightmare as she saw it. It was difficult because to me, it didn't make one bit of sense. However, leaping on the bandwagon of people that was growing by the numbers daily, each blaming her, didn't make sense either.

The hard edge stepped in for both of us.

"OK! Do it!" I said. "Finish it anyway you can...on all fours if you have to. This thing has been with us from the start. It's time to kiss it off.....PERIOD! No matter what they say, they're too far into it to shut it down. I can tell you for a fact that there's no completion bond on this picture. Stopping IT will stop their whole operation."

I was guessing at this, but it seemed reasonable.

"How do you know this?" She asked, her mood shifting slightly to a positive direction.

I slid back from my "executive position."

"Answer me in one word. Are you my girl?"

Her head dipped slightly, a trace of a smile ebbing through the confusion.

"If you still want me like this..."

"Marilyn! I said ONE WORD!"

She nodded her head and the smile broadened.

"Yes."

I now placed the hard edge on the shelf.

"When your girl goes off to some, God knows where, desert, for some God knows what kind of film, with a plane load of men, you get to wondering what kind of chance does she have? I made it my business to find out. Remember, I do this for a living too. Well I found out. That's how I know about the completion bond."

It was more a prayer than a lie.

She wiped a tear from her eye, but the smile remained. "You make it all sound so simple." She whispered.

"Honey, Marilyn...it IS simple." I finally got her complete attention. "People make it difficult. You get up, you go to work, you finish your work, you come home. We grab a bite of dinner, listen to some soft music, I throw you on the bed, and we make mad passionate love until we go to sleep. The pills go into the trash and knock out the rats at the dump. That's it!"

She began to laugh. No music could have sounded sweeter. I pushed my finger into her nose. The lines of her face seemed to be disappearing, or at least trading places with the new laugh lines.

Then she got serious on me.

"Where will you be?" She asked.

"It's not good for me to stay here." I answered. "You already have enough problems and so does Huston."

I gave her the most reassuring look I could muster.

"I'm going home, to our beach." I said. "I'll be there every night. I won't take any assignment that would upset that timetable. Now you call me anytime you need your back scratched long distance. Anytime you feel yourself slipping...Got that?"

"Yes sir!" She saluted.

We had gotten through it again. She reached over to the lamp, and switched it off. In the glow of the outside light source, the moon and a street light, I could see her unbuttoning her blouse. The location made me just a bit nervous.

"Honey, this isn't New York!" I said, concern in my voice. "We're not that far from people who just might not understand."

I must have been talking to myself, as she continued her actions steadily, positively, definitely. She then reached for my shirt and began a similar routine.

"Tonight, we're both going to get some sleep, just like you said." She said, now with a grateful lilt to her voice. "Maybe we'll even knock out some rats in the bargain. I know one of the two-legged kind, and if the whole town breaks in on us, let them!   Tomorrow, I'll be on time for the shooting, and they'll all wonder what happened. And maybe, just maybe, I'll just tell them!.."

It can be the greatest of all illusions, because, in a world of two, the dream goes on, sometimes even to the story-book ending.

Again, rapture and enchantment took us over. My Marilyn was home again, and neither of us made guess work for the other as to how much each had been missed. Were I indeed the possessor of a third eye from which to observe the dark clouds surrounding our last moment in the sun of night, perhaps I could have seen more clearly. Could I have even suspected that this might be the last time I would ever hold her, I believe I would have stepped on that set the next morning, and announced myself.

She had convinced me that she could get through it, and as a sign of that trust and faith, I had to believe her. Passion had overtaken common sense, and the moment was now. Who of us, after all, consider the worst of things during the best?

We rose at 6:30 am, and she had been right. It was the best sleep we'd both had for months. She would probably give ol' John Huston a heart attack that day, being first on the set.

A knock on the door had us both exchanging looks. She hurriedly slipped on the nearest article of clothing, her Roslyn dress from the film.

Cautiously opening the door, I beheld the grinning face of the unknown crew member I had recognized who had obviously done likewise. He stood on the porch with a tray of coffee.

"I thought this might look good to you, Mister Collins." He said.

Without ever asking his name, I turned to Marilyn, who proceeded to burst out laughing. I think she must have laughed for three minutes solid. In a moment we joined her. So much for secrecy, at least among friends we hardly knew, and never realized we had.

Marilyn's mascara had run on my shirt from the first tears of last night, and our unknown partner-in-crime was quick to notice it. He ran to his car and returned with a western shirt that had been used by Monty. It was the kind of shirt I never would have bought in my life, but it was clean. We stood on the porch, almost oblivious to a group of people who were wandering by shooting pictures of everyone they could spot. The cameras went off in our direction as they aimed at Marilyn, and this started her laughing again. Our entire scheme was falling apart in front of our eyes, and it suddenly made us feel wonderful. What a beautiful state Nevada had suddenly become. Poetically I would be given that snapshot many years later by a friend of my step son, whose grandmother was the lady who shot it. A sad reminder of our final moment in the sun.

There could have been many days like this, many bursts of laughter, and enough love to last a couple of lifetimes. Rachman had been right. We could have, indeed, been the "couple of the century." Indeed, I loved her so very much, and just as indeed, I still do.

Chapter Twenty One

Broken Dreams

The epic that followed us for nearly all of our days together, THE MISFITS, was finally completed on November 5th of that year. Mr. and Mrs. Arthur Miller were divorced on the 11th. On the surface, it had been a victory, but just as with many victories, the price was anything but a bargain. The human mind is a wondrous mechanism, but it has yet to understand itself. When it works in collusion with the human heart, the results can be trickery in its finest hour.

Marilyn had called during and after production, and her voice had been optimistic. She would remain in Hollywood for dubbing, but would soon be home. I had been asked to return to England for a simple 2 week arrangement of contracts with my friends across the seas. The studio would distribute their films for seven years, and they felt I should be there. With Marilyn's assurance that she was fine, and near insistence that I go, I did.

Unlike my previous returns, unknown horrors had taken place, and surprises of a different nature waited for me. In Miller's bitterness over the divorce being instigated by Marilyn and not himself, he had begun to use the press to vent his fury. The press, of course, was eager.

He blamed her for everything. Marilyn's earlier belittling him in public, worked against her. He had been smart enough to call her names in private. With the same "intelligent words" that had first attracted her, he now condemned her. He had accused her of doing to him what he, in fact, had done to her. It was a very neat rearrangement of the facts.

From where we sat, our phone conversations possessed a different sound. The more I offered logic, the more frustrated she would become. The last physical conversation I had with Marilyn was via a cold, insensitive telephone.

"You and I are the best." She said. "The very best. It may take us some time, but it will work out. You are so very special to me, and I love you very, very much. I don't think you really know how much. I'll always be yours, if you'll have me."

The Miller tirade continued, and then Clark Gable died. The phone calls ceased. On calling her private number, knowing what Gable meant to her, I was greeted by a dis-connect.

Confused, and a bit frightened, more for her than for me, I waited. Unlike a script, I could not veer off on page one-hundred-and-thirty-one, and make things work out.

Then one night, in my habitual checking of the mail, I received a letter as filled with contradiction as our lives had been:

> It is now important that I sort things out in my own way. Everything I love, dies. Being real is too painful right now. When the time is right, I will come home. Until then, I will be with you wherever you go. All you have to do is close your eyes. I love you very much,
> Your Marilyn.

My mind continued to placate itself with delusion. Somehow, she would be alright. The justification was a deliberate attempt to convince myself of something that I knew wasn't true. I had been watching the signs for months, but hadn't paid them enough attention. While it is true that "nothing succeeds like success," it is also true that the greatest lies are those you tell yourself.

As the years would pass, I began to see it as another sign of her wisdom being much greater than mine. She could have come home right then, but maybe as the kind of moral cripple she despised. Maybe she knew that. Maybe the love that we had was the very thing that frightened her the most. *Everything I love, dies* could have been a clue to that.

Although I had been born there, New York had grown cold to me. It had now become a city of memories. Memories of Marilyn. The park, the deli, Times Square, Macy's - even my beach apartment. Her scent remained with me during the long nights, but her touch was gone. The phone remained silent, much like my heart, it had ceased living.

I offered my resignation to a boss who wouldn't accept it. I knew she had moved to California, and that is where I was going. If I had to keep vigil from a distance, then I could, at least, shorten that distance. He made a few phone calls and arranged work for me on the coast when I wanted it. As Marilyn used to say, "Friends are something you just don't find that easily." Well, he had been one to us both.

The then head of 20th Century Fox, in an effort to help, gave me her new address. Of course, I could not use it, as the letter had been clear enough. Bursting in on her would have been an act of mistrust, and something she clearly didn't want at this moment. Then too, I felt hurt. It seemed she didn't trust *us* enough to fight this thing together.

I began to think she might have been right. Maybe we did need some space to regroup. Self-justification is wonderful. If you try real hard, you might even begin to believe it. For me, a new life had begun. There were new women, new friends, part-time lovers. Nothing serious, nothing lasting.

I had designed it that way. None of these new acquaintances had a clue to what had just transpired in my life. To them I was a nice lookin' guy from New

York with a fancy car. There was a certain peace in keeping it that way.

I met a middle-aged graduate of both Yale and Harvard while very briefly attending Pasadena Playhouse. We decided to "room" together, and within a short period of time, moved to Hollywood. He became a good friend, and many pleasant hours were spent between us dissecting the world of show business. As far as he was concerned, he wanted to be an actor, and assumed as much for me. It was only the typewriter that finally gave me away.

My life, beyond that would fill an additional volume, and now is not the time.

Marilyn's name came up from time to time, the usual pictures of her with a variety of people doing whatever the pictures suggested. It seemed that Marilyn had finally succumbed to that fictional character, and was living it to the max. Her appearance at Madison Square Garden on the occasion of her singing *Happy Birthday* to then President John F. Kennedy, said it all. "Bugs Bunny" had clearly taken over, and I believe it was her way of saying "I give up."

To the world, Marilyn Monroe had become a paper doll. And as everybody knows, paper dolls don't cry.

I had begun to suggest to myself, defensively, that it had all been a kind-of "fairy tale." The day-dreams of a young man who was getting older by the minute... Maybe even Walter Mitty had a hand in it. Thoughts of her "coming home" as she had said, seemed totally impossible.

So often we had spoken of another time and another place, but as the weeks and months went by, those pleasant dreams just dropped off into memories of a land of make-believe.

I was no longer the idealist she had accused me of being, and had become a realist. Nothing is more despicable than self-pity, and at this moment in time, I was wallowing in it. That very same weakness was, again, making me someone I wasn't. Only this time around, not even a warped plan could justify it.

In early 1962 or late 1961, a new woman entered my life. I really don't remember when she made her first appearance, as the entire episode is still somewhat blurred. She had been a former Miss USA, and in fact, a famous one. What had made her famous was that the title had been taken from her the day after she received it, by a then jealous husband who was quick to point out that she could not be a "Miss" anybody, as she was married.

She was statuesque, incredibly beautiful, and drawn to me in moth and candle fashion. In what now seems a gesture of getting even, of showing Marilyn what I could do without her, of forgetting everything that even remotely spoke of love and caring, we were married sometime in July of that same year of 1962.

As publicity followed her wherever she went, we decided on Phoenix, but the media word got out anyway, as it so often does. Once again it was "They look so good together!" And once again that meant nothing.

We had some good times, and some bad, and a daughter was the result. That daughter is this day among my favorite people on earth, as what she had to go through would create more than one book.

A bitter, heavily publicized divorce would follow about a year later, and this statuesque, incredibly beautiful former Miss USA would accuse me, in print, of having "treated her like a sister." She would be right, although never by deliberate plan. I cared about her, even worried about her, but love simply never entered my mind.

One of the most dangerous things you can do, when in this state of revengeful self-pity, is hurt a whole lot of people who don't deserve it. You don't mean to, it just happens.

By August 1,1962, I had come full circle. All my life I had defended a truth within me as reasons for my behavior. And because it was a truth, it finally carried me to Marilyn. She had become a reward for that truth, and even that seemed as right as it should be. By this date, I was clearly involved in a lie, and it was a lie that would hurt myself and those around me. I was pretending to be happy, pretending to be satisfied, boasting of my situation, wearing a false pride on my sleeve and a prime victim of self-delusion.

Inwardly, a huge part of me was missing, and only stupidity kept me from seeing it. For those few insane moments, I had managed to delude myself into thinking Marilyn didn't matter anymore. I was convincing to all but myself.

The song on the radio seemed filled with a lyric that, in some ways, resembled Marilyn's life. Dusty Springfield was singing about "Silver Threads and Golden Needles" things that couldn't buy the truths of life. Things that meant nothing, and were only substitutes, and poor ones at that, for anything worthwhile.

I don't want your lonely mansion, with a tear in every room.
It was a strong song, with a most appropriate message.

I was driving on the Hollywood Freeway to a meeting in the San Fernando Valley. The news came on the radio, but I was first remembering the lyrics of that song. I stopped trying to remember them when the newscast came,

Beloved Screen Legend, Marilyn Monroe is dead at 36.
was all he said. It was August 5th, 1962.

There are things you refuse to hear, or doubt that you heard them.

You pray that you have confused the message.

The broadcast continued, and the details began. At 70 miles per hour, on a crowded early morning freeway, there is little you can do to react. My vision blurred, my stomach tightened, moisture was gone from my mouth, and the cars speeding to the left and right of me were-closing in, or so it appeared.

The reality of it was that I was swerving from lane to lane. Somehow, an unseen hand guided me to a soft shoulder where I sat, trembling and very very sick. I could not stop my hands from shaking. All I kept repeating was "Oh God, Marilyn..Oh God, Marilyn..."

Tears poured from my eyes. I made my hands into two fists, and began pounding myself in the head. I finally jumped from the car and released the contents of my stomach. As I leaned on the car for support, I noticed two flashing red lights coming from behind me. My behavior had not gone unnoticed.

An officer stepped from the black and white CHP vehicle, and approached me. His tone was sympathetic. Did I need help? I assured him I was alright, and had just gotten car sick.

He never asked for my license or registration, but only wanted assurance that I would be able to drive. He received it.

Instead of my meeting, I went to Echo Park and sat on a bench, staring at the lake. I really didn't want to meet with anybody. I began feeling guilty about everything, including my selfish delusion that she no longer counted.

I still loved her with all my heart, and now she would never know that. I'd walked her through so much, but when the real test came, I hadn't even been there.

I couldn't even cry on anyone's shoulder, because no one in my present company of friends even knew. Those who did, were in New York.

I couldn't go home, I couldn't go anywhere.

I checked into a motel, got a copy of the evening paper, and locked the door. Thoughts of joining her crossed my mind, but she wouldn't have wanted that. That would have been only one more mistake in an endless barrage of mistakes.

As I lay in that dark motel room, with only the lights of the street as illumination, a kind of peace suddenly filtered in through the blinds.

There had to be a God. Look at all He had done for us. Remember the hours we had. Remember too, that the world as we know it, is only a stepping off place, enroute to a better one.

I remember saying one prayer, "Please just take care of her."

Then her voice, fixed in my mind, came through loud and clear: "When the time is right, I will come home."

I believe she finally had.

Chapter Twenty Two

Coming of Age

With age comes wisdom. That is the very least you can expect, sometimes in spite of yourself. We all think we know so very much about so many things, when, in truth, the more we learn the more we discover just how little we know about anything. By the time we are old enough to figure it out, we are too old to do anything about it.

Out of a possible 18 months or so, Marilyn and I borrowed about 50 days, give or take a few minutes. Not a very long time indeed. By no means long enough.

We had dreamed into years but had been granted of those years, only minutes. The love we shared which began on that rainy night in New York so very long ago, was no accident. That is only as we perceived it.

Affairs of the heart and indeed of the spirit are never really accidents. They simply appear to be as we are not yet ready to begin to understand the hows and whys of it all. It then is more convenient to consider them part of life's surprises. It is easier.

We were a necessary ingredient to both of us at that time, and planned by an author far more intelligent than I. WE had to exist as alone we were teetering on the brink for so many different reasons.

We needed a partner to share with and dream. For me, it took me off a self-destructing merry-go-round. For Marilyn, it allowed her a few steps backwards to permit Norma Jeane a young love that had first passed her by.

My own beliefs need not be the subject of this writing, but understand only this, to me she remains a presence to me, she simply still **IS**.

It is the most wondrous of all experiences and one that can finally be shouted from the rooftop. I am, as always, so very, very proud of her.

Reflecting back on the "secret" of it all, I now do not think Arthur Miller or "the script" had anything to do with it. I believe it was Marilyn's way of keeping us completely out of it all. Keeping us private.

It was her way of creating a refuge far from the tabloids and flashbulbs that generally followed her. A place just to be.

When she signed that last note *Your Marilyn*, I know now it was a truism. No one had ever seen her this way. And no one ever would.

My memories of her are unlike any that have ever appeared in print. She was wise. Much wiser than I. Nestled in my arms, she made me feel as though I were shielding her from the world, when, in fact, it was she who protected me. She knew that then. But it has taken me some time to figure it out.

On many a dark night, the sound of her voice softly whispering, "I'm here!" made everything alright. I have seen all of the books, looked at all the pictures, listened to all of the stories, and read all of the lies. Nowhere are we a part of any of it. She made that scenario work.

Her final comments to me and that note that so burns in my memory was her way of expressing the sad fact that the dream was over, at least for that time. The further pursuit of it, would have certainly seen it destroyed.

The thoughts and emotions I have tried to convey in the telling of this story have been those that I then felt. That has been difficult, as it is hard to remain innocent after 57 years on this planet. The friends that cheered us on during that period were among the best we'd ever have. They were believers in long-shots and knew the incredible odds we faced. Whether the head of a major film studio or the guy who slung hash at a local deli, all wanted us to win. They would be proud to know that we did in the greater sense.

We all stray from our destinies, from time to time. Take side trips, if you prefer. Go against the grain of what must logically occur. Take a breather.

Look again, for a moment, at the stars. Certainly her time on earth ended on August 5, 1962. That is a matter of record. Certainly a part of me died on that same day. That is unbound logic. Pursuing that logic, I have no comments on what finally did happen on that night so long ago. My personal feelings dictate it was an accident. One last pill for the road. I believe she simply lost count. It is something we will never know and now, at last, belongs only to Marilyn and God.

We do have some small minded people on this planet, those with intelligence levels from zero to below. Those that think a heart is only an organ that keeps you alive. It is for those to ponder and speculate mysteries and impossible theories, all preposterous in their conceptions. If even a shred of truth can be found in the maze of conjecture, it will be for a much higher court to punish the guilty. Perhaps it already has. Dragging her memory through it, can serve no purpose.

I am more than slightly disgusted by the constant re-telling of her human faults as though we, somehow, were removed from such things. The need for some to continue to exploit in words and pictures of condemnation rather than of praise.

Put your accordion away and release her from her chain. Retire her tin cup. Don't you honestly think she's performed for you long enough?

Glow in the warmth of her image. Destroy the snapshots of her weakness. Grant to her the peace she never had. Love her again for who she was, not for what some try to make of her.

If you would have seen her as I did, you would have no

difficulty in that pursuit. Return to her the dignity she so deserves. That which has been so often taken.

Love honestly goes with you and is returned in a million tiny displays of affection that you seldom recognize. For me, it now comes in the eyes of my wife, a girl who, in so many ways, possesses the same spirit as was ours over a quarter of a century ago. The same loving loyalty. The same hands to touch that somehow make it all bearable.

It's Marilyn saying, *"Hey buddy, snap out of it. Nothing's changed. I know you can't see that now, but it's true. We'll get our act back together, and maybe we'll take some of those great people with us. What a time we'll have...all of us. So don't worry so much. I'm ok now. Remember the dreams we had? Well, guess what! Here's where they all come true. You just keep doing what you're doing. Keep making me proud. Trust me, it's going to be just fine."*

She once suggested that I close my eyes and see her. Well, I have. I would, of course, re-open them, and she'd be there.

Today that isn't so.

But, as she said then, it takes *practice*. Over the years I've had that practice. And while it has not permitted my touching her hair, or gazing into her eyes, it has been a somewhat acceptable substitute under the existing circumstances. I know that someday, when I close my eyes for the last time, and open them in a world much greater than this one, she will be there. I also know that those we love and who have loved us, will join us.

Whatever your beliefs, I will leave you with one last thought:

A person who is remembered, never really dies.

For me, it remains, until next time...

Epilogue

Pandering to the lowest common denominator

It has so often been said and paraphrased that "All the-world's a stage...." and we the players. Some of us get to "star" while others remain in supporting positions.

All of us leave prints in the sand, some larger, some smaller. These impressions, left for the new generations, are not based so much on WHAT we have done, but for the exposure we have had doing whatever it is we did.

For myself, rather than the "stage" suggestions, I see life more as a circus, with huge spotlights signaling "key" moments, at least for a time. Those same spotlights move about the arena in search of new targets, and focus on those targets for as long as it takes. During the lulls, they introduce us to the clowns to liven up the action.

When all else fails, popcorn and hot dogs are served, as the standing rule applies that something must, at all times, be bought, sold and consumed.

In this year of 1995, we are governed by a monster that would put the mythical "Godzilla" to shame. This creature, made up of thousands of tiny smaller creatures is called "The Media." And it, or they, manage to arrange our lives as they see fit.

We are told what to think, how to feel, what is really right and wrong, even against common sense, and where we are going.

Whether we care to believe it or not, their input dictates our lives and how we live them.

I personally subscribe to the "pendulum" theory, and find it to be the most trustworthy. Picture, if you can, this huge pendulum swinging above the world in a slow, steady, rhythm. When it finally gets to its furthest position to the right, when excess in that position has reached the point of as much as you can stand, it then begins its slow move to the left. On the way to that LEFT is order.

Once it has reached that far left position, extremism again takes hold, and "order" is lost. It must then begin its return to the right.

Truth exists between both extreme points, never at either.

History will substantiate that we have, quite often, been creatures of extreme. When we are already saturated, we insist on taking that "last one for the road," which generally becomes a bottle more so than a glass.

The Media continues to pour, and it is sometimes as a last resort, in our state of inebriation, that we grab the pendulum and pull it back. Having reached that point of frustration, it is then that even the clowns cease to be funny.

Speculation in our society has a way of becoming fact. It seems less important that we search for the truth, then we arrange it to suit our purposes.

Since the time of my adoption, at age 3 weeks, things were made extremely easy for me. In the early stages of my career, work came just as easily. People, great and small, speak of struggles, of failures, of moments both high and low, and of grasping at things just beyond their reach.

No such scenario was mine. For me, whatever I reached for was there. Whether the prettiest girl on campus or the shiniest car.

This is perhaps the main reason why, in my youth, I could never tell the difference between gold and brass. As far as I could see, they both shined. I saw everything with a price tag, and so often paid it without ever considering its actual cost.

I was never affected by either the good or bad genes of the Media, as I paid little attention to either. The pendulum came so close as to trim my hair, and yet I never saw it. The circus performed all about me, but I saw myself as a casual observer rather than an active participant. Indeed, I was the most laughable clown of all.

Then something, and some ONE happened.

A child reaches for the brightest colored balloon, the one way on top. He nabs it, and holds to it possessively. In a moment of unthinking triumph, the string from the balloon slips from his hand. Before he can grab it again, it flies away.

Somewhere, far away from him, it bursts.

All that remains for him is the knowledge that he held it and let it go. For that, he cries.

Sadly, tears will not bring it back.

It is, for this experience, that the child finally begins to grow. He will never, ever, forget that balloon.

The person known as Marilyn Monroe died in 1962. Her physical body is gone. Fortunately for myself, and, indeed a large portion of the world, only her "coat" lays in that crypt.

Some things, those precious intangibles, never really ever leave.

In finally writing this diary, it was my hope that, through it, those who have come to remember her with positive thoughts would know that she deserved each and every one of those thoughts. It was never my intention to add my own "speculations" relating to what may or may not have happened during her last days.

It seems more than enough people are trying to do that.

Her death occurred some 20 months after our final moments together, and only the weakest of uneducated assumptions could bring me to any conclusions. It would be a physical impossibility for me even to suggest on what path she walked during that time. Yet I am always asked, and now, with the revelation of this diary, even more.

From where I sit, I would prefer to remember her strengths, those that so dwarf her ever-replayed weaknesses. One comes to mind that speaks so clearly for so many others:

I remember children reacting to her in a park or on a beach. I remember seeing their smiles and watching hers return to them. They were able to see so very much more clearly that something special, that something very real that eludes those in the adult world. They never read the gossip, and something inside them would have told them it isn't so if they had.

Perhaps, it would be wiser for all of us to remember her this way, and retire the "the organ grinder." Perhaps it's time for the extremists to call a truce, for the Media to re-direct, and for the pendulum to pause for a moment in tribute.

I suppose all of this can begin with my taking off that writers' cap and speaking to you now and lastly as just a man.

I guess I probably spent the last 30-odd years fighting, winning, and getting beaten. After a while, I don't suppose it mattered which. I've had my opinions about a lot of things, and sometimes they've been as dead wrong as any could have been. The few that may have been right helped keep the scale, at least halfway balanced. I've made enough mistakes to fill a book three times this size, and that would be the condensed version.

Recently when trying to find many who participated in this story, I was saddened to find they had died, leaving me once again, the youngest of the bunch, and now, damned near the last.

One thing I do know now is the difference between gold and brass.

I guess, considering I am in my 57th year, that's not a hell of an accomplishment. I also know that with the new generation, and in fact, the new century, there will come the "new" Marilyns. And Heaven help you, a few new Peter's.

Maybe they will be a bit smarter than we were. Maybe everybody will someday begin trusting each other again, and that includes feelings inside of you that might just be let out in time. God, I hope so.

Standing tall for unimportant badges of ego and self-pity aren't worth a whole lot. What does count is a belief in each other, and for one to die before you can accomplish this, is a hell of a waste and makes for a lonely victory.

This diary happened just as I have said, allowing for a few errors in dates and times, sometimes only hours. I guess the facts contained herein give me the one big advantage over the rest of those who have tried to piece her together. Even that fact becomes less than a reason to applaud.

See, I cheated. I didn't need any research tools, and didn't have to hear anything second or third hand. The only documentation is the one I carry inside me. I will also never need anyone to tell me just what she was like, and just how greatly she is missed. The hand she held was MINE.

I believe that says it all.